SCIENCE FICTION:
An Oral History

SCIENCE FICTION:
An Oral History

Dialogs with Prominent Authors of the Golden Age and New Wave, 1930-80

Interviews conducted by
D. Scott Apel
and
Kevin C. Briggs

Edited by D. Scott Apel

Published by The Impermanent Press

v05

ISBN 978-1-886404-25-0

DEDICATION

For Kevin C. Briggs
(1952-2007)

"Tuck up your sleeves and loosen your talktapes."
—James Joyce, *Finnegans Wake*

CONTENTS

Preface to the 2014 Edition 9

Introduction 13

1. The 1930s: C.L. Moore 17
2. The 1940s: Leigh Brackett 35
3. The 1950s: Theodore Sturgeon 61
4. The 1960s: Philip K. Dick 91
5. The 1940s through 1970s: Fritz Leiber 137
6. The 1970s: Roger Zelazny 165
7. The 1970s: Norman Spinrad 191
8. The 1980s: Robert Anton Wilson 227

Afterword 253

Bonus Interview: Gene Roddenberry 261

PREFACE

to the 2014 Edition

Science fiction is currently one of the most popular forms of literature around the world. It's hard to believe that just a couple of generations ago it was considered a literary ghetto, supported by a relative handful of fans and dedicated readers. Even under these less-than-ideal conditions, a number of talented writers, laboring in virtual obscurity, produced a significant body of speculative literature.

During the past fifty years, however, science fiction has evolved. The most obvious evolutionary leap was from page to screen. Starting with *Star Trek* in the late 1960s and turbo-boosted by *Star Wars* in 1977, the genre has grown to dominate visual, effects-driven media. But "sci-fi" as a literary genre also evolved during this period. The work that emerged is different from its techno-adventure roots: more complex, more wide-ranging, more mature. During this period, the literature of science fiction evolved from cult novelty to mainstream popularity and, occasionally, even art.

In 1973, Kevin C. Briggs and I set out to perform in-depth interviews with key figures in each era of modern science fiction, from its inception in the 1930s through its ghettoization in the '40s and '50s, to the "New Wave" revolution of the '60s and mass acceptance in the '70s. (Since the interviews for this book were completed, we've moved through several additional eras of sci-fi writing, including the Cyberpunk movement of the 1980s as well as several as-yet undefined decades.)

The result is *Science Fiction: An Oral History*—a document of the development of the genre in the writers' own words. Through these interviews with some of the most prominent figures in the field, we get first-hand insight into the changes in style, subject and society that shaped the evolution of the genre over its first half-century.

While the career of each writer included in this book spans several decades, these interviews have been arranged in a chronological order based on the peak years of the author's career—the decade in which the writer did his or her best work, or work that had the most significant impact on the field. Calendar decades are used only as rough guidelines, and the authors are presented as representative of the style or activity of the field in a particular era.

In this way, a major figure from each decade of the history of modern science fiction is represented, from the 1930s through the 1970s—a fifty-year span that saw the genre blossom from the "scientific romances" of Verne and Welles, and Gernsback's "scientifiction," into the vehicle of choice for exploring the technological, moral, and philosophical future of our species.

Our choice of authors was painfully deliberate. After long debates about our favorites, we eventually narrowed the list down to those who met three criteria:

- Each played a significant role in some aspect of the development or history of science fiction as literature.
- Each was an erudite individual, capable of both critical insight into his or her works and analysis of his or her place in the history of the field.
- Each has made a significant and lasting creative literary contribution to the genre.

Each interview covered a minimum of two hours, which afforded time enough to delve deeply into numerous topics. In order to achieve a consistency of theme among the diverse voices, each of the authors was asked to discuss several specific topics, including:

- Their working habits
- A brief autobiography, both personal and professional
- Literary influences
- The science fiction field in general, including definitions of science fiction and the differences between "mainstream" fiction and science fiction
- Science fiction as modern mythology
- An analysis of their major works

While it's clearly impossible for only eight authors to describe a half-century of development of the field—particularly when we wanted to cover so much additional territory with them—we feel this selection is a good first step toward a more comprehensive oral history, which will be left for some younger, more energetic, enterprising writer to accomplish.

Until that time, please join us in conversation with the stellar figures whose efforts defined a genre and whose work we greatly admire.

INTRODUCTION

by
Kevin C. Briggs (1980)

This started out to be a history of science fiction. It only took one weekend to transform into an oral history.

Over the 4th of July weekend in 1973, Scott Apel and I attended the science fiction convention Westercon in San Francisco, specifically to interview people whose work we admired. In those days, authors were rarely given the opportunity to express themselves directly and in depth on the topics we thought were of major importance in the field.

Westercon proved to be a very positive influence on this work because we got so many interviews of such a high level of quality. We quickly realized the history of the field could be told anecdotally, by the people who were actively creating the genre, and that this would be much more interesting than a date, event, and title-based narrative. We decided that even though a book of this sort had never been published, there must be a market for one, however small, given that so many hardcore fans attended numerous conventions where they could hear authors speak firsthand and get to know them personally.

Thankfully, the authors were more than willing to cooperate, often going out of their way to sit with us. We did the bulk of the interviews at two conventions, and the best results we had were in just approaching people directly and saying, "Would you like to do a two-hour interview? Here's the project we're working on; here's the topics we'd like to discuss." And every time we did that, they agreed immediately and always found time. You have to consider that these were people we were just approaching off the streets, so to speak. They were very kind.

One of the purposes of this book, and one of the reasons I'm so pleased with the way it turned out, is that in addition to the historical aspect, we also wanted to provide an analysis of science fiction as literature. While critics might provide an analytical point of view, it's often an outsider's point of view. We wanted to give a voice to the practitioners—the people actively engaged in creating the form. By allowing the authors to contribute to this discussion, we discovered that science fiction is in fact a very coherent art form, with major and minor themes that are being artfully exploited by its writers. I feel that the people at the top of the field—many of whom are included in this book—are fully as capable of dealing with the Grand Themes of literature as any writer in the world.

Science fiction has always been a vastly exciting way of viewing ourselves. As they say in the Russian film *Solaris*, "We don't want other worlds, we want a mirror." What's happened in the last twenty years in science fiction [1960-1980] is perhaps the most important jump in literature since Joyce and Faulkner promoted the internal monolog as a technique of self-understanding. There is an increasing number of solidly mainstream writers who are using science fiction concepts in their work, once they discover that they can best illustrate modern consciousness using the existing encyclopedia of sci-fi tropes. The idea that "reality" is not a linear concept, and that a much more authentic view is to illustrate "reality" as a multi-dimensional experience, for example, is just one of the ideas mainstream fiction has borrowed from SF. This is a point of view that we couldn't have come to philosophically or couldn't understand easily but for the millions of us who grew up on ideas like that by reading science fiction.

To a large extent, I think that in an age dominated by future shock and increasingly aware of the effect of ever-evolving technology on the human psyche, it's comforting that we have a literature that so precisely and on so many levels deals with those topics.

What I feel we have in this volume is much more than a simple oral history of the Golden Age and "New Wave" of science fiction.

It's a glimpse into the minds of some of the pivotal personalities that created that era—the artists who reflected our society and humanity in a truly modern manner, and who, by doing so, changed the course of modern literature and social discourse.

C.L. MOORE

Interview conducted at The Octocon
Santa Rosa, CA
October 1977

Catherine Lucille Moore was born on January 24, 1911, in Indianapolis, Indiana. Seriously ill as a child, she spent many hours reading classic fantasy of the era. During the Great Depression, she dropped out of college to work as a secretary, and wrote her first story, "Shambleau," in 1933 as an attempt to improve her typing skills. It was accepted by the pulp magazine *Weird Tales* and launched her career as one of the first women to write in the science fiction genre.

Moore met fellow writer Henry Kuttner in 1936; they married in 1940 and thereafter wrote most of their stories in collaboration. The collaboration proved very popular, and they turned out a steady stream of stories throughout the 1940s, using their own names or as many as 18 different pseudonyms. Several of these stories are considered classics in the field, with Moore's emphasis on emotion, sensation and romanticism tempering Kuttner's more energetic and intellectual approach.

In the 1950s, the team began concentrating on mysteries and television scripts. Moore also returned to college, graduating with a B.S. from the University of Southern California in 1956, and earning an M.A. in 1964. In 1958, Kuttner died of a heart attack at age 44. Moore continued to write television scripts until she remarried in 1963, at which time she quit writing altogether.

For a few years in the late 1970s and early 1980s, Moore attended fantasy and science fiction conventions, and was guest of honor at a world convention in 1981. She died in a Hollywood convalescent home on April 4, 1987, of Alzheimer's disease complicated by pneumonia.

In his groundbreaking book *Seekers of Tomorrow: Masters of Science Fiction* (1966), author Sam Moskowitz wrote that C.L. Moore was “the most important member of her sex to contribute to science fiction since Mary Wollstonecraft Shelley wrote *Frankenstein*.”

CATHERINE MOORE

Apel: First of all, I'd like to thank you for participating in this interview, and to let you know what great admirers of your work Kevin and I have been for many years.

Moore: I love to hear that. *(Laughter)*

Apel: The first question we usually ask is about the artist's working habits, but since we've established that you aren't writing anymore, let's skip that and discuss the days you were writing. How did you get started in science fiction?

Moore: The first writing that I did, beginning with "Shambleau," was done in a very helter-skelter way. I wrote "Shambleau" and sold it, first bounce, probably not because I was a genius, but because I had read a great deal of fantasy. I'd even read some science fiction at that point. I've mentioned this so many times it's probably not worth repeating, but very briefly: I had a job during the Depression, and I had to look busy whether I was or not. I had to make that typewriter noise a lot, and "Shambleau" came out of the typewriter. I sometimes wonder if Shambleau didn't create me, or if, alternatively, anybody had been sitting there it might just have come out of the typewriter. It didn't give me a bit of trouble; it just came rolling out.

Apel: Starting out an almost perfect scene, the "red, running figure" followed by the crowd. It has a beautiful dreamlike quality.

Moore: Wasn't that great? I just love it. I take great credit to myself—no, to the typewriter—for that. *(Laughter)*

Briggs: You liked the typewriter so much you made it a character in the story. *(Laughter)*

Apel: Tell us what it's like to work in collaboration with Henry Kuttner.

Moore: I met Hank Kuttner through my writing—we wrote for the same magazine—and eventually we were married and we wrote for a living then. When you write for a living, you have to write a tremendous lot of copy. Three days before the rent is due, if you haven't got any money in the bank, you write a story, regardless. Then you rush down and give to the publishers. By this time, we had formed a very happy association with several publishing houses in New York, and they would take the story in and read it quickly and give Hank a check. He would walk home because we didn't have an extra nickel for the subway, and then we would go out and have roast beef and Yorkshire pudding for dinner in celebration. We lived hand-to-mouth and it was great fun, because we had no doubts whatsoever that we could always turn out another story. And we always did.

As for collaborating, we would sit down and I would say, "It's time." He always liked to have thought that maybe we could start tomorrow, but I was a little more nervous than he. We would kick the table, smoke cigarettes (back in the days when we all had that vice), talk to the cat, watch the boats go by on the Hudson River. We had a house up on the Hudson, right after the war, and that's a delightful place. But sooner or later the time came and we had to drag those two chairs out on the front porch and ask, "Well, what shall it be this time?" And one of us would say, "Well, I've always liked the story about, oh, the little man with two heads." We never wrote a story about that; that's just a general example...not a bad thought, though.

Apel: Well, they are better than one... *(Groans)*

Moore: Now you stop that!

Apel: Pardon me...

Moore: I believe we did do a story called "Better Than One" with a two-headed something in it...

At any rate, we would just simply kick the idea around until one or the other of us said, "Well, I think I can take it from here," and would proceed to do so. Pretty soon that person would stop, and ask, "What should happen next?" in a hopeful sort of voice, and the other was fresh enough on it, after reading what had been written, to take over. That is how we collaborated, and how we turned out a tremendous lot of copy. We almost never touched one another's copy. For some reason it seemed to fit in; it flowed together pretty well. The most one would do would be perhaps to rewrite a sentence or two in order to make the styles meld together a little better. That was the way it was done, as a rule, though now and again one of us would sit down and hammer out something entirely on our own. But it's difficult to remember exactly what is whose from almost four hundred titles.

Apel: Under several different names.

Moore: A great many names. Eighteen different names.

Apel: Did you use all those pseudonyms because you wrote for a living in a limited field and needed to have stories published every month, sometimes two or more in the same magazine?

Moore: Right.

Apel: People wouldn't buy a magazine that featured three stories by the same person.

Moore: It would look kind of ridiculous.

Apel: The way it appears to me is that you assigned certain types of stories to specific pseudonyms, so that a reader seeing a "Lewis Padgett" story, for instance, would expect elfin humor in stories that were rather obscure.

Moore: They were. The pseudonyms were mostly family names, sort of crisscrossed. "Padgett" was my grandmother's maiden name, and "Lewis" was Hank's mother's maiden name, for example.

Apel: There's one specific story on which I'd like to check the authorship, and that is "The Children's Hour." I've seen it printed in three different places; once under your name, once under "Moore and Kuttner," and once under the "Laurence O'Donnell" byline. So before I compliment you highly on that story I want to make sure you were responsible.

Moore: That was mine entirely.

Briggs: I love that story.

Apel: Me, too, that's why I asked. I think that's one of the best things you ever wrote.

Moore: I'm very fond of that story, and so was Hank.

Apel: I'd like to thank you personally for that story; it had me thinking for days. The theme is a minor one in my first novel, in a way, and is an idea of major interest to me, but I've never seen it stated so poetically or so well. "What is mature to humanity may be childhood to a higher race."

Moore: I love hearing that. I'll have to reread it; I haven't read it since I wrote it.

Apel: Let's jump into themes. I want to tell you what I think about "Shambleau," but I do this with some trepidation. I don't want to anger you by telling you that I think the first thing you published is one of the best short stories ever written.

Moore: *(Laughing)* Oh, I've heard that before. "You'll never top that!" they say.

Apel: Well, you did in fact. I think there are many things in "Shambleau" that molded the field more than might be immediately apparent. For instance, one of the things that we've been talking about in all of these interviews is how science fiction is fast becoming this era's mythology, and "Shambleau" stands as a perfect example. Here is an ancient Earth myth, the Medusa, retold in perfectly idiomatic terms on another planet. In this story and others you've provided a great amount of evidence that the symbols of classical mythology can be easily translated into science fiction.

Moore: That's very true.

Apel: You've said that your early influences in reading were Edgar Rice Burroughs, the Oz books, and Greek mythology. There's just so much mythology that shows up in your works, especially in some of your best works: the medusa in "Shambleau"; Danaë and the Golden Shower in "The Children's Hour"; "No Woman Born" mentions in rapid succession the Abelard and Heloise legend as well as the myth of the Phoenix and the Frankenstein story, which in turn was based on the myth of Prometheus. Many other classical myths are mentioned in your works as well. Do you believe that the symbols of classical mythology are similar to the symbolism of science fiction?

Moore: I'm sure they are. I wasn't conscious of doing this myself. I hadn't thought of it until just now. But I think so. We're personifying the unknowable in terms of characters like Shambleau. I hadn't really thought it through to that extent, but I feel that it's probably true, up to a point. It seems so self-evident.

Apel: I pick this up as a very strong aspect of your work, especially in "The Children's Hour," where the whole plot runs parallel to the story of Zeus and Danaë. You've even gone so far as to use the name "Comus" in Doomsday Morning, pointing out that Comus, once a god of mirth and joy, had now degenerated into a rigid and sterile slave-making machine. These and many more examples have added to my appreciation of the depths of your stories in portraying mythology in modern terms.

Moore: That's very satisfying. Any children you may have, lock them in the closet with copies of Bullfinch, *Alice in Wonderland*, and one or two other things...

Apel: The Oz books?

Moore: Yes, of course. The entire set that Baum wrote. I still have my copies of those, containing my first staggering attempts at writing my name on the first pages.

I don't think anyone consciously writes mythology; if they tried it wouldn't come off at all. It has to take place down in the midbrain somewhere before it will come out right.

Apel: Perhaps that's why "Shambleau" was so successful, springing as it did full-blown from your midbrain. That story is a beautiful illustration of Jung's depth psychology, too, showing contact with the negative side of the anima, with its dark fascination.

As long as we're talking about this fatal fascination, we might mention another major aspect of your writing, that being the emotional tone of seductive danger. "Black Thirst" is a good example of this, as is "Shambleau." Most of the Northwest Smith stories contain this element. So does "Bright Illusions," in which love conquers death, and also sections of *Judgment Night*. And "The Black God's Kiss." And on and on and on... That feeling of ominous eroticism really seems to pervade your work.

Moore: Well, now, that I can't comment on; it had never occurred to me before. I feel it's quite valid, but I'd have to think it over. I feel that it's entirely true. I must reread some of them to see where it all began. I'm glad you mentioned it.

Apel: That erotic undercurrent is one of the most-often mentioned illustrations of how you helped bring sentiment, or emotions in general, into what had been the strictly cold, intellectual writing in the field before you. And you started out with some of the most mature emotions there are. That erotic undercurrent is one of the most engaging aspects of your work, to me.

Moore: Well, thank you.

Apel: You've also stated that the theme you've written over and over again was that "Love is the most dangerous thing that exists." Have you changed your mind since then?

Moore: Nooooo, it still is! *(Laughter)* It's wonderful, but anything that can be so overpoweringly important and is not under one's control is definitely very frightening...to anybody, I should think. I have never had any personal problems in that department, except by death. But that in itself is a menace.

Apel: That's a fascinating way to view relationships. Some of your best work uses that theme: "Vintage Season," *Judgment Night*, "Bright Illusions." That's a fascinating story, the way they use their love to transcend death itself. That idea is something I've seen very, very rarely in literature, outside of *Antony and Cleopatra... (Laughter)*

Moore: Oh, I'm in great company!

Briggs: One series of stories that are favorites of mine are the Jirel of Joiry stories—a beautiful picture of a liberated woman in unliberated settings. How did you come to develop Jirel?

Moore: I was probably sick and tired of being chained to a typewriter all that time, and it was fun just to make up wild adventures in which I could imagine myself in part as Jirel. It's a good way of expressing that spirit of adventure while being safe behind a typewriter. That's an awfully humdrum explanation; I wish I could think of something more interesting. If anything over occurs to me, I'll drop you a card.

Briggs: Did you find any resistance to your being a woman trying to succeed in a field which, up until your appearance, was populated entirely by males?

Moore: Not the least bit in the world. It's a boring story; I hate to repeat it. But I didn't want anyone at the bank where I worked during the Depression to know I had an alternate source of income—even though nobody could possibly have lived on the income the stories brought. The bank was rather paternalistic, and kept many more people on its payroll than it really needed. I felt the need to hide, and so I wrote under the name "C.L. Moore." The chances that anyone there would ever see a magazine with my name in it, or connect me with that person were remote, so it was probably an alarmist reaction. When the science fiction world found out I was a woman, everybody was very pleased. I never had the slightest bit of down-putting because I was a woman.

Briggs: That response leads us into another one of the things we've been talking about with the writers we've been interviewing, namely the relation between the science fiction writer and science fiction fandom. It seems that science fiction is a field where writers get more feedback than any other area of literature, so we were wondering what kind of relationship you've had with this vocal readership.

Moore: In the last five years or so, I just suddenly thought it might be fun to get acquainted with a group of science fiction people. I had never done it before, and Hank and I never had anything to do with fans in the days that he was living. We had way too much we wanted to do and talk about and think and say; places we wanted to go together. After his death, I was busy with other things, and just never developed an interest in fandom. And then one time I went to a meeting in Los Angeles, and was well-received, and from then on I just began to go out and to see more of them. I think they've improved since the early days.

Apel: We're trying.

Moore: I'm sure you are.

Briggs: Since you are just getting back into this milieu, do you find it a little like coming back to a life you left behind you long ago?

Moore: No, because this was never a part of the kind of life I had before. The only association that Hank and I ever had in science fiction, aside from one another, was with a group in New York that met once a week in a bar, to sit around and talk and drink beer. I think they called themselves "The Fictioneers." Ed Hamilton was a member, I think.

Briggs: Do you find it odd being suddenly presented with a group of people who think you're an "Old Master"?

Moore: Oh, goodness, yes. I feel I should be sitting at my own feet, asking myself questions. *(Laughter)*

Briggs: That's OK...we'll sit at your feet and ask questions.

Moore: That wouldn't work. I'd like to sit at my own feet and ask myself the Ultimate Question. If I could think of it. *(Laughter)*

Apel: Maybe you could just think up the Ultimate Answer, and dispense with the Question entirely...

Moore: Oh, stop that! You're not supposed to top me that well! *(Laughter)* That was very good.

Briggs: Did you ever think that you weren't making the money you might have been making because of the label "science fiction" or "fantasy"?

Moore: I never thought about that. It was the only way we had of making a living...certainly, and with great pleasure, and with great ease. It never occurred to us to take a chance on turning out the Great American Novel, then finding out after a number of years that it wasn't the Great American Novel after all. It was just sort of a routine, workaday method of making a living, and nothing else. We had no desire to go in any different direction, or to go any further. There wasn't any further. A group of us were at the top of the heap, and it was a nice heap to be on. We had a comfortable living. We traveled around as much as we chose, and everything was just great. It was a very good way to live.

Apel: Another couple of people who were at the top of that heap were Leigh Brackett and Edmond Hamilton. It's interesting that you four should become such good friends, as each of you had a very different approach to the same field. Leigh relies mostly on male heroes, for instance, while you have many female main characters. And you and Kuttner collaborated continually while Leigh and Ed Hamilton only once in their long careers worked on a story together.

Moore: I didn't know that! I'll have to talk to her about that. You know, I worked at Warner Brothers years after Leigh left...

Apel: Now, that I didn't know. Were you working on *Maverick* scripts, by any chance?

Moore: Yes, and, oh, that was such fun. I wrote *77 Sunset Strip* scripts, too.

Briggs: There's another interesting parallel, because Leigh has written so many Westerns and detective stories.

Moore: Yes, she's very good at that.

Briggs: Do you think that this other work has helped your science fiction? Do you see any exchange between the fields?

Moore: Only in the sense that we developed a sense of how to build a story: what to do and what not to do; how to keep it moving and how to keep the fat out of it. If we got bored, it was ruined—we couldn't finish the story. So it was much to our own advantage to tell a tight, fast-moving story. That transfers; in television, however, it's a different area completely. Leigh was miles above me in the studio area, because she wrote complete feature films. I humbly wrote television shows, and much of what I wrote was changed by the directors or producers. But it was fun; whenever you got tired you could always go out to one of the sets and watch them shoot films. It was great fun.

Briggs: Do you think that with the new, revived interest in filming science fiction and fantasy that you'll be approached to do something for the screen? Would you like to do something...if you ever got desperate and hungry again? *(Laughter)*

Moore: I don't know. I'd probably like to think about it. Nobody's ever approached me. I don't think that anyone's aware of me now, as I've been out of the "center of the stage" for so long. I would probably agree, if anyone asked me. Ted Sturgeon was suggesting that there's an open market for this now. It might be kind of fun to switch over. I'm kind of tired of doing the "lady of leisure" bit. *(Laughter)*

Apel: Well, we'd all be looking forward to whatever you chose to do.

Moore: Bless you; that's lovely to hear.

Apel: I'm delighted to hear you're considering doing more work.

Moore: Well, if it's in television, it won't be me who does the work. "The hand is the hand of Esau; the voice is the voice of Jacob." *(Laughter)* Now that's wonderful—I've never said that before! I must remember it...I do appreciate myself. *(Laughter)*

Briggs: Ambrose Bierce described "yourself" as "The person who gives you a compliment when no one else is around."

Moore: What was your guys' first interest in science fiction? Were you real little kids, or more or less mature, or what?

Briggs: I came to it by a very classical route, one I've heard you and Leigh, in particular, speak of. The first science fiction novel I ever read—or heard, more properly as it was read to me—was Burroughs' *The Land That Time Forgot*, when I was about five. And I decided, Why bother to read anything else? *(To Apel)* But now you tell us the story of the first science fiction novel *you* read.

Apel: I was raised on children's fantasy, mostly, because my parents thought science fiction was unhealthy—

Briggs: And it is...

Apel: Yes, thank...whoever. I read Dr. Dolittle and the Oz books. And then when I was seven years old, I went unaccompanied to the movies and saw *Forbidden Planet*. Talk about your "first contact" stories... Suddenly, nothing was the same anymore. *(Laughter)*

Moore: How daring! Isn't it funny how prissy parents were in those days?

Briggs: Now that's a thing I don't understand. It was my father who read me Burroughs, and he just created a monster in me—

Apel: In more ways than one...

Briggs: My mother would read me mythology, and my father read me Burroughs, and the next thing I know, I'm saying, "I have to have more of this stuff." Were your parents strict in this way or permissive?

Moore: I was allowed to read *Alice in Wonderland*, of course, but mother disapproved very much of Tarzan and Edgar Rice Burroughs in general. One cousin of mine and I were very puzzled as to why Tarzan should have such parental disapproval, and we decided there must be some bad words in there somewhere. We couldn't see anything wrong with it. But we knew there were bad words around that we weren't supposed to say or hear. So we went through the books very carefully, and finally we found a bad word. It was *belly*. You said *stomach*, you didn't say *belly*. *Belly* was, well...

Apel: Not refined.

Moore: Right, right. Tarzan crawled on his belly. So I'm happy to say that that's why parents disapprove of Tarzan.

Apel: It's nice to see that so many writers at the very top of the field were repressed in that area as children. It's almost as if they were somehow driven to it by being denied it.

Moore: Of course! The forbidden fruit is always the most interesting. I didn't realize that so many parents felt that way.

Briggs: I used to talk to people who claimed that letting their kids watch, say, *Godzilla Versus the Mushroom People* would give the kids nightmares. And I'd think, Geez, I could give you stories that would send you gibbering into a padded cell, you know? *(Laughter)*

Moore: But you didn't.

Briggs: My pure heart prevented me... Do you read much science fiction anymore?

Moore: Well, that I can't really answer. I'm not in that sort of focus right at this point.

Briggs: Of your contemporaries, then, is there anybody you particularly admire other than Kuttner?

Moore: I love Leigh's work. And I don't know why; it just does something that I enjoy very, very much. I'm sure there were others, but it's been so very long since I've read even my own work, let alone anyone else's.

Apel: What do you read now for pleasure?

Moore: I go to the libraries regularly. First of all I go to the current mystery shelf. I like novelists who have an unusual approach. I can read Agatha Christie over and over again. But much of what I borrow I return unread, and even those I finish don't make that great an impression on me.

Briggs: What is it that made you want to write science fiction? You said that you rarely reread what you've written, so it can't be the desire to write stories that you want to read. And there were any number of available genres for you to write in to make a living at that time—gothic, romance, mystery, western, etc.—yet you chose a fledgling field and stayed with it. Was it because of the science fiction and fantasy you read as a child, perhaps?

Moore: I had a very restricted childhood, on account of I was ill a good bit of my childhood, and I was kept out of school until about the 5th grade and tutored at home. I was kept in bed, staring at the ceiling or reading whatever could be found or was given to me. I was very bored a good bit of the time. I suppose it was a kind of reaction to this being restricted in mobility and in association and just general experience that made me want to bust out in other directions and go as far as I could into Wonderland, or Barsoom, or whatever. I wonder how many science fiction writers—in particular, science fiction writers—have had some kind of restricting experiences in their childhood that were enough to make them feel the need for getting outside the bounds of their illness?

Apel: This is a very interesting question, and seems to relate to the psychological repression that we were talking about earlier.

Briggs: Agatha Christie wrote her first novel because she was very ill and sitting around. Her mother came into her room and said, "Why don't you read a book?" and she said that she had read all the books around, so her mother said, "Then why don't you write yourself a story?" And so she sat down and wrote *The Mysterious Affair at Styles*.

Apel: Robert Anton Wilson was very sick as a child; he had polio twice. Ted Sturgeon, was also ill as a youth. He was going to be a circus gymnast, but got scarlet fever, which enlarged his heart and made any great physical exertion out of the question.

Moore: I had scarlet fever and an enlarged heart, too. Actually, I had a continuing series of illnesses. They just wear you down to the point where you've got to escape into fantasy. If you can't get out of the bed, you can at least get out of the world. *(Laughter)* It reminds me of the Indian Yogis who have themselves buried and come back having had wonderful adventures inside their minds, or outside their bodies.

Apel: Is there anything that we haven't asked that you'd like to comment on?

Moore: I will think of that for the next interview. *(Laughter)*

Apel: We're giving our competitors a head start.

Moore: Well, you've gotten some from the previous people; it's only fair to pass it on down the line. *(Laughter)* I wish I could think of something; I love to talk about things like this. But unfortunately, I've about talked myself out, even on that fascinating subject, me.

Apel: OK, then, one last question: Do you intend to do any more writing?

Moore: That's like asking me if I intend to have a car accident on the way home. I don't know. I really have no control over these things.

Apel: And if your typewriter starts talking to you again someday...

Moore: Now that would be very interesting. It may be chattering away right now and I don't know about it.

Apel: Well, I certainly hope it does happen someday.

Moore: I do, too; I love it. I just don't have the pressures on me, but who knows? I may become vulnerable to a whole new set of pressures.

Apel: Would a petition signed by five hundred of the top names in science fiction change your mind...? *(Laughter)*

Briggs: How about if we *threatened your life... (Laughter)*

Moore: Anything is worth trying.

Apel: Well, then, thank you very much, Catherine Moore. It's been delightful.

Briggs: Yes, thank you.

Moore: Thank you, sirs. I enjoyed talking with the both of you...and I especially enjoyed talking about myself! *(Laughter)*

LEIGH BRACKETT HAMILTON

Interview conducted at The Octocon
Santa Rosa, California
October 1977

Leigh Douglass Brackett Hamilton was born in Los Angeles, California, on December 7, 1915. She published her first story, "Martian Quest," in 1940 and began a long career with a string of Edgar Rice Burroughs-inspired adventure stories appearing in the SF magazines of the era.

In 1944 she branched out into hard-boiled mysteries, which led to a job collaborating with William Faulkner on director Howard Hawks' big screen adaptation of Raymond Chandler's novel, *The Big Sleep*. She would go on to collaborate with Hawks on several more films, including *Rio Bravo* (1959) and *Hatari!* (1962).

She married fellow Golden Age science fiction writer Edmond Hamilton on December 31, 1946, and continued writing genre fiction, including science fiction, mysteries, and Westerns, as well as screenplays and TV scripts. Her fluency with both the hard-boiled mystery and space opera adventure fused into a style that was colorful, energetic and character-driven.

As just one indication of her professionalism and her dedication to her craft, in early March of 1978, Brackett handed in her first draft of *The Empire Strikes Back* to George Lucas, then checked into a hospital in Lancaster, California, and died of cancer at age 62 a week later, on March 18.

LEIGH BRACKETT HAMILTON

Apel: First off, I'd like to thank you very much for allowing us to interview you; it's really a pleasure and quite an honor to meet you. You have a long-established reputation for quality work in the field of science fiction; on the personal side, we've both been reading you most of our lives and have enjoyed every word.

What we'd like to do is to start with something basic, namely, How do you work? What are your typical working habits? Do you have regular office hours, or some kind of a system?

Brackett: Yes. I got into this very early on. I hit the typewriter early in the morning. I'm an early riser; I have my morning coffee or tea, whichever it may be, then I get to the typewriter. If I don't get it done in the morning, that's a gone day. I used to work, always, from early morning until lunchtime. The afternoons were for running around and doing errands and things. Then very often I would work in the evening. Those were the days when you were turning out pulp stories, trying like mad to meet the deadlines, and you worked and worked and worked. I used to do some of my best work at night, because it was quiet, and I didn't have any other little fiddle-faddle to do. But in recent years I do not have quite that much pressure, so I really don't work at night much anymore...unless I have a very pressing script. Television is another matter. When you've got someone on the phone yelling, "I need the script by yesterday!" or "We're shooting tomorrow!" you do it.

Apel: That's five days a week? Six?

Brackett: That's seven days a week. Sundays, holidays, you name it; everything.

Apel: OK... Let's move right along to your predecessors in the world of literature—the people who have influenced you, both within and outside of the science fiction/fantasy field. I know that Burroughs played a significant part in your development; are there any other others or any specific books you would single out as being major influences on you?

Brackett: Yes. There are a number of them, and first of all I would have to say Edgar Rice Burroughs. I was given a copy of *The Gods of Mars* when I was eight or nine years old, and the world was never the same afterwards. I think I was committed right then to being a science fiction writer. You know: The curtains had gone up, the lights came on, and the band played, and all of a sudden I'm aware of a whole cosmos out there—the concept of other planets, and all these marvelous possibilities. The chills still go up my back when I think about it, because it was a marvelous "opening up" of things.

I've often laughed about it since, because I had a terrible fight with my grandfather in the kitchen of a tiny little beach house. (It used to be cheap to live at the beach; we lived at the beach because we didn't have any money. I loved it.) I said, "I want to be on the first spaceship that goes to Mars." And my grandfather said, "There will never be a spaceship going to Mars. There's nothing out there but vacuum. What would it push against?" At that point I had nothing to refute him with, but I remember pounding my fist on the counter and saying, "I don't care! I don't care! It will, it will, I know it will!" I've often laughed at myself, because I had only just arrived on this planet, and I'm frantic about getting to the next one! *(Laughter)*

After Burroughs... Well, there were many influences. Kipling was a great influence; I knew *The Jungle Book* by heart before I cut my eye teeth, I think. In later years Haggard, Dunsany, Merritt. I had a great passion for anything that was mythology, or ancient history. They gave us Breasted's *The Ancient World* [probably referring to James Henry Breasted's *Ancient Times—A History of the Early World*, 1916] in about the seventh or eighth grade in the small school I went to, and that, too, opened up a whole new vista of fascination. I've been an ancient history buff, and an archeology buff, and an anthropology buff ever since, which has brought me a great deal of pleasure. It was so wonderful when we had the chance to actually go and see so many of these places, and there're still many places I want to go. We went to Egypt and had a marvelous cruise down the Nile, stopping at every old stone. We were signed up to go to Mohini Darau and the Indus Valley, and then Edward developed something that had to be surgically repaired, so we had to cancel that trip and never made it. But I'm still hoping.

Briggs: Visiting places like that is amazing. I went to see the obelisks at Karnak, the Celtic ruins in Britanny...

Brackett: I've never been there. I'm dying to go there.

Briggs: Oh, it's beautiful. There's this all-pervading sense of this being old, ancient. Remarkable feeling.

Brackett: I want very much to go there. I know when you stand at Stonehenge, even crowded with tourists, and listen to the wind whistling over the plain, and look at those stones, it does something to you.

I should get back to what we were discussing. These people were influences in my very early formative years, and on up. After I began reading science fiction, Edward Hamilton was a great influence. I loved his stories. And Jack Williamson's too. Henry Kuttner, as an individual and as a writer, I think, did more for me than anyone else, because Henry was working for the Dorsey Literary Agency when I was first trying to sell. Everybody told me, "Don't write science fiction, there's no money in it. It's a miserable little field, it doesn't pay anything, there's no prestige. Go for the big markets." Well, of course, in the big markets I'm bucking Talbot Mundy, John Patchen, Christopher Wren, all these people who've been all over the world and know exactly what they're talking about. All I could do was get it out of books—I was pretty young and had never been anywhere or done anything. I didn't know anything. And of course all the women in my family said, "Why don't you write for nice magazines, like *The Ladies' Home Journal* and *Woman's Home Companion*?" I said, "I'd love to, because they pay beautiful, beautiful money. But I can't even read those magazines, so I certainly can't write those stories. I really don't care who loves who." *(Laughter)*

I was always for the adventure stuff; as Ed used to say, "Birds that lay eggs as big as mountain ranges" *(Laughter)* and the Arabian Nights type of thing. So I finally decided the heck with it; science fiction is what I want to do. I've never been to Mars, but no one else has either, so I can write stories about Mars as well as anybody. I'll make up my own Mars, and there's nobody can come around and say, "It isn't like that!"

So I started sending in these first feeble efforts, and Hank was reading for Dorsey. He took a very special interest in me because I was writing science fiction, and went out of his way to give me personal help, personal criticism; to tell me where I went wrong. You talk about writing courses... The funny thing was that Hank used to be able to tell me what I did wrong, but he couldn't tell me how to do it right. I had to find that out for myself. These are areas where there are no black and white; no diagrams that you can draw.

Apel: If he told you how to do it right, then he'd be writing the story.

Brackett: Right. Then it would be his story; it wouldn't be mine.

I've never forgotten the day when I'd been out all afternoon with my mother, and I came back and my grandmother said, "Your friend Mr. Kuttner called, but wouldn't leave a message." Well, Mr. Kuttner never called, he always wrote. So I had this feeling in the back of my mind that it must be important, and the only thing that would be important enough is if I sold a story...but *I mustn't even think that! (Laughter)* You know, *It'll go away if I think that!* So I sweated for nearly two hours before Hank called again, and his little voice came over the phone, and he said, "I just wanted to tell you that John Campbell has bought 'Martian Quest' for *Astounding Stories*." Whereupon I all but fainted dead away. I don't remember whether I screamed or what. Anyway, it was one of those pivotal moments of one's life. Then a week later Campbell bought another one. So that was two stories in one week to *Astounding*. But then it was a long time before I sold anything else. It was the most frustrating period, because I wanted to know what was I doing right then that I'm doing wrong now?

Apel: Obviously you discovered the answer...

Brackett: Finally, yes. I finally began to sell. Unfortunately, Campbell was not a market for me. I admired the man and the magazine; it was a prestige magazine and I was extremely proud of having sold it. But I didn't know enough hard science. Frankly, I had no background in chemistry, engineering, or any of these other things, and I couldn't write the type of story that he liked. Everything I wrote had a logical explanation, based on some scientific principle, but it was the adventure, the color, the strange people and the strange animals... I still had that extreme fascination with Mars that had never left me. Burroughs bibliophiles were kind enough to make me the Guest of Honor in Miami this year [1977]; what I told them when I made my little talk was that in later years I realized that I was telling myself Martian stories. I had so loved the Burroughs books, and the Burroughs Mars; they had been so much a part of my youth, that I wanted more and there wasn't any more, so I had to go out and do it myself.

Apel: You must have started very young.

Brackett: Actually, the first attempt I made at writing was when I was quite small. I was a tremendous admirer of Douglas Fairbanks, Senior. I thought he was just—*oh!* I can't remember what movie it was, but I wanted more, and there wasn't more, so I decided, I'll write it myself. I scribbled on little sheets of paper—and I didn't get very far with it. But I had the idea; I was starting. I always had this lunatic compulsion to keep empty copy-books around me. I had this terrible feeling that I must have more blank paper, because I have to fill it up.

Briggs: You work mostly in the novel length...

Brackett: Yes. I was never too much of a short story reader; I was never happy working in the short story length myself. I had very few of what I would call good short stories. I need the elbow room, whereas, say, Ray Bradbury was a born short story writer. Absolutely perfect. Edmund was unique—or at least unusual—in that he would trot from one to the other with the greatest of ease. He'd write *The Star Kings*, then he'd write these marvelous, sensitive, beautiful, lyrical, poetic short stories which nobody gave him credit for many years—stories like "Requiem." His big, thundering space operas were always the novel length; in the short story length he did the cameos, the really beautiful bits of lapidary work. I'm just not geared for it.

Apel: Do you read much science fiction now?

Brackett: Yes. I don't read the magazines too much anymore, and I know that I miss many good things that way. Some of the young writers coming up are really brilliant. I read their stuff with great enjoyment.

Briggs: As long as we're talking about people in the field, perhaps we could also ask you what your relationship with fandom is like.

Brackett: Oh, it's always been just beautiful. I love them dearly. I don't know what I would have done without them all these thirty-seven years. Fandom is such a unique creation; you wonder where it sprang from, really. In no other field of writing do you have this business. I didn't know there were fan groups until after I had sold several stories. Then Hank introduced me to Forry Ackerman and Ray Bradbury, and all these people in the Los Angeles Science Fiction Society, and suddenly I had people to talk to. Everybody in my family thought I was nuts. *(Laughter)* It was so nice to have a group that you could fit in with. We all spoke the same language, and it was marvelous. It brought me my husband. It brought me years of very happy and enjoyable work. I love it. You can travel the world and have ready-made friends everywhere you go. We went to Australia a few years ago, and they really rolled out the red carpet for us. I'm very proud of us; it's a very warm and wonderful business.

Apel: Shall we jump right into the heavy stuff now?

Briggs: Yeah—now we're going to take our gloves off.

Brackett: All right.

Apel: One of the themes of this book is the interplay between science fiction and mythology, and the theory that science fiction seems to be this age's mythology. You are a person who very consciously works along those lines. You wrote in the foreword to the first anthology of *Planet Stories* material that you thought that what happened was that primitive people told stories to explain how they could survive in the midst of these overwhelming and uncontrollable forces of nature surrounding them. These stories were handed down through generations and eventually filtered down to the 20th century as the same basic hero figures now facing new unknowns: the depths of space, the reaches of time, myriad exotic worlds, and so on. I wondered if you'd like to comment on this opinion that you're writing what, to another age, would be epic tales.

Brackett: Yes. This is, as you say, kind of a heavy question. I think science fiction has been exceedingly valuable to modern culture because—while I won't say we're responsible for the space age—science fiction provided the medium through which ideas like a "space age" could be disseminated. In other words, a whole generation of people grew up reading science fiction in which it was taken for granted that you could go out to other planets. When I started writing, this was still rather a daring idea. When Ed started writing, practically nobody did it. Even John Carter got there by some strange supernatural transference which was never explained—but no spaceships. A whole generation grew up reading about space flight and travel to other planets, and they got used to the idea of the planetary ships and interstellar ships that ran on faster than light drives, and cross-cutting space through subspace, or hyperspace, or whatever. They get used to all these concepts, and now we find we've actually got spaceships, and we've actually been to the moon, and we've got probes going out, and a lot of people in these programs are old science fiction readers.

Briggs: Carl Sagan, for instance, said that Burroughs' *Princess of Mars* was the book that decided him to become an astronomer.

Brackett: Yeah, I read that. He had *Princess of Mars*, I had *Gods of Mars*. What science fiction does chiefly is stretch the mind, to give it concepts that your average education did not, in those days, give you. It's made people more receptive. We didn't have the hardware, the technology; in many cases the idea came from science fiction. Hugo Gernsback described television long years ago. I think Ed "invented" radar. He invented space suits.

Apel: He wrote the first story about travel outside the solar system, too; a notable symbolic achievement in addition to his contributions to its hardware.

Brackett: Right. It was. He was a mover and shaker.

Briggs: He also wrote "What's It Like Out There?" which I think is one of the most realistic stories ever written.

Brackett: Absolutely beautiful.

Apel: And that was a perfect example of a "New Wave"-type story, too; he was able to keep up with the times at every turn.

Brackett: Right. He had an amazing talent which never, never hardened. It was always going on, moving up. Right until a few days before he went into a coma, he was still eagerly reading magazines; reading about the latest find of clay figures in China; still learning. To him, learning was the most important thing there was.

But I think science fiction is important in this way. This gets back to the mythology. Humanity has always seemed to need heroes. We've been going through a very anti-heroic period, you know, where everybody was cynical, they were slobs, they were cowards, they were everything that was rotten, which you're supposed to admire instead of the tall, ept, kempt, coifed hero who wouldn't go back on his word and wouldn't strike a man when he was down, et cetera. Wasn't it G.K. Chesterton who referred to humanity still driving stark trade in heroes? We just need them, which is why Superman was such as hit. Everybody said, "It's impossible. What can you do with a man who's absolutely invulnerable and able to do anything?"

Apel: You can look up to him.

Brackett: Right. And look at *Star Wars*, which is heroes and villains, good guys and bad guys...

Apel: Nothing but.

Briggs: Since you brought up *Star Wars*, what do you feel about that movie? It's so much in the vein of things you've written over the years.

*(Note: Keep in mind this was October 1977—*Star Wars *was a brand new phenomenon at that time.)*

Brackett: I think that this is because Lucas cut his eye teeth on science fiction; he's been reading it for years and years. He's one of the few producers in Hollywood who knows science fiction. Not, maybe he's read one book by Isaac Asimov or one by Heinlein, but he's read the whole field, and he came to it knowing all the things to throw in, the stuff which is all a part of the matrix. And he threw it all in with no apologies whatsoever. He wanted a spacebar with all these marvelous creatures—

Briggs: Yeah, that in particular reminded me of descriptions of yours...the "low space dive with continuous entertainment," and strange life-forms...

Brackett: Oddly enough, I'm very happy to say, it turns out that Mr. Lucas is quite an old fan of mine. It was just a great film, I thought; just beautiful. He didn't try to teach anybody anything;

it's not beating people over the head with what terrible people they are and how they're ruining the environment, or telling us we must all get down and wallow in our shame and beat our breasts. With no apologies to anybody, he just took us back "a long time ago" to "a galaxy far, far away," and did one hell of a rousing adventure story. Beautiful! So much of it was "throwaway" lines or shots. You know...momentary shot of a skeleton of a sand-worm; "Hello, Frank Herbert."

Apel: Yeah, yeah. You see Obi-Wan wandering through the corridors of the Death Star, and it's "Hello, *Forbidden Planet*."

Brackett: So it has echoes...

Apel: Right—all the best elements of a number of popular science fiction images put together in Lucas' own unique way.

Brackett: I'm so frustrated... Nobody in Hollywood connects me with science fiction, because nobody in Hollywood reads science fiction. They associate me with hard-boiled detectives and Westerns. So recently my agent says to some producers, "You know, Leigh's been doing science fiction for years," and they all say, "Oh, has she?"

So I did a script, and actually got something that I was pleased with. But I discovered they don't know anything about science fiction. They're afraid of it. They just wanted a good, warm, family picture. Science fictional, but no monsters, no hardware, no spaceships; in other words, nothing science fictional; just a good, warm, family story.

Apel: Walt Disney from Mars.

Brackett: Yeah. It was hard to do. Every time I'd throw in something that was the least bit technical, I'd get, "Oh, the audience isn't going to understand that."

Briggs: Not if they never get to see it, they won't.

Brackett: That's right. They'd be surprised, because the audience is generally miles ahead of them. I think *Star Wars* is a great thing, and I think *Star Trek* is a great thing, too.

(Note: A week after our conversation, Leigh Brackett met with George Lucas, and he offered her the job of scripting the second film in the Star Wars series, The Empire Strikes Back.*)*

But to get back to the topic: I've always drawn very strongly on mythology—particularly the Celtic and Norse mythologies—for my own stories, because I've been fascinated by those since I was knee-high to a pup. They're marvelous stories, and marvelous characters, and marvelous interplays of personality and morality, with a good bit of philosophy embedded in them. And they're basic human patterns. It all goes back to the primitive nature myths, really; the slain god, the birth and death of the seasons, the sowing of the crops and new life starting, and so on. You can follow it through every mythology in one way or another. We're born and bred of this planet, and we move around carrying our original seawater in our blood. People in the cities tend to forget. They're cut off from nature. I've been living in the country for many years, and I grew up at the beach, which is about as basic as you can get. I used to sit at the end of a big long jetty with my feet in the ocean, and feel it breathe, and look out over the horizon and think enormous thoughts. Huge. I think this is something basic; that any kind of critter you find out anywhere in the universe that achieves intelligence will have some kind of a mythology.

Apel: There are even specific mythic patterns we can find in some of your works. The one that comes to mind immediately is "The Moon That Vanished," which is a beautiful representation of the Hero's Journey. Here's a man who gets on his ship, sails off to a distant land where few men have been before, fights the demons of hubris, with the revelation that all his god-like creation on this island is illusory—just more webs of maya. So when he finally returns to human society, it is with a gift of transcendental consciousness, immediately recognizable to those around him, and combined with the great humility not to misuse his new "godhood." It's a beautiful story, and well told. I love it.

Brackett: Thank you.

Apel: Thank *you. (Laughter)* In the same breath I might also mention *The Big Jump* as an excellent novel with the same major theme. A little more downbeat ending, though.

Another theme we've detected in much of what you write gets its name straight from mythology—the Pyrrhic Victory. Defeat in victory. A man will set himself an impossible goal and somehow manage to attain that goal, yet upon its attainment he'll realize that it just wasn't all it was cracked up to be. *The Long Tomorrow* is a good example...

Briggs: Or "The Last Days of Shandakor."

Apel: "The Moon That Vanished"; although I don't want to overuse that as an example, it still fits. *The Big Jump*, too. There the hero attains virtual godhood yet denies that attainment, thinking that it's just not right for humans to be gods.

Brackett: I don't know just why I've got this particular bent except that it appeals to my sense of drama. The typical fantasy is, "If you get everything you want, then it's all perfect." But the older I get, the more I realize that it just ain't so. You never get everything just the way you want it, and nothing is exactly as you expect it to be. Fate has a strange way of quirking things a little bit, so that you never quite get all of what you want, and you learn to be very thankful for what you've been permitted to have. *(Laughter)*

Apel: The idea that you use that theme so much seems to make you uniquely suited to adapt Chandler's work...

Brackett: Well, that, of course, was Chandler's concept, and he characterized Marlowe as a loser. He and Sam Spade had much in common, because they were both rather seedy men in a seedy occupation...

Briggs: There's a major difference in their characters, though, in that Spade was a bastard and Marlowe was a romantic at heart.

Brackett: Spade was that way in the books; the way they played him in the movie was a little more sympathetic. You're right, though; Marlowe was never a bastard, he was a very soft-hearted character with a tough exterior. But in both cases, there was one thing that you were not going to sell, and that was your pride, your sense of decency.

Apel: Your integrity.

Brackett: That's right. There were some things you wouldn't do even if they killed you. This is what makes Marlowe such a brilliant character.

Apel: There were some depths to which he would not sink.

Brackett: Right. "Up these mean streets a man must go who is not himself mean." It was a lonely character. Chandler was a tremendous influence, speaking of influences on my work.

Apel: I think that really shows in *The Big Jump*. The title echoes Chandler's titles, and the main character is very much Philip Marlowe in a science fiction setting. I liked that book a lot.

Briggs: Well, the big motivation for his involvement in the plot is friendship: "I have to find this guy; he helped me out."

Brackett: Yes. A good theme; one I've used in the Stark books more than once. I like this business of obligation to somebody, rather than saying, "Well, sure, he saved my life, but what the hell." *(Laughter)*

My first and greatest passion was for science fiction, but I also very much like the hard-boiled detective stuff—Chandler, Hammett, and so on—and I wrote a good bit of what you might call "Chandler well-water" for the hard-boiled detective pulps. I greatly enjoyed doing them, and I found that the style carried over very well into science fiction. That lean, hard-boiled prose was kind of a refreshing way to do science fiction. It worked very nicely.

Apel: You mentioned your early association with Henry Kuttner; something I'd like to ask you about is your relationship with Catherine Moore. She predated you in beginning to publish by only a very few years, and since then you've both become top women writers in the field—and by that I mean top writers who also and incidentally happen to be women. Did her writing or her success affect you in any way?

Brackett: Oh, I love her material. I flipped out when I read "Shambleau," and I loved the Northwest Smith stories. She has such a beautiful way with language. She and Hank and Ed and I were always dear friends; she made a trip back East with us, cross-country, one time, and we had a perfectly marvelous time. Catherine and I have long been dear friends; I'm a tremendous admirer of her work.

Briggs: When you started out as a writer, did people actively try to fool the readers into thinking you weren't a woman?

Brackett: I don't think so. Of course, I've got one of those unisex names—and it's my real name—but they made no secret of my sex. They'd run those little biographical things in the science fiction magazines, you know. People would write into the letters column and say, "A woman cannot write science fiction, and the Leigh Brackett story is the worst in the issue." Well, the Leigh Brackett story was the worst in the issue—not because I was a woman, but because I wasn't a very good writer. *(Laughter)* As soon as I learned how to write a decent story, I didn't get all these complaints anymore. I even sold to the hard-boiled detective pulps, which were almost entirely male, and they never made my sex a secret even there. What strikes me as funny now is some of the radical feminists who ask me, "Weren't you discriminated against?" and I say, "They welcomed me with open arms." You know, here was another lunatic coming into the fold. *(Laughter)* There were so few of us they were just happy to get another nut who could talk science fiction. It wouldn't have mattered if I'd had four legs and a tail. So then these women say, "Well, you should have been discriminated against; the only reason you weren't was because you sold out to the male establishment and wrote the kind of stories they wanted." Well, I wasn't smart enough to sell out to anybody! If I had been technically competent enough to sell out to anybody, I would have sold out to a market that paid more than science fiction! *(Laughter)*

Apel: It seems that as a woman welcomed into the field that you contributed to a long line of literary descendants, too. We can trace a direct line from you and Catherine Moore down through women like Joanna Russ, and recently to another generation, like Tanith Lee, for instance, all writing adventure or swords and sorcery stuff.

Briggs: Tanith Lee's work reminds me a great deal of yours; I think in a lot of ways, she's been influenced by you.

Brackett: Possibly, but certainly not slavishly. She's got her own style. She's a brilliant new talent. So is C.J. Cherryh. I'll tell you another one I think is brilliant, and that is Doris Piserchia. She fascinates me. And she doesn't owe anything to anybody.

Apel: We were talking earlier about your hard-boiled heroes, so that might be a good excuse to talk to you about some of the movies you've written. I have to now once again adore you... *(Laughter)*

Briggs: We'll now take five minutes out for adoration...

Brackett: Thank you...thank you. I'll sit here and look lofty. *(Laughter)*

Apel: All seriousness aside... *Rio Bravo* is one of my three or four all-time favorite Westerns, and I've been watching Westerns since before I could talk. I watch *Rio Bravo* with rapt attention every time it comes on television.

Brackett: It does hold up very well.

Apel: It probably always will. It's history, a slice of the West, and that won't change. But at any rate... You worked on both *Rio Bravo* and *El Dorado* with Howard Hawkes and John Wayne; the single word I might use to characterize all three of you is *professional.* No room for any amateur mucking around of any sort...

Brackett: No. You're right. Wayne is a professional to his fingertips; he is always on the set on time, always ready. Howard and he worked beautifully together because they trusted each other. There was no business of one trying to impose his ego on the other. They both wanted to get the best they could out of a scene, and they'd run through it before they started shooting, for an hour sometimes.

Howard had a beautiful sense of pacing. You go along in a film like this where you have relatively calm periods, where you have some fun, some laughs, some good people scenes, a man and a woman scene, maybe, then all of a sudden *wham!* The action pops, then it's over. And you have got the audience going, "What happened?" So many directors will lead up to a gunfight, then keep it going for fifteen minutes, until everybody's eardrums are numb, and the thrill wears off. Howard's method was just to pop it, and get it over with. You always knew more was coming. I've seen a lot of movies where the director didn't do this, and I'm beginning to appreciate that Hawkes was right.

Apel: *Rio Bravo* was nice that way—as a background to every "quiet" scene, the audience knew that another confrontation was imminent, and that each outbreak of hostilities would be worse than the last. Peak upon peak—the pacing and suspense are marvelous.

Briggs: Another film you did that I have to tell you I think is brilliantly paced—and in one of my favorite movies of all times—is *The Big Sleep*.

Brackett: Oh, yes. That was brilliant.

Briggs: There's not a lost motion in that film. If you ever miss more than, say, five minutes, you're just lost.

Brackett: Howard was always a genius at that. When you write a film, it's totally different than writing a novel. When I sit down at the typewriter and write a novel, everything comes out of my own head. When I sit down to write a movie, things have to come out of everybody's heads. I've got to do what the producer wants, I've got to do what is possible to stage and won't cost too much, which was a problem with *The Long Goodbye*; all these problems that you don't have when you write a novel, like when you actually go to cast a part, who're you going to get to play this? Infinite amounts depend on the director, on the film editor, on the cameraman, on how it's all put together... *Man's Favorite Sport* was practically put together in the cutting room.

Apel: Is that the Rock Hudson film you wrote and weren't credited for? I thought that was a pretty funny film.

Brackett: I didn't get any credit on that because two boys had done the script and it wasn't quite what Howard wanted, so he had me do a polish on it. He told me it would be a three-week job, and I ended up there for four months, writing right ahead of the cameras. *Hatari!* was another one like that—I'd be pounding out at 9:30 or 10 at night the scene they'd be shooting at 9 the next morning.

Briggs: Peter Bogdanovich says in his book on film that *Hatari!* is the best American movie made.

Brackett: I didn't know that. Bless his heart!

Briggs: I always wondered how you wrote lines for a rhinoceros. *(Laughter)*

Brackett: Actually, I didn't try to write lines for the animals...

Apel: Leave that to Dr. Dolittle.

Brackett: Yeah, right. (And I loved those books, too; I just adored them.) It was amazing that they got most of the animal footage for *Hatari!* just as it was needed. A few things they couldn't get, which I knew when I wrote it. I often used the phrase "If this is possible..." This was dealing with a lot of things over which a writer has no control, like reality. *(Laughter)*

Briggs: Yeah, you can't explain to a rhinoceros that he's supposed to hit his mark. *(Laughter)*

Brackett: Yeah, he hasn't read the script. *(Laughter)* I'll tell you this, though: The rhino wasn't supposed to get away. But when he did, they just kept the cameras rolling. I've seen the original footage, where they were trying to tie the rhino down, and Duke is jumping back and forth to avoid the rhino's horn...and Big Duke isn't saying what it says in the final print! He was saying bad words...he was speaking *rudely* to that rhino! (*Laughter obscures the next few lines of conversation.)*

Briggs: I think we can tie in another of the questions we've been asking for our book here, which is the practice of writing in collaboration. You've written in collaboration with William Faulkner, among other people...

Brackett: Technically, yes; actually, no. There was no possible form of collaboration there. I checked into work at the studio as a young green writer, practically crawling in apology for being there, while Faulkner was a great, famous writer; a major American figure at the time. I'd never even been away from home before. I was used to working in my little room with the door shut, with nobody watching. It took me years before I could take part in a story conference; the idea of getting up and voicing my ideas made me choke. I just couldn't do it. I didn't know how we were going to work this. He met me, said, "How do you do"; then he plunked the book down and said, "I've decided how we're going to do this; we're going to do alternate chapters. You do these and I'll do those." And that was how it worked. I don't think I spoke half-a-dozen words to Mr. Faulkner. He was in his office and I was in mine; I wrote my pages and handed them to Howard's secretary and he did the same; I never saw his stuff and he never saw mine.

Apel: Then they pieced it together and in the final form there's no difference between your part and his.

Brackett: Well...I have to say it. I was sticking very close to the Chandler dialog, and when I had to write bridging scenes, they were as pure Chandler as I could make them. I remember Bogie came up to me one day on the set and said, "Hey, Butch, did you write this?" And he showed me a line of dialog about a page long, full of clauses, and I said, "No, I didn't." He said, "I didn't think you did." Faulkner was writing Faulkner dialog, and I don't think any actor could get his larynx around it without strangling. They changed a lot on the set. There was a canard around—probably a vile and base one—about William Faulkner being famous in Hollywood as the one writer who had never had a line of dialog on the screen. *(Laughter)* I don't know if that's true or not. He was a very remote and solitary man, a very, very private person, so I think a lot of the writers rather resented him.

Apel: The story I thought you were going to tell was one that might also be apocryphal. Someone supposedly told you that a remake of *The Big Sleep* was in the works, and your alleged reply was, "Why? It's perfect already." *(Laughter)*

Brackett: I never said that. But I'm very curious about it. It's being made in England, so I want to see how they translate Chandler's Southern California to London. It's a very interesting experiment. But I think *The Big Sleep* was so good simply because of the expert direction. As far as my own personal involvement with it as a writer, I was simply putting Chandler into screenplay form, which was perfectly simple, because he wrote screenplays, really. I stuck very closely to the book; what came out actually was the expert acting, the expert directing, the expert pacing. I was dealing with the works of a master; I would not have dreamed of committing violence on it.

Briggs: You said earlier that you thought that years of writing detective fiction expanded your horizons in science fiction, since infusing the detective style prose had an interesting effect on your science fiction. Do you think that writing in films has helped your writing science fiction?

Brackett: It's helped all my writing in one very important way. I was always a perfect dub on construction. Ed was born with one of those minds where he always knew the last line of a story before he wrote the first line. We early on discerned that we could not collaborate; I'd start out with a character, or a setting, and was so impatient to get to all the wonderful things that I was dreaming up that I couldn't be bothered working out the story. That killed it for me. If I've told the story, then I've told it, and I don't have to write it. It was just a blind spot—partly laziness, and partly that I just couldn't construct a plot. I couldn't put the bones together and then put the flesh on later. Living and working closely with Ed I learned an enormous amount about construction. But basically, I think I learned more of it from screenplay work. I learned very painfully. It's very strange. When you sit in a room and you have input from three or four different people, it's a lot like building a brick wall: You've got people saying, "Well, let's pull this brick out and put it in over here, and then we'll move these bricks over here..." But you've still got to remember what the shape of the wall is. You have to look at the technical side of things. I was always one for language; I loved describing people and landscapes; I loved writing. Well, in the movies, you can forget about that. Except in dialog, style means absolutely nothing. What really means something is the construction of the thing, the bones, and I got to be pretty good on construction. So now I do it in my head. I don't write an outline, but now I have to know where I'm going before I start. I'm able to do that now, where I wasn't able before. Sometimes, of course, you throw yourself and think you see the way clearly, but you get up to page 53 and can't get on to page 54 and you know that somewhere back about page 31 you did something wrong.

Apel: Mark Twain had that problem with his book *Huck Finn and Tom Sawyer Among the Indians*. He got about a hundred pages into it and realized he had come to an insoluble dilemma. Huck and Tom being captured by Indians could lead to only one or two logical conclusions that would have been totally wrong for Twain and for the book. Torturing them or killing them was out of the question, and escape would have foiled the whole premise of the novel, so he just dropped the book and never did finish it. He reached a dead end...or a brick wall.

Brackett: I have an awful lot of half-stories that started out just beautifully, but then I'd write myself right into a box canyon where I couldn't get over the walls. But film work has been greatly instructive. I can sit in a story conference now and I can give ideas and I can say what I like and what I don't like and not be all choked up with self-consciousness and fear the way I was before. I used to think *My God! Tell Howard Hawkes and Humphrey Bogart and William Faulkner what to do? Heavens no!*

Apel: I read one story that I loved about you being talked down by Wayne and Hawkes...

Brackett: Oh, yes. Now that actually happened. The three of us were working on *El Dorado*, sitting in Howard's office discussing a scene, and I said, "Howard, we did that scene in *Rio Bravo*, word for word." Howard said, "Well, what's the matter with that?" Duke looked down at me and said, "Yeah, if it was good once, it'll be just as good again." At that point I could have done one of two things: said good-bye to the whole project, or rewrite the scene and try to make it as little like the first one as possible. So I rewrote, and we got away with it. A few people who were very knowledgeable about films asked me, "Hey, how come you remade *Rio Bravo*?" And I'd say, "Go ask Hawkes and Wayne. They made me do it." *(Laughter)*

Apel: One thing we specifically wanted to talk to you about was a point we've brushed on here and there already, but bears stating: Of all the people we've talked to, you are perhaps the best qualified to give an objective view of the field of science fiction. You've been in the field practically since its inception in modern form, and—although you've said it's your first love, to which you continually return—you've worked in many other areas—television, films, detective fiction, the historical novel, and so on. Is there any special insight into the genre "science fiction" that you've gained from the outside looking in that you'd like to pass along?

Brackett: Philosophically?

Apel: Well, that, or practically—anything you might have to say about the relationship of the mainstream world, the "real world," to our world.

Brackett: In a way, the science fiction world is a very real world, because it embodies the dreams and hopes—and, in recent years, the fears and nightmares—of a great many people. One thing I have learned to abhor in science fiction is people who overnight become great and important and then begin laying down rules and laws, saying, "Only this is science fiction, and nothing else." Ed and I were wiped out more than once, because these people would say, "That rotten old space opera stuff is all through, finished, and done with. We're not going to have any more of that foolishness, we're just going to write beautiful, significant, good and true stories about the human condition." Well, OK. My own opinion has always been that there should be room enough in science fiction for both, and much more. They ruined the mystery story that way; it was as rigid as a chemical formula: the least suspected person, the three clues, all those other elements that had to be there.

Briggs: That's what moved Chandler to write *The Simple Art of Murder*.

Brackett: Right. It wasn't until I read Chandler and Hammett that I felt I could write a detective story. I enjoyed reading them, but I wasn't going to strap myself in that straight jacket to write them. Forget it. Usually a genre will break out of that, because once you try to harness it, you kill it. I absolutely detest any attempt by anybody, including myself, to say what science fiction should or should not be. I think there's room in it for every point of view, for every type of writing. I get a little bored with polemics, with people trying to instruct me. I want to know what exactly are your qualifications, you know? I'm not saying they shouldn't write it; I'm just saying it's not exactly my cup of tea. I've always written for the entertainment, and what messages I've dropped in have mostly been unstated. Like: There are certain things you don't do. You don't kick a man when he's down. And, if somebody's your friend you come to his aid and don't cop out when the going gets rough. You don't sell out. You never surrender your self-respect. Somewhere along the line there's got to be an ethic you believe in, otherwise you're nobody. I like the colorful action-adventure story. And I think that one very great thing that every writer in every genre has to do is not to lose his sense of humor and become too convinced of his own over-riding importance. Suddenly, someday, he'll find himself surrounded by people who don't think he's all that important, and it's a terrible shock to his ego.

Apel: It appears we're almost finished here; the thing we generally ask at this point is if there's anything you'd like to say.

Brackett: Wonderful. I was anticipating this.

I think science fiction's chief function in society at the moment is to educate people to avoid the type of "future shock" that so many of them got when Sputnik went up. I was astounded at the reaction among people who considered science fiction "that junk." All of a sudden there's this little thing up there—

Briggs: A little *Russian* thing...

Brackett: Right...a little *Russian* thing up there. It was as though someone had torn a hole in the sky and who knew what might be looking in? And they were practically panicky. We'd been telling them about this for years, and they just wouldn't listen. I think science fiction is important as a forum where these ideas can be disseminated and where people can become used to the concepts. It's absolutely astounding to me, because when I first began writing science fiction the atom was considered indivisible, it was impossible to get a radio beam out beyond the heavyside layer, et cetera. You reach a plateau, then rise from that to reach a new plateau...

Apel: Like FTL drives... They've always been a staple fantasy invention of science fiction, until a few years ago when tachyons, particles that theoretically move faster than light, were postulated by physicists.

Brackett: Yes. And when they found some in the cyclotron, they said, "Oh, it's an optical illusion." *(Laughter)* Like when they found the duck-billed platypus, and some scientists still insisted it didn't exist.

Apel: Those scientists graduated from the same school as the ones who said it's aerodynamically impossible for bees to fly.

Brackett: And that heavier-than-air flight was impossible, and that trains would never go over 30 mph...

Briggs: ...because the acceleration would push you back in your seat and squeeze the life and breath out of you.

Brackett: Poor old Goddard was trying to put his little rocket up, and he didn't dare say anything about space because he knew they'd slap him into a loony bin. He had to call it "high altitude research." The fact that just the very words "starflight" and "FTL drive" can be spoken in public today is very encouraging.

Apel: Well, that about wraps it up, unless you have anything else...?

Brackett: No, except thank you very much for doing me the honor of interviewing me.

Apel: The honor is all ours. Thank you very much.

THEODORE STURGEON

Interview conducted at The Octocon
Santa Rosa, California
October 1977

Edward Hamilton Waldo was born on February 26, 1918, on Staten Island, New York. At age eleven, after his divorced mother married William Sturgeon, his name was legally changed to "Theodore Sturgeon."

Sturgeon's mercurial early years almost define the archetype of a born writer. His first choice of career, circus acrobat, was derailed by a bout of rheumatic fever which left his heart permanently enlarged. At 17, he became a merchant marine for three years, and began writing in his free time at sea. During the following decade, he sold refrigerators door-to-door, managed a hotel in Jamaica, worked construction in Puerto Rico, wrote copy for an advertising agency, edited various publications, and founded a literary agency. All these experiences would work their way into his fiction.

He sold his first story in 1938 and his first genre story in 1939. He was a prolific short story writer throughout the decades of the 1940s and '50s, but is perhaps best known for his trilogy of linked novellas, *More Than Human*, which won the International Fantasy Award in 1954. In the 1950s he was the most anthologized English-language author alive, and garnered much critical acclaim for his accomplished style, even though "science fiction" was generally considered a literary ghetto during that and previous decades.

Modern sci-fi fans might know him better for his contributions to the original *Star Trek* TV series; his two scripts for the series introduced such Trek tropes as the Prime Directive, the Vulcan mating ritual "Pon Farr," and the phrase "Live long and prosper." He will also long be remembered for "Sturgeon's Law"; although variously recorded and repeated, the version he related to us is:

"Ninety percent of everything is shit." (We feel he was generous in his estimate.)

Sturgeon's work was always character driven, often concerning sex and other (for the times) edgy, unconventional and occasionally downright taboo topics, as well as more philosophical explorations of the nature of love. A Hugo, Nebula, and International Fantasy award-winner, his work never came easily, mostly occurring in spurts of intense production followed by long bouts of writer's block. And yet throughout his work runs a deep, almost pixyish sense of humor, of fun, and of delight in tweaking established, conservative thinking.

Sturgeon died of lung fibrosis at Sacred Heart General Hospital in Eugene, Oregon, on May 8, 1985. Six of his seven children, and his fourth wife, Jayne Tannehill Sturgeon, were at his bedside.

THEODORE STURGEON

Apel: First of all, I'd like to thank you very much for participating in our little project here. I'd also like to say that it is an honor to meet you, definitely. We've both long been admirers of yours.

Sturgeon: Thanks very much. But I'm the one who should be saying thank you, because, after all, whose ego is getting stroked here? *(Laughter)*

Briggs: That's an interesting question. *(Laughter)*

Apel: We could open things up in one of two ways. The usual procedure we've been using is to talk to the artist for a few minutes about his or her working habits. But the one I'd really like to try is a Theraveda Buddhist exercise called "What brought you here tonight?" Is there a short biographical correlation between your birth and this evening and event?

Sturgeon: That's an interesting question, why I should be here tonight. This is a series of conventions I've been going to, having avoided conventions for many, many years. Virtually never did I show up at a con, unless I was guest of honor or something. I just did not go to conventions. But recently I decided that was a bad decision. And the feedback from the people that I write for—and that is essentially who I write for—was incredibly rewarding. I'm not talking about ego-stroking, but about the clear embodiment of what it is that I do, and how it reaches people, and what difference it makes to them. I've had some extraordinary experiences in that vein. It's been well worthwhile. But I'll probably stop going in a while.

Briggs: Does that decision relate to your computer-model of the mind—varying the input, et cetera?

Sturgeon: The model I have for the mind is a hopper and a processing machine. You take the inputs of all kinds—physical, social, spiritual, and "X"-type inputs—and they all pile up in the hopper. Then this machine sorts and matches every bit—in the exact sense of computer "bits"—against every single other bit that exists in your memory banks. Most don't match at all, and they're thrown back into the pile. Occasionally they do harmonize or resonate against one another, and that sets up a whole new sequence which can be very interesting, and lead to a story or something like that.

Sometimes it comes in what I call the "pigs with wings" syndrome. It's non-sense, with that important hyphen. It's that quality of human beings which enables them to put the concept "pigs" with the concept "wings." This is why it's very good to have lots of input of lots of kinds—sensory, sensible, intellectual, spiritual.

I think the "pigs with wings" syndrome is the very essence of creativity. I think that all creative ideation since the dawn of intellect has come from that ability of people to put pigs with wings, or ham with pineapple. *(Laughter)* Or eating raw oysters. The guy who ate the first raw oyster must have been the most courageous guy who ever lived.

Briggs: I always wanted to meet the guy who discovered you could eat artichokes.

Apel: Or Brazil nuts, where you have to break three separate shells to get to the meat. Somebody spent a lot of time on that one.

To dig into this same topic we began with, we could go back from convention attendance to longer biographical details. Someone once said about you—derogatorily, I think— that you are a person who lives your own biography...

Sturgeon: Yeah, that was Phil Klass, who frequently turned a phrase because it was a particularly well-turned phrase. Groff Conklin once referred to me as a "slight and bearded satyr." Whether or not I'm a satyr, I'll leave to my heirs to judge; there's no question that I'm bearded; whether I'm slight, however... *(Laughter)* This is a word that came so fortuitously into the phrase that Groff used it. "Living his own biography" falls into that category. Phil's a most extraordinary man, and a dear friend. There's only one like him in the whole world. He's terribly prolix, except that once in a while he comes up with a *mot* so *bon (laughter)* that it really flattens you. He's a super-brilliant guy; a living legend at Penn State.

Apel: Let's approach this subject of biography from a different angle. I read a quote of yours to the effect that the only reason you wrote was to justify all the things you didn't do in life. And yet, when we look at the list of things you *have* done, it tallies to an extremely wide range of accomplishments...or at least experiences.

Sturgeon: That's a nice way to put it; what I actually said was that if I wasn't a writer, I'd be a bum. *(Laughter)* I have done a great many things, and have failed at a great many things. I've done some things to keep myself alive that I wouldn't possibly give my life to, like being a short order cook, or selling refrigerators door-to-door. I never got particularly good at any of these things, although I did acquire some skill as a heavy equipment operator, because I loved it a lot. But at the same time, I knew I wasn't going to give my life to that. I can take apart radios, tape recorders, et cetera, and fix them, but I don't have what it takes to be an electronics technician.

The only thing I am really good at is writing, and that's not so much a skill as a talent. There is a distinction, a very important distinction. A skill you can brag about; that's something you've worked at and studied hard.

Apel: While a talent is a gift?

Sturgeon: A talent is a gift, exactly. Anybody can be a wire walker, although for some people it would take years of training, and even then they'd never be top grade. But some people are perfect at it the second time they step out on the wire. That's the difference between a talent and a skill. Anyone has a right to brag about his skills. Nobody has the right to brag about his talents.

I knew a guy at one time who was 6 foot 4 inches and 230 pounds. He'd walk into a room and say, "Six-foot-four, 230 pounds." Sometimes at that point he'd crook his arms and rip his shirt up the back. He'd take another step into the room and say, "SixfoottwoahundredeightypoundswhenIwas-twelve." It came out like one word. He had to do these two things before he felt comfortable walking into a crowded room. And neither of these two things was anything he had a damn thing to do about, and yet he had to present himself this way—as if you couldn't notice it. *(Laughter)* A very dumb guy. It was compulsive, bragging about his talents.

Apel: Why don't we talk a bit about your working habits. Do you follow a particular regimen?

Sturgeon: I can't give you a clear answer to that question at all. I really can't. There's no way of working that I have not done or do not do. For example, at a time when I thought I didn't want to write, I tried to arrange things so that I *did* want to write; I mean really and truly *want* to write. I was working at the time for Time, Inc., so what I did was come home from work every day and write one page, double spaced. One page, that's all; that's less than 300 words. When I reached the bottom of the page I'd stop—in the middle of the sentence, even in the middle of a word. Well, after the third or fourth day of doing that, all I wanted to do was finish. So in 28 days I wrote a 28 page story. It was very consistent in tone. The title was "Shadow, Shadow, On the Wall." That technique was so successful that I never used it again. *(Laughter)*

I am the world's greatest authority on writer's block. One time I had it for six years. And when you have a wife and children on your agenda of responsibility, it gets a little rough.

Apel: So you can reveal the secret of how to break through writer's block?

Sturgeon: That's a little like asking how one breaks through the sniffles. Or cancer. It's a whole matrix for things that can come from a variety of causes. There are certain simple tests you can make to find out in what general area your writer's block is located. One is the "four typewriter" technique. Or use one typewriter; it'll still work. Say you have a story in one typewriter and it just won't come. So without wasting too much time on that, you take it out of the typewriter altogether, and start on a completely different, brand new story.

Apel: Richard Francis Burton and his wife used to write like that. They had a room set aside for writing, where they would be working on as many as seventeen different books at one time, each laid out on a separate table. When they grew bored of one, they'd just switch tables and work on another.

Sturgeon: That's right. If, however, you find that you can't write that second story, then you take a story that you have written but are not satisfied with, and begin to rewrite it, and clean it up.

If you find that you literally can't do that, then you get the telephone book, and set it beside the fourth typewriter, and start copying names.

If you discover you can't do that, you've discovered you don't have a writing block, you've got a *doing* block. If you're in that condition, you'll find that you probably haven't washed the dishes, or brushed your teeth, or taken a bath, or done anything. And that has nothing at all to do with writing; that's depression.

That's one reason. Another reason is the amateur's perfectionism. The amateur hits one phrase that he can't get right and sits for two weeks working on it. This comes from his conviction that everything he writes is etched in steel and can never be retracted, and that he's going to be blamed for it. He's afraid to confront that.

Apel: What about the other side of that? Salinger and Capote both write that way, agonizing over each word and phrase. Does your theory include them, too?

Sturgeon: Yes, absolutely. It's probably that subliminally they don't like the story, or the market, or the editor, or being writers, or something else entirely.

Briggs: I had a teacher who maintained that that was true; that perfectionists didn't really want to be writers. Someone called him on it and said, "Well, what about Hemingway? He wrote the end of *The Sun Also Rises* twenty-seven times." And the teacher said, "And he *still* didn't get it right!" *(Laughter)*

Sturgeon: It gives you a really high altitude to be a perfectionist. What you're writing has to be worth perfection; it has to be really good, or this is just bullshit. I don't for a moment mean that you should be careless. What I mean is that it is all wet clay; it's all malleable. My advice to students who come up with that particular difficulty is feel free to do it wrong. I've said this over and over and over again. Feel free to do it wrong...but do it.

Apel: One of the most valuable pieces of advice I ever got relates directly to this: a wise friend of mine told me, "If you write enough shit, then pile it up and stand on it, you can see a long way."

Sturgeon: That's right. Concerning this malleability: suppose you write a story and sell it. Well, you can still change it if you call the editor and explain your changes. If he's any kind of editor and can see the improvement, he'll say, "By all means, go ahead and do it." Even after it's in print it's still wet clay, because if it's any good, it's worth anthologizing, and you have that opportunity to change it again.

Apel: Jung had an agreement with his publishers that he could rewrite right up to the time they set the plates for his books.

Briggs: And Yates rewrote his poems throughout his life.

Sturgeon: There are many other ways of curing writer's block; some of them get into the most subtle psychoanalysis-type thing, and some of them just come down to sheer ass-kicking, and nothing else. You can joke people out of it sometimes; sometimes you can fight them out of it. You can get them to argue their position of why they're not writing and just have them reiterate their arguments as if you don't understand, until you have them screaming at the top of their lungs and they themselves realize how stupid it is.

Apel: Act as a mirror.

Sturgeon: Correct. But there's no one cure, because there's no one cause. Writer's blocks are like bellyaches—they could mean anything.

Another thing I tell my students is that writing can be a matter of simple arithmetic: If on New Year's Day you start writing 500 words per day, on June 30th, you'll have a novel...60,000 words. If on the first of July you start again, by New Year's Eve you'll have a second. If you write two novels a year for five years, you'll have ten novels, and if they're any good—good enough to remain in print—by that time you would have made $50,000 in advances, plus your ownership rights, plus subsidiary rights—movies, TV—plus your royalties. Robert Silverberg, for instance, made more money than God at two and three cents a word.

Apel: Phil Dick, too, who did it to survive, knocked out three or four novels a year for many years.

Sturgeon: It goes beyond arithmetic by that point, too. If you assign yourself to produce and produce and produce; to write one short story a week—

Apel: The Bradbury Gambit—

Sturgeon: It is not possible for any writer, however bad, to write fifty consecutive bad stories. He cannot do it. So if you write fifty short stories and two are brilliant...well, writing two brilliant short stories in a year is something any writer would be proud of. If you went on with that process, I don't think you'd stay bad. This long-haired business of "wait until the muse hits you" is for the birds. However, I am going to say in the same breath: I can cure anybody's writer's blocks except my own. I am a lot better at it now, though, from self-examination and from helping other people. The only time I ran across a person whose block could not be broken was Manfred Lee, half of the "Ellery Queen" duo. Manny never asked anybody to help; he didn't want to write anymore, that's what it really came down to. Clearly, that was the situation. I didn't much blame him; he was locked into Ellery Queen for years.

Briggs: Your Ellery Queen novel, *The Player On the Other Side*, is a favorite of mine.

Sturgeon: Yes, I could have gone on with Ellery Queen and made a bundle, but I would have had to devote myself exclusively and totally to that for the rest of my life.

But to get back to the original question, which is my work habits as such: I've written a lot of stories by goofing around for weeks then sitting for twenty hours at the typewriter, not eating, not sleeping, not going to the bathroom just typing, one draft, until I was done. Then I'd collapse for fourteen hours, gather the pages up, and mail them off.

Or another method: After my little boy Andros was born, we moved into an old house with very poor water pressure, so I made frequent trips late at night to the laundromat. And while I was there, I'd take out my pencil and notepad and add a little piece each time to a story, and over the course of five or six weeks I finished it. That story was called "Slow Sculpture," which won a Hugo and a Nebula both, and has been translated into seven or eight languages.

Apel: Beautiful story.

Sturgeon: There's one strange way of writing that happens sometimes, and it takes a Robert Anton Wilson to understand what's going on. And that is to sit down and write something, and when you reread it be absolutely flabbergasted that you didn't write this.

I have a passage in my new novel *Godbody* involving an artist who is kind of a hermit. She lives by herself up on a mountainside, and she does virtually everything for herself: she grows her own food, makes her own furniture, such as it is, and she paints, and she has her own way of doing it. Now, I happen to be one of those people with absolutely no skill in the graphic arts at all. I profoundly envy people who can do it. I can't. Yet that passage contains absolutely informative material that I did not know when I wrote it. It goes further than that about her techniques; it goes into what she calls her "Art Secret," and goes into the mind of the graphic artist: Why the artist sees things the way she does, and does things the way she does. In addition, her idiom—her cadence, and sentence structure, and so on—are quite different from anything I've ever written before. My feeling about that passage is one of real astonishment. It's beautifully written, yet I can't really claim authorship of it. The first time I read it to an audience, the impact was stunning—they were thunderstruck. And it had the same effect on me. If you'd like to hear it, it's on an Alternate Worlds recording of me reading some of my stuff. Very short passage; only about five minutes long. Anyway, what amazes me is the feeling that I had nothing to do with it, in style or in substance. It's happened to me once or twice before; all you can do is leave yourself open to it and hope for the best.

Apel: As long as you mentioned Robert Anton Wilson in this connection, I might mention that he's got a whole group of poems which he swears were not written *by* him, but *through* him; the transcendental consciousness of the Black Virgin of Guadeloupe, where he was visiting, used him as a vehicle for the expression of these beautiful poems, he says.

Sturgeon: Wilson tries to explain everything that happens. I don't. I'll report it, the way I just did this, but I wouldn't even try to explain it. To use Fletcher Pratt's phrase about flying saucers, I want hardware and bodies. The data will speak the truth if we can only gather data and have it revealed to us clearly what the data are, without any foregone conclusions that they are defense secrets, or white-robed people, et cetera. The data will give us the answer.

Apel: The data seems already to be reaping some results. Jacques Vallee has done a lot of interesting work correlating data in books like *The Invisible College.*

Sturgeon: Yes. Wilson goes into this in his excellent book *Cosmic Trigger.* But Vallee tends to jump to conclusions rather than just lay down data. One of the most impressive books on the subject is Aime Michel's *Flying Saucers and the Straight Line Mystery.* He'd put a dot on the map for each sighting around the world close temporally, and found these things would, say, be sighted in Scotland, then England, then France, and so on, in a straight line. That's the kind of data collection I really am impressed by; that's the kind I really like. The data will produce the answer.

Apel: As long as we're concentrating on external details, we might ask you about your relations with other people in the field. You are one of the most respected writers in this field and are admired both by your peers and by the general readership. Do you find your relations with fans and editors are, on the whole, congenial?

Sturgeon: Yes.

Apel: I couldn't help overhearing—because I was eavesdropping—just snatch of conversation between you and Phil Dick this afternoon; you were saying something like, "I've waited fifteen years to have this conversation with you," and proceeded to talk with him for half an hour or so. Is this kind of thing typical?

Sturgeon: Occasionally. It depends very largely on the people. That conversation had been holding fire, building up in me, for a good long time. It a fascination experience, when you three walked in here and I launched into this, precisely like one of those kids diving off the cliffs at Acapulco, without any preliminaries. Off we went. There are a lot of things that I have been very sure about for a long time that I feel Phil has been bumbling into and out of, into and out of, for a long time, without any clear delineation of what it is. I think Phil recognizes that I knew what it was, too. It's a whole universal concept which I don't think I'll go into in great detail right now. I'm too curious to see what Phil is going to do with it. But it has to do with my whole idea of the cosmos and intelligence, that is to say, entity intelligence...

Apel: If you want to go into it in great detail, that's what we're here for...

Sturgeon: Well, as I say, it's complex, and I don't want to use up the entire interview time with this; it's too large. But it was a fascinating experience, to be able to talk with him about this. I've really only gotten together with him twice before. Once was when I lectured I Fullerton, but I couldn't spend much time with him. Another time he came up to the house; he just blew in like a northwest gale, surrounded by flying icicles and withered leaves; he roared in and roared out, and that was that. On the other hand, I've read a lot of what he's written and am profoundly impressed by it. He is one of the great talents around. It's a wild talent, but there's a reason for that, too. I think he's on the very verge now of confronting who he really is. The kind of thing that Phil Dick does reaches very deeply into his readers, and actually dictates their actions and their thoughts to a great degree. And Phil is willing to take responsibility for that. He wants more than anything else to be free to write, and life keeps piling things on him, making him afraid, making him wary, and sometimes making him aggressive. When he drives away devils, sometimes the devils are there...but sometimes they're not, and he drives them away anyway, which makes it a little rough on his surroundings. A writer like Phil ought to be a writer who writes.

Apel: Is that how you consider yourself?

Sturgeon: I have just reached the position of being a writer who writes, and I credit my Lady Jayne [Tannehill] with that. I met Jayne in July of 1976 at a convention in San Diego, and ever since then my life has been straightening out. She's perfectly incredible. She's a gigantic organizer; she can get things really straight. But she does this without nagging. It's difficult to even describe the extent to which she's been a help to me. She's one of the few human beings who I really and truly want to be with twenty-four hours a day. Whenever she isn't around I feel I've been amputated and I'm waving a little stump; it hurts and it bleeds until she gets back. This has been consistently true and there's no sign of it dwindling at all. Jayne is a psychic, she knows the I Ching, she's a Silva Mind Control graduate—she can cure your headache over the telephone—she teaches children, she's been with the San Diego school system for twelve years as a reading specialist, and so on. Amazing abilities.

When I went to do the recorded version of the middle section of *More Than Human*, it took me six months to adapt it. It had to be cut fifty-two percent, and it was like amputating my baby's toes, one by one, without an anesthetic. So when we went to do a second album and decided to include the first section of *More Than Human*, Jayne suggested I make two copies so she could edit one. So I took my copy, looked at page one, knocked out a "the" and an "and" *(Laughter)*; Jayne, in six hours, did what took me six months to do before. And she did it so clean that I took her abridgment over to Capitol records and recorded it in under two hours. It so impressed the producer that he hired Jayne to do abridgments, and in the past two weeks she's done *Tender Is The Night* and has begun to work on Jane Austin's *Sense and Sensibility*. What's more, she's marvelous with children...

Briggs: One of the things that I think is striking about your work is that you portray children so well.

Sturgeon: I have a clear ambiance with children. I can evoke a smile out of infants just days old with no effort.

Briggs: I used to be a professional Santa Claus. I like children. I think they're in far better shape than anyone ever gives them credit for.

Sturgeon: And so beautifully straightforward. Lying comes so difficult for them.

Apel: The way you portray them is always at least sympathetic, as in, say, *More Than Human*, or "Bulkhead." But sometimes it goes even deeper than that, like the society in *Venus Plus X* that literally worships children.

Sturgeon: That book was twenty years ahead of its time. It's just coming into its own.

Apel: It strikes chords not only of contemporary society, in its sexual liberation, but also of Crowleyan occultism, as we are supposedly in the Age of Horus, the "crowned and all-conquering child." By the way, I'd just like to say how pleased I am to hear you speak so highly of Jayne. It seems only fitting that a man who has spent most of his life writing about the hazards and rewards of love should find himself in such a rewarding situation.

Sturgeon: I certainly feel that way. I've never been happier in my whole life. Really, this is what I've been searching for, almost finding, time and time again. We fit. In many ways, our relationship bears striking similarities to those discussed in a novel entitled *2150*.

Apel: *2150 A.D.*? The "Macro Love Story"?

Sturgeon: You know the book?

Apel: Inside out. A great book. If you'll allow me, I'll give you my analysis, then we can get the "professional opinion"... *(Laughter)*

Sturgeon: By all means. I'd like to hear what you have to say.

Apel: Thank you. I think a little background is probably necessary, though, to explain why I feel so close to that book. I wrote a Utopian novel myself, but because of the limitations of the real-life characters I was working with, I couldn't talk much about either sex or violence. So when I read *2150 A.D.*, I immediately saw it as the opposite side of the same coin I was working with. It deals graphically with violence and intimately with sex. I don't think it was very well written, but the ideas contained in it are so important and—specifically—so archetypal that it didn't matter that the author wasn't Shakespeare. The book is larger than the author and seems almost to have been written through her, as we were discussing earlier. *2150 A.D.* is one of the three books I recommend unequivocally to people who are looking for books on consciousness expansion. Now the professional opinion.

Sturgeon: Well, a little history is necessary first. One of Jayne's high school students recommended it to her, and when she read it, it absolutely blew her away. It was so much what she had been looking for, inwardly, that she began teaching it, in a class on American Folklore. She wrote to Thea Alexander to ask about a quantity discount, because she couldn't get the book cleared by the district in time to order it through them, and Thea wrote back saying that they'd work out some price, and included a P.S.—"The books are on the way." Even before they agreed on the price, there was that trust. Jayne has also run seminars on *2150*, on her own, and has traveled to Arizona to meet with Thea for an afternoon.

Now switch scenes: I was guest of honor at a science fiction convention in Tucson, and one of the other guests was Thea Alexander. So when I arrived, I was standing in the lobby, and from sixty feet away the door opens and there was Thea. I'd never seen her before. She's a beautiful woman; absolutely radiant. God, what charisma that woman has got! She came straight across the lobby to me and said, "There's a great deal that you and I don't have to explain to one another." She paused for the barest fraction of a moment, then continued. "They gave me half a suite," she said. "Why don't you ask them for the other half?" Which I did. And we were actually inseparable for that weekend. I've known that woman...forever; for hundreds of years. Since then I've seen Thea several times. Jayne and I went to one of her encounters, and her encounters are something else. The people who leave two or three days later are not the same people who arrived, and the change is permanent and irreversible; you can see that. We've come to know her well indeed, and expect to see her again soon.

So much for the history of our relationship. As far as the philosophy is concerned, I agree with you. A novelist she ain't. She doesn't pretend to be. I urged Phil to read *2150*; I feel the philosophical structure is what he's looking for. It's an extraordinary concept she has; very large, too. What it amounts to, basically, is that we are all asexual entities who are literally outside of space and time. We kind of circle around this great ball which involves both space and time, if you can draw that kind of model, and we say to ourselves, for example, "I would like to have the experience of being an aborted fetus." And we drop down into this "ball" and experience the whole thing, from beginning to end, of our own free choice, and come out again and say, "Hey, that was a real knotty experience." There are a number of things which she brings out in the book which I think are extraordinarily wise. For example, the Macro interchange between people is a huge experience, transcending anything we know in the micro world. It surpasses orgasm, or anything else you can imagine.

Apel: The way she writes about it, it's intimately connected with orgasm, at least in the early stages. Quite similar to some Tantric Yoga beliefs and meditations.

Sturgeon: It also resonates nicely against Tolkien. The power is potent, but unreliable. One can get trapped in it, trapped by it. In one scene in *The Hobbit*, Bilbo is leaving the caves and depending on the ring to make him invisible. He's just about out when suddenly he realizes he's visible again. The ring simply deserts him. In that lies the thinking behind the entire book. Everything in the trilogy ultimately refers back to *The Hobbit*.

Anyway, this Macro power makes it possible for these entities to "inject" themselves into human beings. They are, in effect, writing a script, which is to say, they know in advance what a life is going to be. They just want the experience of living it. They've written a script and are determined to play it through. Therefore, what you are is what you have chosen to be. And to be angry at anyone for their effects on you or for their lifestyle...well, don't criticize another actor for doing such a superb job. That spun my head around.

So the fatalistic idea, or the idea that after death we'll move on to a better land, is just hearsay. There's no basis for that. You must take responsibility for who you are and where you are and what happens to you. You have chosen it, so don't criticize the people who have made the whole thing so very real for you.

Briggs: Robert Frost had a story about a farmer sitting on a fence, and a man comes along the road and says to the farmer, "I'm thinking of moving to this town up the road. What kind of people live there?" And the farmer asks, "Well, what were the people like where you came from?"

"You've never seen a bigger collection of bastards," says the man.

"Folks in the next town are just the same," replies the farmer, and the man moves on.

Ten minutes later another man comes down the road and stops and says to the farmer, "I'm thinking of moving to this town up the road. What kind of people live there?"

"Well, what were the people like where you came from?" asks the farmer.

"Great! Beautiful people; very helpful and friendly."

"Folks in the next town are just the same."

Sturgeon: He was absolutely right. You are what you choose to be, and so is your whole environment. Thea brings up another point, too, which I think is very interesting. We're all familiar with the type of person who makes the same mistake over and over again in his life. One bad marriage after another, or some such thing. Thea says that some entities make the same mistakes over and over again not just in one lifetime, but life after life, because they have forgotten that they are these Macro entities. So Thea says you will never recognize who you are as a Macro entity until you can remember your past lives, which is to say you must recognize the mistakes you've made. When you do realize, when you can remember your past lives, you are then free to leave and go on and go outside and start over.

Briggs: Dashiell Hammett used to call that "getting to see the guts of things"—some experience, like seeing a safe almost fall on someone but miss him, which would be like having the back of a clock ripped off and seeing how things work for a brief instant, only on a universal scale. You get a fleeting glimpse of the intricate interconnectedness of the universe.

Sturgeon: Yep. This whole concept has crystallized a great many things in my life. For one thing, I've stopped repeating a lot of errors. Secondly, if you really understand this mechanism, or embrace this particular model, the whole matter of death becomes less and less meaningful. I've reached a point now where, literally, if I'm breathing my last and I see it coming and you're there, I'll just say, "See you later." It's not finished, it's just a transition. But so is tomorrow morning a transition.

Briggs: I like the Hatha Yoga meditation that says you die with each exhalation and are reborn each time you inhale.

Sturgeon: I can go with that, too. I had an insight while I was talking to Phil this afternoon which ties in to all of this; this is very much a part of what we were talking about. All space and time is here and everywhere simultaneously. There's synchronicity for you.

Bob Heinlein many years ago wrote a story called "All You Zombies." He maintained to me—and I don't think he's ever written this anywhere—that it was not a time-travel story; that was not the point he was trying to make. And he gave me this model: Say you've got an LP record with a great many selections on it—one's martial music, one's a speech, the next one's a waltz, and so on. The record looks like a series of separate concentric circles, but if you look closely enough, you notice it is in fact one continuous groove. And that single groove exists on the record, at all times, all at once. No matter what the contents of the individual selection, it's all on one groove. All the individual selections exist simultaneously, as parts of that same line. What selection gets played at any point is just a question of where you put the needle down.

Heinlein came very close to the whole *2150 A.D.* thing in that story, when you think about it. Anyway, the insight I had in talking with Phil—he was saying he did indeed remember some past lives; one then, one before, then one before that... And I said, "Phil, you're tied into sequentiality there. They're all occurring simultaneously."

Apel: May I suggest a book to you? It's called *Adventures in Consciousness* by Jane Roberts, who does the Seth stuff.

Sturgeon: I haven't read Jane Roberts at all.

Apel: I talked with Phil about this for a while as well. She—or Seth—expresses this same view; it's not a line of lives, but a circle, all lives occurring simultaneously. From the center point, the "self," you draw experiences from each of these lives as you need them, in any order. Projective geometry is a good model to understand this.

Sturgeon: But I still haven't gotten to my insight yet *(laughter)* which was that Phil must have experienced future lives as well —

Apel & Briggs *(in unison):* Oh, he has!

Sturgeon: He pointed out that he got some Greek words in dreams that his wife Tessa translated for him. The point is that our past does have documentation lying around—glyphs and manuscripts, and stuff. The past has left traces; the future has not.

Briggs: Maybe that section of *Godbody* that you received rather than wrote is a message from your future.

Sturgeon: Very possibly. That ties into the insight, yes. On top of that, if the future has left things you can remember, they'd be comparatively meaningless to you.

Apel: Right—you might pick up a future language, but it would sound like foreign gibberish.

Sturgeon: As I said to Phil: "You could not at this point describe solid state circuitry or total diodes or the transistor to someone in 1927, let alone 1727. It would be utterly meaningless. Here is the future, sending back things impossible to trace now. So naturally, unless you are aware and wary of this, you're going to get locked into this idea of sequentiality of past lives. The future ones are coming in, too, only they're comparatively meaningless and very difficult to interpret." At which point Phil began to remember some future ones, which was very interesting.

Apel: I'm sure that if anyone can, Phil can.

Sturgeon: And there's only one area in which to look for future memories: science fiction.

Apel: Which leads by a circuitous route to something we would like to ask you. One of the themes we've been developing in this book is that science fiction seems to be the way this culture expresses many things that other cultures have expressed in myth. It seems as though science fiction is our modern form of mythology.

Sturgeon: Indeed it is.

Briggs: One reason we wanted to talk to you was because you seem to be very conscious of this.

Sturgeon: I haven't always been conscious of this, but I have become so, without question. First of all, the mythmaker is necessary to the culture. Second of all, we are the contemporary mythmakers. And there is no doubt about that. None.

Apel: There is an aspect of this that I would like to discuss with you, but I approach it with some trepidation, because it involves me talking at you, instead of the usual interview process. Judith Merrill said once that she felt responsible for you beginning to teach writing by letting you know how much you know about writing; I've been very conscious of your use of psychology, and would like a chance to let you know how much you know about this area.

Sturgeon: By all means.

Apel: Great. We can start out with the "easy" psychology, Freudian psychology, which is illustrated in *More Than Human.* The three divisions of that book correspond exactly to Freud's concepts of the id, ego, and superego.

Sturgeon: I never had a conscious blueprint of that at all.

Apel: It came out perfectly.

Sturgeon: Yes, it did.

Apel: Lone, the main character of the first segment, represents the id, attempting purely material survival for this gestalt-individual. In the middle section we've got a character who is this entity's ego, who draws them together and give them a goal in the world. By the final chapter the ego has become the egoist, outliving his usefulness and destroying the entity, until the character representing the superego forces him into a moral showdown and defeats him. Only then, with the control of the gestalt entity firmly under the guidance of the higher-minded goals of the superego, is the entity allowed to communicate with the "Galactic Culture" they're developing into.

That's the easy stuff. *(Laughter)* Freud never got much deeper than the subconscious—the personal unconscious. But Jung picked up the ball and discovered the next level of depth in the human psyche, which he characterized as the anima—the image of a perfect woman in each man's psyche—or the animus—the perfect man within each woman. You write many, many stories that deal with anima contact. "Slow Sculpture" is an excellent example of an animus contact.

Sturgeon: It is?

Apel: Surely. A woman in deep trouble finds this mysterious, fascinating man who solves her life-or-death problem and also gives her the ability to form opinions and formulate goals, which is the function of the integrated animus. Her opinions at the end of the story are about relationships, and her goal is to have one with this man. She has thus symbolically accepted her own masculine side, learning what it has to teach her by relating to it without fear.

Sturgeon: It will be interesting to see what kind of work I do from here on out. All those "anima contact" stories are expressions of The Search, and I seem to have found my woman now.

Apel: "When You Care, When You Love" is another one—especially the "Author's Note" at the end, talking to men in their early 20's—"Did you ever feel as if there was a girl in your life who was mysteriously plucked out of the script?" And others come close to being perfect illustrations of anima contact in idiomatic science fiction terms—"To Here and the Easel," "It Wasn't Syzygy," and so on. Shall I continue?

Sturgeon: By all means.

Apel: The function of the animus or anima, as Jung defined them, is to lead the conscious mind to a still lower level of the unconscious psyche, the collective unconscious: the realm of the archetypes; the instinctual desires to organize thoughts and experiences into mythological patterns. There is one story of yours that I would consider a perfect expression of the major archetype of the male psyche, the Hero's Journey, or the Sacred Quest. That story is "If All Men Were Brothers, Would You Let One Marry Your Sister?"

Sturgeon: I find this absolutely fascinating. You're getting into the very core...

Apel: Now we're getting into the really interesting part, down near the core of the psyche.

Joseph Campbell, many years ago, wrote a book entitled *The Hero with a Thousand Faces*, in which he attempted an analysis of the single mythic structure dominating the masculine psyche—the "monomyth" he called it, after Joyce in *Finnegans Wake*. There is one pattern, he discovered, that underlies all stories of a hero's quest, and he considers this sequence the pivotal myth linking the spiritual adventures of ancient heroes with the modern search for meaning. This Hero's Journey has three main stages—Departure, Initiation, and Return—with various substations along the route. A "hero" figure, who may typically start out as a fairly average man, gets a call to action and separates himself from the everyday world of his society, plunging headlong into the depths of the unknown, however that might be represented. In medieval literature, this might be symbolized by chasing a stag or a hawk or an arrow into the darkest part of the forest, or finding some clue that the Holy Grail is nearby. Once the hero-to-be is in the thick of things, he encounters dragons, weird demons, or strange monsters of some kind—

Sturgeon: That's the Orpheus myth.

Apel: Exactly. It's also the Ulysses myth, the Easter myth, the Holy Grail myth...it's the monomyth. Once the hero destroys the monsters which threaten to devour him, he wins his boon. Orpheus gets Eurydice, Jason gets the Golden Fleece—

Briggs: Tarzan gets the Jewels of Opar... *(Laughter)*

Apel: The final stage in the Journey is for the hero to ascend from this dark world and rejoin his society, to try and teach them what he learned. Mostly they don't listen, but that's another story...

Now, I told you all that so I can tell you this: Your story "If All Men Were Brothers, Would You Let One Marry Your Sister" is, step for step, stage for stage, a perfect representation of the Hero's Journey. Charlie Bux gets his call to adventure in a very prosaic way, by noticing certain anomalies in the shipping records from the planet Vexvelt; this spurs his curiosity, and he decides to investigate. Once he gets to Vexvelt, the monster which threatens to destroy him—or threatens at least to destroy his "world view" that this planet is a paradise—is the incest taboo, a dragon in his own mind. This mental monster drives him to beat up another character and actually makes him sick at one point.

Sturgeon: If this had been a dreadful society, he could have understood the incest. But it was a perfect society.

Apel: The price for perfect social harmony on Vexvelt was social ostracism on any other inhabited planet. Nice paradox. But Bux finally does overcome his revulsion and wins his boon—the love of all the beautiful people around him and the peace and contentment of this utopian society. The last stage in his full journey is completed by going back to Earth to try to get the government to listen to his experiences and idealistic ideas about Vexveltian society—which doesn't work, and hasn't worked in the past for those few others who, it is implied, have made the trip to Vexvelt and have gone through the same things Charlie Bux has.

There are many more details to the Hero's Journey, and almost an infinite number of personal flourishes. And your story is one of the few detail-perfect examples I can find that illustrates the theory that science fiction is the modern mythology. That story is the Hero's Journey, told in perfect science fiction terms.

Sturgeon: I find this all absolutely amazing. I really do.

Apel: So do I! *(Laughter)*

Sturgeon: I have to tell you, first of all, I've never been to college; I don't have a high school diploma; I've read only a smattering Freud; I've never read Jung at all.

Apel: You hardly need to. You're illustrating him.

Sturgeon: I'm not particularly knowledgeable in Greek mythology, although after seeing that beautiful, beautiful movie *Black Orpheus* I went running to the encyclopedia to get my head squared away as to what I had just seen. My whole education is so full of great holes and blanks that I'm anything but proud of it.

It's amazing to me that you come up with these sharply focused exemplifications... It really and truly astonishes me, because I have not been educated in these areas, I haven't studied these areas, and yet you give me a whole series of incidents...

Apel: Well, I'm glad to be able to contribute something to your art. I've been waiting for months to give you that specific rap—

Briggs: He has. He's been practicing.

Apel: Yeah, in front of the mirror... *(Laughter)*

Sturgeon: Scott, that's a very fascinating thing. I have no standing as far as being a student of these things is concerned.

Apel: You're a teacher.

Sturgeon: I think you have to be a student to be a teacher, really.

Some other things have happened which have always struck me as strange; for example, I wrote a book called *Some of Your Blood* —

Briggs: May I take a brief moment for adulation? I very much liked *Some of Your Blood.* I think it's an excellent book for a number of reasons. That was one of the first things I ever read by you, and I read it because it was "shocking" at the time. I was vastly impressed with that book.

Sturgeon: I always remember the New York Times review of that book—by Tony Boucher, bless his heart. He said, "Mr. Sturgeon has succeeded in smashing two of literature's most unbreakable taboos, and he has done it with what can only be called excessive restraint." *(Laughter)* Tony was a marvelous, marvelous man. I was so shook up when he died. I just couldn't believe it; it was a totally wrong thing to happen.

Apel: It is in anybody's case... What a lousy way to end your life, by dying. *(Laughter)*

Sturgeon: But especially Tony. I'm angry about having him withdrawn. It's just not right. I really loved that man.

Anyway, I mentioned *Some of Your Blood...* I got an awful lot of mail on that book, and most of it wasn't from science fiction fans, except those letters screaming, "How dare you write a mainstream novel!" Science fiction is my best friend and my worst enemy; I've said that many times. I've seriously been thinking of publishing *Godbody* under a different name. I've got a special agent for that book alone. I must say that the only reason I've stayed within the science fiction matrix is that there's only one other form of literature in which you're so free.

Apel: Poetry?

Sturgeon: Poetry, exactly. I want that kind of freedom, that kind of wingspread, and you don't get it anywhere else. I suppose I could, but up to now I just haven't, although I have done a lot of mainstream work. *Sturgeon Is Alive and Well* is half mainstream stories. It makes a lot of people angry, utterly furious, that this is mainstream.

Apel: That book is a beautiful string of pearls. If I were to go through that book and make a list of my favorite stories, I think they'd be the mainstream ones. "The Girl Who Knew What They Meant" is very touching, and very mainstream.

Sturgeon: Very mainstream, yeah.

Apel: "Slow Sculpture," of course; "Suicide"—I am in awe of that little piece —

Sturgeon: "It's You"...

Apel: Yeah... and "Take Care of Joey"; I love that one. Perfectly controlled writing in so many of those.

Sturgeon: Harlen decided he did not like that book; he called it something like "a piece of shit by Sturgeon." Most of the review was an absolute rave, particularly about "Take Care of Joey," which is an Ellison story if ever there was one. *(Laughter)*

Anyway, what I was going to say about *Some of Your Blood*: There was a long passage of psychotherapy in that book, and the mail that came in came from psychiatrists, doctors, and psychologists, all over the country—and from England, and France, and all over the place. And essentially what most of them wanted to know was What was my school? This is the taxonomist at work again; he's got to find out, Was it Jungian? What was it? So I handled it the way I handled most of my correspondence until Jayne came into my life, which is by not answering it at all. The therapy involved there—although I've never written it up for publication before—was early Dianetics. The first third of the first edition of the first book.

Apel: There's a healthy dose of Dianetics in *More Than Human* as well.

Sturgeon: Yes, there was. But about the mythology, it's absolutely fascinating that you come up with these things. I've not studied these things, I've not read these things, you must believe me.

Apel: No, I don't believe you! *(Laughter)*

Briggs: You've been doing it secretly when we're not around... under the covers, with a flashlight. *(Laughter)*

Sturgeon: From the time I left high school, sometime after the twelfth grade, after having been there six years—I didn't graduate, I was released—I was not in school again (except when I was President of the PTA in Woodstock, New York) until I started lecturing in colleges and universities. It amazes me indeed, because of the structure of academia, to see people getting those brownie points for their post-graduate degrees by burrowing through my works and coming up with conclusions not quite as well expressed as yours. Strange things with titles like "The Emergence of the Nietzschean Superman in the Works of Clifford Simak." *(Laughter)* Or "The Philosophical Limitations of Science Fiction."

Apel: Now, there's a two-word thesis: "Ain't none." *(Laughter)*

Sturgeon: "The Use of the Semi-Colon in Sturgeon's Works." But you really have blown my mind with that one.

Apel: Thank you. I've enjoyed your work for so many years that it's nice to be able to repay you in small some way.

Sturgeon: Things like that spook me a little, though—like discovering my work is being used for graduate and post-graduate degrees. I suddenly visualized myself sitting in my little room, being what I thought I was, a writer who writes. And suddenly all the walls and the ceiling are studded with eyeballs from the future, all watching my every move. Talk about writer's block! *(Laughter)*

Apel: "Eyeballs from the Future"...great *Planet Stories* title...

Sturgeon: I happen to have a deformed toe—the little toe on my left foot sits on top of the fourth toe—so that when I walk on the sand, my left foot leaves an imprint of only four toes. Some posthumous post-graduate is going to go through all of my work looking for references to feet, and finding out what influence my one deformed toe has had on the corpus of my work. Makes me feel very invaded.

Apel: Yeah, and they'll put in an appendix to discern if you were influenced by statements like Salinger's reference to deformed feet in "A Perfect Day for Bananafish." Or maybe an appendix about your appendix.

At any rate—is there anything we haven't asked that you'd like to be asked? Any statement you'd like to make in this open forum?

Sturgeon: I can't think of anything that I haven't already gotten into print.

Apel: We talked a little over the phone about alternate energy sources; you seemed quite adamant about keeping things ecologically pure.

Sturgeon: Yes, I do feel very strongly about it, and I do feel there is no reason at all not to eliminate fossil fuels altogether. The petrochemical industry can make a classic buck by sticking to dyes and lubricants, medicines, and the like, and keep the hell away from fuels. There are so many alternatives. Los Angeles produces enough solid waste which, if turned into methane—not a complicated process—could power the entire Western tier of states. I'd love to see sewage, paper, certain plastics, wood and shavings, and all kinds of things reclaimed for their methane content and turned into methanol. With certain assists from wind and solar power, we could do alright.

One reason I'd like to make a classic buck—and I've avoided making a classic buck for years—is that I've got six notebooks full of ideas for research and development in this area.

So that's my message, if I have a message at all: *Get rid of the fossil fuels*. I've been saying this for years. Get rid of the fossil fuels. We don't need them. They're expensive, they're filthy and they're killing off people and filling babies' lungs with lead, and so on. We really and truly can get rid of them.

Apel: Well, I guess that about wraps it up. Thank you very much; it's been a genuine pleasure.

Sturgeon: You're welcome.

PHILIP K. DICK

Interview conducted at the home of Joan Simpson
Sonoma, California
June 20 and July 23, 1977

Philip Kindred Dick was born on December 16, 1928, in Chicago, Illinois. He and his twin sister Jane were born six weeks premature; six weeks after their birth, Jane died. Although he could have no conscious knowledge of the event, the trauma of her death haunted Dick for the rest of his life, often appearing as a "phantom twin" theme in his work.

The family moved to the San Francisco Bay Area, but when his father was transferred to Reno, Nevada, and his mother refused to move, his parents divorced and his mother was awarded custody of Philip. She moved to Washington, D.C., where he attended grade school, then returned to the Bay Area when Phil was about ten years old. He graduated from Berkeley High School in Berkeley and briefly attended the University of California, Berkeley.

Dick published his first story in 1951 and his first novel, *Solar Lottery*, in 1955, during which period he began writing as a full-time career. Although he was a prolific and popular writer—in his first two years of writing, he published nearly 50 stories, and in the ten years between 1955 and 1965, he wrote 14 novels—his work was financially unrewarding, forcing him and his family to live a low-rent lifestyle for decades—a difficult task for a man who would over the course of thirty years have five wives and three children. And even though he completed several "literary" novels in an attempt to be recognized by the mainstream, no agent or publisher was interested in anything other than his science fiction.

Dick would eventually publish some 44 novels and more than 120 short stories, winning a Hugo and the John W. Campbell Memorial Award. He himself identified his major themes as the questions "What is really real?" and "Who is really human, and who is merely masquerading as human?" His work is often political, with a clear liberal and anti-war bias, and just as often philosophical, with a heavy emphasis on the metaphysical. His protagonists are most often common working people, usually craftsmen, caught in a web of oppression by authoritarian governments, soulless corporations, or unexplained shifts in the nature of their reality, who must nonetheless perform some heroic action against nearly impossible odds. A deep empathy for his characters and their plights, foibles, and character flaws is everpresent in his work.

Outside of his writing, Dick is perhaps best known for a series of unusual experiences which occurred to him in February and March of 1974—experiences which he variously attempted to explain as everything from medication-induced hallucinations to a "divine invasion" of his mind by Russians, aliens, the prophet Elijah, or by an entity vastly superior to the human race. Some of these experiences were integrated into his final books; in addition, they spawned a million-word, multifaceted attempt at analysis in his Exegesis (published as *The Exegesis of Philip K. Dick* in 2011). (The most complete description of these experiences can be found in the obscure and eccentric volume *Philip K. Dick: The Dream Connection.*)

Following a series of strokes, Dick died of circulatory collapse in Santa Ana, California, on March 2, 1982. He was 53. His reputation as a philosopher disguised as a sci-fi writer continues to grow following his death, as has the number of his works adapted into movies. Clute and Nicholls, in their *Encyclopedia of Science Fiction*, credit the "brilliantly inventive" Dick as "one of the two or three most important figures in 20th century US science fiction and an author of general significance," noting that "in all his work he was astonishingly intimate, self-exposed, and very dangerous. He was the funniest sf writer of his time, and perhaps the most terrifying."

For a more detailed biography, we suggest *Divine Invasions: A Life of Philip K. Dick*, by Lawrence Sutin

PHILIP K. DICK

Apel: We're in interview today with noted science fiction author Philip K. Dick. I guess the first order of business is to thank you for consenting to this interview.

Dick: My pleasure.

Apel: We've been starting out most of these interviews with a simple, basic question that allows us and the readers to grasp some kind of reality before we go on to talk about themes and opinions; the question which is foremost, therefore, would be: What are your working habits? Are there definite guidelines you've given yourself as a writer for getting a book produced?

Dick: My working habits fall into two distinct groups. The first group was when if I didn't write three or four novels a year I'd starve to death, and so I wrote three or four novels a year. Mark Hurst, my Bantam editor, says I wrote something like sixteen novels in five years. I don't know if that's true.

Apel: You didn't keep count?

Dick: Well, I just wrote all the time. I remember typing the words "The End," pulling that page out, and putting in another page which said "Chapter One." I calculated I had typed...well, two drafts on a book would be six hundred pages—and I do two drafts minimum—that's twelve hundred pages in three weeks. I was beginning to show real signs of wear. I had an electric typewriter, of course; everything to facilitate a large output.

Then there came a point where there were two factors involved that changed. One, the simple factor of fatigue. You just cannot go on forever doing that much, even if you have the ideas. The physical condition that you find yourself in prohibits it. This was all around 1964, after I won the Hugo for *The Man in the High Castle*. I said to myself, "Strike while the iron is hot," and I wrote.

I was a writing fool. Sixteen novels in five years. Now how long a life span would you want to give a person that tried to make that a professional working schedule? I didn't run out of ideas; I just ran out of energy. I was depleting myself.

Then another thing happened. Terry Carr said to me, "All your novels are exactly the same." Boy, do I remember this; this really got put in my long-term memory banks. He said, "Whenever you pick up a Poul Anderson novel, it's completely different from all other Poul Anderson novels." (I'm not willing to concede that that's correct, but that's what he said.) "Whenever you pick up a Bob Silverberg novel, it's different from all other Bob Silverberg novels. But pick up one of your novels, and they're all the same. And the fans are grumbling," he says. "Why don't you stop trying to figure out what reality is and asking what reality is, as you continually do, and *say* what it is." And I thought: *Golly*! That is pro*found*! I *have* written that theme perpetually: What is reality? And now They—and by "They," you know who I mean...those giant figures that surround you all the time.

Briggs: *Them.*

Dick: *Them.* Yes. *They* say I have to say what reality is, and I never had any intention of doing that. And the reason I never had any intention of doing that is that *I don't know*—I have no knowledge at all of what reality is. All I can do is plaintively inquire, "Hey, gang, what is really real?" And then here is Terry Carr—the great anthologizer—and a major figure in the field—and he says, "All right!" and he blows on his little whistle, like the Recreation Director at camp has... "All right! Time to write about what reality is!"

Apel: "Everybody outta the pool! Honeymoon's over!"

Dick: "You have asked the question, now you have to answer it."

Apel: You're duty-bound.

Dick: Yes. Right. I had a moral obligation. He got me from my Protestant, moral obligation side.

Briggs: Crept up on your blind side, eh?

Dick: So I discovered—as amazing as it may sound—that it was a lot harder to *say* what it was than to ask what it was.

Apel: What was it?

Dick: Damned if I know! *(general roar of laughter)* But I thought: *I'll fake it.* So in 1970 I started working on *Flow My Tears, The Policeman Said.* And it was my intention to resolve the problem by the discovery of what reality really was. So that meant there was a three-year ellipsis in my writing...

Apel: When you had to go out and find out what it was?

Dick: Yeah. Well, I just sort of sat there at the typewriter. I did *eleven drafts* of that novel. I mean literally; I'm not using that as hyperbole. I had a complicated code system worked out so I wouldn't start feeding the old drafts back in, in which case I guess I'd still be there today.

I decided the thing that was really real was *love.* Then I thought, *Y'know, somebody else said this. Now who the hell was it that said this?* Well, actually, a lot of people have said it. My revelation which I'm about to lay on the world is not going to come as a complete surprise.

Apel: St. Augustine said it, and Aleister Crowley...

Dick: St. Paul said, "If I have not love then I am jack shit"... or something like that. So anyway, I worked for three years on *Flow My Tears*, then when Terry Carr wasn't looking, I began to go back to the question of what is real. But another thing happened then—because your question had to do with working habits. Working all those years on *Flow My Tears*, doing all those drafts, changed my working habits. I'd never done more than a rough draft and a final on a novel before. And there were *eleven drafts*. God—I was reshaping it word by word. Once in, never out; I couldn't go back to doing a rough draft and a final draft, just like that. So the next novel was *A Scanner Darkly*, and it took years to write *Scanner*; it just took *years*. The idea came to me in the early part of 1972, and it wasn't until '76 that I sent the manuscript off to Doubleday. And I wasn't trying to say what was real; I was just no longer able to dash stuff off at the rate I had done before.

The novel I'm working on now for Bantam, which is called *VALIS*... They gave me a 45-day deadline to go from the rough draft to the final draft. And I didn't read my contract. I signed the contract when I got the first payment from Bantam. And I was prepared to work a couple of years between the rough draft and the final. Then I looked and saw I had 45 days—that would have just given me time to do the physical job of typing, really. I couldn't believe that my agent would pass that contract on to me, then I read his letter, and he said, "You'd better read this contract." Jesus Christ, I've been in this business 27 years and I still have to be reminded that I should read these things before I sign them. I couldn't produce a final draft under those circumstances. It would have just been a correct typing; a polished form of the first draft.

So I began to play a very complicated game with Bantam. They then gave me a few extra weeks, but at that point it might as well have been 24 hours, because what I discovered in *Scanner* was that when the final draft was completed, after several years from the rough, it was much better than the first draft. The book was *so* much better. The difference was incredible. And so once that fact had been correlated in the processing center of my brain—that if you work on it a couple years you get a much better book—I could hardly reject this and go back to the old system. So I said to Bantam, "Do you want the fastest possible book or the best possible book?" Now of course the answer is contained in the phrasing of the question. They can't very well say, "No, we don't care if it's rotten. What the hell do we care? We're just a word factory." *(Laughter)* Of course they said they wanted the best possible book, sensing as they did that they were falling into a trap. I says, "Fine. I'll have it for you when it's finished," or some such tautology. I'm still working on it. I did a rough draft last October, and this is now June. I've got, like, two years of work left to do on that damn book before I'll be satisfied with it. I've had to get people in the business to go into Bantam and assure them that I'm really working on it.

This happened with *Scanner*; it was so funny. I sent off an outline of the first four chapters, and then I didn't come up with the final book for several years. Even my agent was saying, privately, to people he doubted if there really was a completed manuscript.

Apel: *The Maltese Scanner.*

Dick: Yeah. But of course I did have one. So my work habits now are: I work very slowly and I do a lot of research—and I'm speaking of several years of research—and then proceed at a snail's pace. The only way I can be secure economically under these circumstances is my foreign royalties. If I wasn't getting money from abroad, I would be doomed.

Apel: Where do you sell best, France?

Dick: France, yeah. I've been told that I'm the most popular American science fiction author in France. I used to say it's because they have very good translators in France...really hip. But the real reason is very simple: I'm feeding back to the French public their own novels.

The novels that influenced my writing, when I was in my late teens and early twenties, were the French realistic novels. Flaubert, Stendhal, Balzac, *et al*...and the Russian novelists who were influenced by them, like Turgenev, and so on. I even read the Japanese novelists who were influenced by them. That was what I really liked, that slice-of-life stuff.

Apel: Was that part of your search to find out what reality was?

Dick: Well, in those days, I didn't know I didn't know. I hadn't even formulated the question yet. I read them because I liked them;

I enjoyed them. I thought Stendhal's *The Red and the Black* was maybe the finest novel I'd ever read. And *Madame Bovary* was a close second.

I wasn't writing novels when I started out, I was writing stories. But the second I switched to novels, this inner template based on the French realistic novels just fired like a circuit board. You can see that *Solar Lottery*, my first novel, is literally like the French novels in that respect: all manner of people in all walks of life...portrayed as best I could. It never occurred to me when I did this that these books would be published abroad. That was not a factor that entered my mind. It wasn't until 1964 that I was approached by a French publisher...and I had been writing since 1951, and writing novels since 1955. It wasn't until 1964, when Editions Opta of Paris approached me with the extraordinary proposition that they would publish every novel I had written. They have a fancy book club edition that they put out, and for this they got a picture of me for the back cover, and an article about me by John Brunner. They sent me a copy of the first book—*The Man in the High Castle* and *Counter-Clock World*—and they had a complete bibliography of my stuff. They had everything, and it was beautiful. Oh, my God! In comparison to, like, Ace Books...*(Laughter)* I used to hold the French edition in one hand and an Ace edition in the other...*Clans of the Alphane Moon* is the one I used.

Apel: *(sarcastically)* Yeah...great cover for that book...the guy with the gun...

Dick: *(also sarcastically)* Yeah, right...it's a book about guns... *(Laughter)* So I said, "Holy smoke! I can see a tremendous difference in the physical qualities of the two books. This is great. And they say they're going to publish all my novels." Well, they did not publish all my novels, because other French publishers bid on them and outbid them for a large number of novels. So Opta just republishes the ones they acquired title to. Somebody told me I have, like, twenty-six to twenty-nine novels in print in France.

So it's really very simple as to why my stuff is more popular in France than it is in America.

Apel: You learned the art from them...

Dick: ...and then I fed it back to them. So I don't take any credit; if I had thoroughly mastered the English novel, I'd probably be terribly popular in England. But it's France's royalties that keep me alive. United Kingdom royalties, for instance, come in in hundreds of dollars, but France's come in in thousands of dollars.

I guess that was one of the smartest things I ever did. I had meant to say this sometime in an interview. I think the most important thing for me in writing was before I wrote novels I very thoroughly read and studied a very large number of what we generally agree on as the "Great Novels."

Apel: You educated yourself as to how you should behave as a writer of novels.

Dick: Yes. In other words, I was not raised on science fiction novels. One of the saddest things that's happened in our field, and has been happening for a long time, is people coming in to write who are just science fiction fans *per se*—that is, they read science fiction, then feed back an eviscerated form of what they've read. It's almost like Gresham's Law—making copies of copies of copies.

Apel: You lose something with each generation.

Briggs: Each one becomes more blurry and less distinct.

Dick: I'm really lucky; I grew up in Berkeley, where it was absolutely natural to read people like Proust. You really couldn't get into a party—you couldn't get in through the door—if you hadn't read things like Proust, and Henry Miller, and...shit, I forget what else. It was really a burden. All these damn books were real long. *War and Peace* is an example. You really didn't dare go to a party unless you'd read *War and Peace*, because somebody'd start talking about the scene where she gives birth to the child and dies, and you'd say *[in a cowboy accent]* "Ah've never read *War and Peace*...and not only thet, Ah've never read *The Brothers Karamazov*." Then you'd go right out the door you came in; you're just heaved right out into the street.

So I'm really lucky; if I'd grown up in Turlock, or someplace like that, I don't think the pressure would have been on me. I mean, I even got to read *Finnegans Wake*, which we were discussing earlier. Reading *Ulysses* was *super*obligatory; reading *Finnegans Wake* was almost optional, but it was important that you tried to read it, and could say something more about it than, "Man, he was crazy when he wrote that! It's utter gibberish!" That wasn't sufficient. You could say, "Well, I think the whole thing is a dream, told from the standpoint of the dreaming mind, which is remembering reality, and that Earwicker is waking up," which was always my theory on it. You have to come up with some theory on it, so you have to have some familiarity with it.

But it didn't enter my mind when I read those books that I was going to be able to make use of this knowledge of those novels myself, because I didn't plan to write novels, I planned to write short stories. When I broke into the field there were—oh, God, I don't know how many—maybe sixteen magazines.

Briggs: You published a lot of stuff in those days, too.

Dick: Yeah. Like, I remember in June of 1953 I went to... to... wherever it was I bought my SF...and there were seven magazines which were carrying stories of mine simultaneously. So I was doing nothing but writing stories. Then in 1954, I met an editor at the '54 WorldCon, and he said, "Novels." I said, "Huh?" He said, "Novels. Write novels." I said, "How come?" He said, "You'll make more money." I said, *"How come?"* He said, "Well, *Astounding* will print them as a serial, and then you can sell it later in book form. So you can sell it twice." I said, "That's terrific. I never thought of that. I'll write a novel!" So I went home and wrote *Solar Lottery*. And it didn't work out the way the editor had said. Nothing that I wrote for any of my early novels got bought by any magazine. They just went into Ace Books, and the revenue was not any greater than if I had written a whole lot of stories. Ace Books paid $1,000.

Briggs: Do you have a Donald Wollheim story?

Dick: Matter of fact, I have. When I was preparing the Ballantine collection, Donald Wollheim wrote to me and said, "I'd like to do a collection of your stories." I said, "I'm sorry, Don, but I'm going through my stories to sell to Ballantine right now." He wrote back and said, "Well, Betty"—Betty Ballantine was still editor—"Betty and I have different tastes. Give me what Betty doesn't want." And that's exactly what he got. Wollheim read them over and became hysterical. He said, "These are Betty Ballantine rejects!" I says, "Don, that's what we contracted for." He says, "Well, the stories aren't very good." And I said, "Yeah, and the price ain't very good, either." He published them, but he was grumpy about it. That's my Wollheim story.

Briggs: For my ever-growing collection.

Dick: Oh, I'll tell you another story. He was late in paying me for *We Can Build You*. I was really broke; matter of fact, I was starving to death. My wife and I were living in Southern California, sharing one can of Chunky Chicken soup a day; that was all we could afford. So I wrote Wollheim this piteous letter: "Dear Don: I must tell you that I have been forced to give up writing science fiction and am going to work at Disneyland as one of the janitors who sweeps things up. The reason is because you have not sent me the money due me on *We Can Build You*." And you know what his answer was? "Why don't you come to New York and go on Welfare?" *(general hilarity)* He said that! Talk about your heart of stone! Shit!

Apel: Speaking of *We Can Build You* and Disneyland in the same sentence, I've wondered for years how many times you went to the Lincoln exhibit on some foreign substance and wondered how you could write a book about it.

Dick: Well, you know—maybe you didn't know this—but my book was written long before Disney proposed building the Mr. Lincoln robot. That book was written in the '50s.

Apel: That book is great; it's one of my favorites of your books. It shows great subtlety and amazing depth in its characters. And the humor is magnificent. Like that scene where the splinter group introduces their answer to the Lincoln robot... God, I just roared. So logical, and still a complete surprise.

Dick: I wrote that novel before Disney even proposed to build the Lincoln simulacrum. I couldn't sell it for years and years and years and years. I wrote it while I was trying to fuse my mainstream stuff with my science fiction stuff, so it's not quite science fiction, in the usual sense of the word. Finally Ted White, who knew of the existence of the manuscript, asked for it so he could publish it in a magazine. Ted added a final chapter to it, because—as is well known—writers are incapable of writing their own books. *(explosive laughter on our part; Phil deadpans the whole routine with perfect sincerity)* If it wasn't for kindly editors, who are your best friends, who'll help you out by adding another chapter, or removing one here or there, or turning one inside out, or changing all the names, or whatever, you'd never have gotten off the ground. Naturally I was very indebted to Ted White, and I let him know. The way I let him know was that when Wollheim published the book, I told Wollheim to remove the final chapter. So one day I ran into Ted White, and he said, "Do you know what they did to our book?" I says, "I know exactly what they did to 'our' book, Ted. They took the 'our' out of 'our' book!"

I have seen the Lincoln simulacrum down there. I cut out the notice in the newspaper that Disney planned to build the Lincoln simulacrum and pasted it up on the wall of my study. I remember doing that because the novel had already been written. So he built it and I went down to Disneyland and looked at the goddam thing...

You talk about synchronicity that governs the universe—coincidence which is meaningful... I rented an apartment in a building where one of the ladies living in the building worked at

Disneyland. I said to her, "What do you do there?" She says, "I reapply the makeup to the Lincoln every night, so the next morning when the park is open, it looks real."

Apel: It has a vinyl skin which actually secretes oil, so they have to wipe it off and put powder and makeup on it. It's very close to human skin in its chemical composition. It can bruise, for instance.

Dick: Can you imagine how I felt, finding I lived in a building with a woman who added a touch of verisimilitude to the damn thing? "Well, let me ask you a question," I said. "You see this thing after the park is closed. How real does that thing seem to you to be?" And she says, "Well, I'll tell you exactly how real it seems to be to me." Now it's important to remember that every part of all the rides are continually scanned by closed-circuit television—to make sure no hippies will leap out of the ship and steal the jewels from the pirate treasure, or rape one of the women the pirates are trying to catch up with...

Apel: If you try to blast a reefer on the water rides they catch you at the end and take you to the Disney police.

Briggs: Guys dressed like the Beagle Boys will beat you up.

Dick: So anyway, she says, "One time I was painting the Lincoln thing and one of the monitors was still on. The guy on the screen saw me and reached over and pressed the controls. And the thing stood up."

"And what did you do, miss," I asked.

"I peed my pants."

"I take it," says I, "that you found a high degree of verisimilitude in this simulacrum."

"Sure scared the shit out of me."

Apel: There are dozens of stories like that about the Lincoln audio-animatronic device. The first time they tried to animate it, it threw a fit, thrashing out with its arms, smashing its chair.

Dick: That's another example of precognition in my writing, the Lincoln robot, or... what did you call it?

Apel: Audio-animatronics. That's what they call it. Down in DisneyWorld, they have a Hall of Presidents—all the presidents done as audio-animatronic figures. More robots in that one room than in the whole rest of the world; more simulacra in that one room than in all your novels put together, I think.

At any rate...onward and upward, from the ridiculous to the sublime. We've spent quite a bit of time talking about one of your main themes, which is "What is reality?" I thought we might go into some of the other major themes that run like threads weaving through the fabric of your work. Since we've been talking about *We Can Build You*, this might be a good time to go into the one you yourself refer to as your "Grand Theme," the question "Who is really human, and who is merely masquerading as human?"

You seem to have established that the dividing line between the two categories is *kindness*: an act of kindness separates real humans from "android humans." When we put this together with the results of your search for reality with the conclusion that love is the true reality, it seems to me almost as if you are echoing or perhaps rediscovering the early Christian concepts of *Caritas*, or kindness, and *Agape*, or love. Do you want to comment on this?

Dick: The way you put it, it certainly sounds as if we're talking about the same thing. I had never really thought of it that way before. You've articulated it very concisely, and the articulation appeals to me. It sounds consistent and coherent... which for me is a big relief, when something of mine sounds consistent and coherent.

There was another quality that I felt distinguished the human being, that being the tendency to *balk* at things which were wrong. I developed quite a strong inner image of this happening.

Taking the worst possible social situation imaginable, which would be Nazi Germany, you can imagine, say, in those days, the ordinary police—not the SS police, the Gestapo, but the civil police—were given lists of Jewish people in their precincts to pick up, and they weren't told what would be done with these Jewish people; they were just told to go get them and bring them to a central point. It's very important to understand that these were not the Gestapo, who had a very good idea of what they were doing; these were the municipal police.

A Quaker, Milton Meyer, wrote a book in which he interviewed five different Germans who had either been Nazis or had lived under them—there was no clear distinction; it was a way of life during those years, and party membership was more of a technicality than anything else, because nothing else was permitted. Meyer talked to a man who had been a civil policeman, and the man described how he had been given a list of names of Jews to go and bring downtown... "downtown," like in all the old detective movies you see...that's where the police always threaten to bring you: "downtown." And Meyer asked him, "Did you know what would be done to the Jews when they were brought there?" And he said, "No." And Meyer said, "Did you have any idea that they were to be taken to extermination camps and killed?" The policeman said, "It never entered my mind that there was anything more than relocation involved."

That made a big impression on me, and I got to thinking about this. Suppose you have a job as a civil servant and somebody hands you a list and says, "Go get these people and bring them downtown." Now the mechanical, the android, element takes place when the person simply takes the list, goes to the door of these people, and says, "Come with me." And then this same android quality shows up tragically—and incredibly—among the very victims, who come along docilely, who don't say, "Well, what are they going to do downtown?"

Meyer said it was quite different than what we had been told in most cases, where the Gestapo supposedly bashes down the door in the middle of the night and grabs them and flings them in the backs of trucks, and kicks and beats and humiliates them. It was more a procedural thing where the local constabulary would knock politely and would say, "Would you get your possessions and come with me."

The idea occurred to me that the human element would come in where the policeman would say, "Wait a minute. I want to know what you're going to do with these people." I got this idea of *balking*; this very vivid picture of a human being suddenly stopping in his tracks, just literally physically stopping, and turning around, and then I had a vivid image of this person saying, "No, I won't do this. I won't go get these people. I don't really know why I won't get them, because I don't know what's going to happen to them...maybe that's why I won't go get them." Or the victim saying, "No, I won't come with you." This is exactly what did *not* happen. Except for the uprising of the Warsaw ghetto, the Jewish people came along. Meyer discovered this, too: everybody just simply did what they were told.

So I got this vivid picture of the human element...somebody, anywhere along the line, balking. Some secretary, for instance, who has to type up the list. All of a sudden she could say to herself, "No, I'm going to leave a name out...or I'm going to leave two names out...or I'm going to give the addresses wrong," or something like that. I got to thinking about this as one of the fundamental constituents of the human being. W. H. Auden put it this way: "There is some shit up with which I will not put." But that requires that you know it's shit you're putting up with, whether it's some humiliating thing or some hostile thing, or some degrading or unjust thing. If you know that these people are going to be murdered and you perform your duty, you round them up, then you are a clear collaborator and conspirator in murder. A court would agree. And you are as guilty as anybody else along the line.

The point is that all five of the people that Meyer talked to really didn't know, and all that really would have been required would have been some balking along the line by people here and there, and the structure would have begun to become unglued.

Apel: This balking, then, is more than just a sense of guilt, correct? It would involve taking action on that moral decision that something is wrong.

Dick: Right. Actually, I got the idea clearly from a book written by Martin Buber's wife, who was in an extermination camp. There were Jehovah's Witnesses there; they're taught to "obey Caesar," but not salute the flag, and so on, and that's how they wound up in the camps: they would not accept the national political authority. Since allegiance is directly to God, they wound up in the camps with the Jews, the Gypsies and the Communists, marked for extermination. At the same time, they were taught to "obey Caesar" whenever Caesar's edict did not conflict directly with God's. And typing up lists of people who were to be gassed that day did not directly conflict with the Bible. So Buber's wife would see these Jehovah's Witnesses carrying lists of people who were to be taken from their bunkers and exterminated, and she'd say, "Why don't you just lose the list?" And they'd answer, "Oh, no, we couldn't lose the list—we were told to take it to Officer So-and-so." She'd say, "All right; I agree that Officer So-and-so is expecting a list, and if you don't show up with a list you'll be immediately killed. But you know those people are going to be killed. Couldn't you leave a name off?" And they'd say, "No, we were told to type up twenty names today, so we put on twenty names."

And I got to thinking that this is the essence of the unhuman. That is it, right there. Frau Buber had put her finger on the core of what is not human. These Jehovah's Witnesses knew the situation; they knew that they and other people were going to be gassed. And yet they were typing lists, and emptying wastebaskets, whatever, as long as it didn't break some damn ordinance in the Bible like "Thou shalt not salute the flag." They'd go to their deaths rather than salute the flag, and yet they'd type up and carry lists of people who were to be exterminated!

Apel: Do you think they would have left their own names off the list?

Dick: No. I really don't. I think we're talking about the android which has passed over into complete insanity.

This raises the other issue of the relationship between being human and being sane, and requires us to define sanity. There is really something insane about this behavior. The android—and of course, we're not really speaking about "androids" in the strict scientific sense of "a human being created in a laboratory"; we're talking about a form of unhuman behavior, with an element of pathology.

Apel: We're using "android" specifically as you use the term in your novels: a parable of a human; a pseudo-human, or a "Xerox copy"; a person that has all the outward appearances of a human being, but is lacking some or all of the psychic components that distinguish humankind from animals or machines.

Dick: Right. Exactly.

Briggs: Gurdjieff would call them "sleepwalkers."

Dick: Yes. One of the things I've noticed is that many people equate insanity with extravagant behavior—shouting, impassioned violence, and so on. But if something is done very calmly and dispassionately, this is rational. "Rational" and "dispassionate" are somehow synonymous, and a person who speaks in a calm, modulated voice is, ipso facto, a rational person. This is a typical Anglo-Saxon fallacy; you won't find this confusion in Greece or Italy or Spain.

This is beautifully illustrated by the Gestapo. Himmler once delivered a very important speech, a major policy speech, to the Gestapo and SS, cautioning them that they must never enjoy the death of the Jews in the camps. They must never get emotionally excited by it, but must view it all calmly and without feeling.

Briggs: A small-known fact about the SS—specifically the Totenkamp branch of the Waffen SS—is that they ran a training camp for people who were going to be extermination camp commandants; who were going to be physically responsible for carrying out the death orders. At this camp, they took German citizens of perfect Aryan stock and no particularly harmful political opinions and had them executed, under the theory that if a Gestapo man could kill a right-thinking German he'd have no trouble with the Poles, and Russians, and Jews, and Gypsies and other wrong-thinking types.

Dick: What Himmler was really saying was this all must be done as if it were rational: scientifically, not as the result of hate or passion. Therefore, I'm sure that to the people who did it, it seemed a rational thing they were doing. But they were making the same error. It's not sane at all. If you remember the film *Zorba the Greek*, there was a great deal of behavior which, from the conventional standpoint, would be called pathological: people dancing around crazily, swilling wine, breaking things. The book was even more that way: he cut the widow's head off, for instance. It was all extravagant, grotesque, hysterical, bombastic—it was not crazy. Being crazy very commonly can be typing up a list of names and turning them over to the officer at the end of the hall. And this can be even more crazy because it is done in such a dispassionate way. This is what first led me to the thought of the machine-like quality of pathology and of the "inhuman." What's lacking is a sense of perspective, a sense of proportion. If you pick up your instructions that morning when you go to work and it says "Twenty people will be gassed today," and this is typed out, and it's all spelled right, and it's on the right order form, and this seems fine to you, then what we have here is not just an insidious pathology, but almost, in a way, the very heart of true pathology. What we have here is a lack of an emotional grasping of a situation. We have here a purely mechanical mind; a metal sphere rotating without any contact with the earth or other humans.

I remember one time I went down to the Department of Motor Vehicles to renew my license. This is always very traumatic for me, because I don't want to take the driving test. I know what I'll do when I take the driving test. I know how many people I'll run over. So I must pass the written test so I don't have to take the driving test, and I get very frightened by the written test. You can make five errors and still pass. So I went up to the girl with my answers, and I handed the sheet to her, and she was grading it, and I said to her, "If I do not pass this test, I am going to kill myself." And she turned absolutely ashen, and she said, "Oh, no, you've passed; I swear to God you've passed. Look, look here—two mistakes—you've passed." And I thought: Here's a real human being.

Another time I went into the bank carrying the largest sum of money that I'd ever had in my possession at one time: $7,800. I said to thc clcrk, "Every cent of this money has to go to the IRS. What do you think of that?" And she didn't say a goddamn thing. I thought to myself, I see a correlation between insanity, lack of a sense of proportion, and something that we encounter very often in the bureaucratic mind, which processes people as things.

Apel: You weren't a human to that clerk, just an account number. That type of insanity seems to me to be an emphasis on form to the exclusion of all content or meaning. Like you mentioned earlier...if the typed form is correct, everything is fine. It doesn't matter or register that the meaning of the form is the termination of human lives.

Dick: Exactly right. The key word is *significance*: what's lacking is an insight into the *authentic significance* of things. If the list says, "These twenty people will be mailed a twenty dollar utility bill refund," you then mail it to them; if it says, "These twenty people will be exterminated," you *balk*, you see. But the true insane person will calmly, very calmly, process both the same way. And this is what I regard as insanity, rather than regarding extravagant behavior—ripping off clothes, screaming, carrying on—as insane. In fact, you get this dispassionate insanity at times where great emotions are appropriate: when someone has died, when some terrible calamity has happened, the insane one will proceed as if nothing of great importance has occurred.

I remember when I was living in the country, my wife and I had a little baby, so we were up at six AM for the early feeding. And one morning I looked out the window, and wild dogs were killing our sheep—they were tearing their legs off. Now, the sheriff had told us whenever we saw this to call him immediately and he'd come and shoot the dogs. They were killing thousands of dollars worth of sheep—or to put it more along the lines of the way I would view it—hundreds and hundreds of innocent animals. Those dogs were being sought by every sheep owner in that part of Marin County. So I said to my wife, "Call the sheriff." And she said, "I'm busy." She was warming the bottle. The thing was, she had planned to feed the baby at six o'clock. If I had said, "Look, a giant tidal wave is washing toward us, carrying all the houses with it, and we're next. Get out the rowboat!" she would have said, "I'm busy." There was a failure to respond to the gravity of the situation.

We're talking about the inhuman as an inadequacy; inhumanity is the absence of something, rather than the presence. We're always looking for the presence of something. Clinically, we're speaking of the schizoid personality, which technically has lack of adequate affect. I have a lot of trust in schizophrenics, for instance. They have an overabundance of affect. They have frantic crying jags, frantic depressions, frantic manias...

Apel: They are the ones most often pointed out as "crazy," because of their extravagant behavior.

Briggs: Your "baseline crazy" is generally a schizophrenic... although paranoia has been gaining in the last fifteen years or so.

Dick: Right. I remember in a Gilbert and Sullivan libretto the directions, "Mad Meg comes out, the picture of theatrical madness."

Apel: Clothes in disarray; large wild smile.

Dick: Yeah. Eyes bugged out. I thought: That's very interesting...theatrical madness. Gilbert was such an astute human being that he didn't say she's the picture of madness; he says she's the picture of *theatrical* madness.

In a way, your schizophrenic is theatrically mad. I had one poor schizophrenic wife who used to paint herself all over with lipstick—circles, designs and so forth—but she was just a sweetie-pie; she'd kiss you and hug you and all that. But she heard the Virgin Mary talking to her, and at Easter she'd lie on the floor with a lily clutched over her stomach until 3:00, then she'd say, "I'm rising now from the tomb; I'm immortal." And I would say, "Yes, dear; I know it's Easter." Obviously she was crazy. Yet I would prefer this any day to the schizoid.

I'll give you an example of *that*. The woman who told me this was working at the Bevatron...a qualified scientist; educated, intelligent, calm and rational. She had this beautiful orange cat, and I came over one time and he was missing, so I asked what happened to him. She said, "Well, we didn't want him anymore, so we drove him seven miles out into the country and dumped him off. Y'know, a month later he showed up with all his pads worn off his feet, having trudged seven miles, and had come back." And I said, "Well, where is he now?" She said, "Oh, we took him and gassed him."

Apel: I learned a lot about sanity from Scientology; they equate sanity with survival. Basically the position is that the better you are surviving—and helping those around you survive—the more sane you are. This agrees with something Robert Anton Wilson's beautiful wife Arlen once said while we were discussing this same point: her criterion for sanity was how valuable you are in an emergency.

Dick: The schizophrenic is not sane because he overreacts to an emergency; the schizoid is not sane because he underreacts. If the house catches fire, the schizophrenic's immediate response might be, "It is God's will that we all perish, for we are all evil!" This is inappropriate...and doesn't help put out the fire.

Apel: Or he says, "Oh, gee, isn't this a beautiful flame..."

Dick: ...and walks into it.

Apel: While a schizoid reaction to the same fire might be something like, "I have to save my library," when his wife and family are asleep upstairs. Another form of choice that's wrong, that's insane, that's anti-survival.

Dick: I'm not worried about the theatrical madness of the schizophrenic, because it's self-evident that the person has disengaged himself from everyday reality. He wears a very bold badge that says, "I am completely crazy."

Apel: What intrigues me about these people is the dream logic that they seem to use...the same sort of rationality you find in dreams, where the most outrageous events are accepted as perfectly natural. I've worked in several asylums, and in one, we admitted a fellow who went around his first week there telling everyone he was a woman. His second week there, he was not only a woman, but he had been raped, and by his third week the rape had made him pregnant. When he didn't mention his pregnancy during the fourth week, I asked him how it was coming along. "Oh, I got an abortion," he said. A perfectly logical, step-by-step fantasy which bore no relation to reality.

Dick: I remember when I worked in a record store, there was a lady who used to come in wearing man's clothes, with her face painted purple, her hair shaved, and her body rubbed all over with garlic. Harmless enough, I suppose, although it could lead to the Charlie Manson thing.

Briggs: Even Manson, to a certain extent, exhibited the cold, schizoid personality. He would have made a first class SS officer—he never got emotionally involved. You're right; those are the guys that are really dangerous.

Apel: The insidious ones.

Dick: Viewing from a global standpoint, from the standpoint of most cultures, the Anglo-Saxon is a pretty cold fish. Your Englishman is a better example than your American, perhaps. The dangerous madness of the Anglo-Saxon is not that he'll go raving mad, in the theatrical sense, and run down the street painted purple with garlic cloves sticking out his ears—the bizarre sort of things—it's this insidious thing which I feel is an absence of the passions of the heart. They're not literally in the heart, of course—they're literally in the thalamus.

So divide it this way: you've got the person with an overabundance of the thalamus, who goes into emotional spasms sometimes, and we treat him with the phenothiazines, which suppress the thalamus; but the really inhuman person for our culture is the overtrained cerebral person. What I'm saying now exactly conforms to Jung's concept of schizophrenia; that schizophrenia is a failure of adequate affect and an overdevelopment of the thinking function, until the thinking function breaks down by an onrush of contents from the unconscious, which are attempting to compensate for the exaggerated use of a single function, the thinking function.

Apel: It's like pulling yourself up by your own bootstraps—the "bootstraps" being the major differentiated function—to a certain height, and when you lose control you fall that same distance, or deeper, into the unconscious. I really like Jung's idea of the psyche as a self-regulating system, where concentrating too much on the major function of consciousness and ignoring the other three vital functions always leads to an attempt at compensation by the unconscious, so that any function overextended too far becomes its own opposite. There's a word for that...what'd he call it? Enantiodromia?

Dick: Like Jung said, you cannot think your way through life, you have to feel your way through life.

Apel: He was a thinking type; that may explain why he said that. He'd have to differentiate his opposite function, his least developed function, the feeling function, as much as possible, then constantly use it, so it didn't slip back into the unconscious. It's still good advice, though...especially for us cold fish.

Dick: In relationships, especially, the thinking function is inadequate. And the thinking function is overly utilized by the Anglo-Saxon. We have far too great a regard for it. I was interested in this business about I.Q. tests, because the ones I've seen are a deformed culture's way of ratifying the adequacy of its deformity; of certifying its own deformity as being adequate. They feed back their own deformity to themselves as a positive value. There ought to be tests with questions like this: If your cat is sick, do you: a.) take it to the vet, or b.) kill it?

Apel: Yeah. Or c.) chant over it to make it well. I agree with you one hundred percent.

Dick: This goes back to the authentic human displaying kindness. Kindness is a very complex act and emotion. It's involved, for instance, with making exceptions. You can imagine this very simply in the paradigm of the Hall of Misery—from which we have all come—which is high school. It's Purgatory.

Apel: Junior high school is the concentration camp of the American school system, then they send you to high school, which is purgatory, but which looks better by comparison.

Dick: I was going to say junior high school originally; I was thinking that my traumas all came from junior high. But gym class is usually where this all happens. *(Peals of laughter)*

Apel: What never failed to outrage and embarrass me was watching the coaches up in their glass booth above the locker room watching the boys take their showers after every class.

Dick: That's why *Carrie* was such a great film. You take your junior high school gym class and you have some kid who's too fat to climb the rope, all that's going to happen is the kid is going to suffer terribly, and be humiliated. The gym teacher who out of kindness "accidentally" skips that kid's name and doesn't require him or her to climb the rope is exhibiting true humanity. This is almost where it begins.

Briggs: I never ever met a kind gym teacher.

Apel: Well, in all fairness to my old gym teachers, I did have a couple who had their shining moments. One guy in my class got out of swimming once by telling the coach it was "that time of the month." But you really had to work at looking pitiful enough so that it registered with them.

Dick: But you can see it in a simple situation like that. The willingness to make an exception is somehow intimately connected with the act of kindness, which is also connected with the act of balking. A person will do what he's told to do, and all of a sudden he will balk, and this is an exception. So you've got the common theme of knowing when an exception is to be made. And an emergency is an exceptional situation, where exceptional behavior of some type is required. There is no formula for this behavior; you can't post rules for it, because by definition, exceptional behavior is something other than formula behavior. Therefore the total brain, on all levels, must be brought to bear—all its functions and faculties.

I remember one time I had ten acres of land, and I was way out in a pasture, and one of my little girls was heating paraffin to make a paraffin puppet. And the troll who was in charge of the class had not told the children that paraffin has a flash point. When that is reached, it becomes a flame-thrower. It's incredible. So I'm standing out in the pasture hoeing weeds, when all of a sudden I see this column of flame in the house that goes from the stove all the way up to the twelve-foot-high ceiling. Just this jet of flame in which my little girl was standing. I run across the pasture, leap over the fence, run into the house, right past the child, without even stopping, and grab the fire extinguisher, yank it down, turn around, and just confront her with it. She was OK; she had stepped back and the flame had singed her eyebrows off completely, but she was not on fire. The point is, there was no time for me to say, "Let's see now... should I wrap her in a rug?" like going through the list of rules, or a formula: "When someone is on fire, you wrap them in a rug." My cerebral cortex never got involved in the situation.

Later, I worked back to what my sub-cortical reasoning had been: If she was on fire, there was no use running and grabbing her and putting her head in the sink; it would probably take the fire extinguisher to put her out. I did the right thing, but never did I think, in the usual sense of the word "think."

I have a great respect for the older, more primitive parts of the brain. I think these are the things that are going to save our lives when the chips are down. Korzybski always talked about that ten-second cortical-thalamic pause. There are so many situations when ten seconds later, when the cerebral cortex cuts in, it's all over; it's all happened. Anybody who drives a car knows that. If you wait the ten seconds to respond—

Apel: —you're dead, about nine and a half seconds earlier.

Dick: The other side of those instinctual reactions are the times when you feel almost preternaturally guided by a higher destiny rather than motivated by primitive survival patterns. There is a figure that occurs quite often in my novels, a figure which I regard as very real; not a metaphoric thing, but a very real thing. And that is the kind stranger who intervenes and then disappears immediately afterwards. You never know who it was, but whoever it was knew exactly what to say and do. It's a mysterious figure who just seems to be there.

I played that role once in a situation, and having played that role even once, I know it from the other side, too. It's been done for me so many times that I have the feeling that there is something of a supernatural quality in this kindly stranger, that this is more than just an ordinary person. I had the very strong impression that what I did did not emanate from the part of my brain that I call "myself"...the "self-system," or the ego, or me. It came from a supra-personal level, which everyone has access to. If the spirit had struck either of you at that time, that spirit might have animated those levels and you might have said equivalent things.

The human brain has areas in it of grandeur, beauty and appropriate knowledge. Wisdom—incredible wisdom—which is not going to show up on those I.Q. tests which test whether or not you've read *David Copperfield.* I sometimes have the feeling that we really contain superconsciousness in other parts of the brain that are not the personality, that we draw on from time to time. I don't care to be the one to make a definitive statement about this.

Apel: You can always refer people to Jung, who says much the same thing. The ego is just a constellation of these contents that remains conscious for relatively long periods of time compared with those relatively unconscious supra-or sub-personality constellations. Jung often used the metaphor of the ego as an island surrounded by a sea of unconsciousness. And a great deal of his work dealt with delineating those other archetypal personalities that sometimes overwhelm consciousness.

Dick: I sometimes have the feeling that if the conscious ego were to dissolve... something we very much fear—

Apel: "I'll lose control!"

Dick: Yes...I'll paint myself purple and run around naked. But we might possibly exhibit an incredible ancestral or primordial wisdom that might then be free to come forth; a wisdom based on thousands of years of reality-testing and problem-solving and coping, and things like that.

We guard our individual egos we build up during our individual lifetimes so carefully, as if it's the total repository of all skills, all knowledge, all experience. It's really a very limited and ignorant creation, very short in duration. What it has acquired in the way of knowledge and skills is very little. There are really fantastic layers that can be tapped. Unfortunately, we don't have reliable techniques for readily tapping them.

Apel: I'm glad you brought up the whole subject of insanity without being asked, because one of the things I wanted to mention was something that I just recently realized. About the same time you were writing several books—*We Can Build You, Clans of the Alphane Moon*, and others—with the theme of situational behavior versus chronic psychiatric categories, there was a revolution occurring along these same lines in the field of psychiatry. R.D. Laing was asking if it is insane to be insane in an insane society; Thomas Szasz was writing about how society manufactures madness and pointed out that single instances of extravagant behavior were not enough to justify the label of insanity; that the situational context needed to be considered as well; E. Fuller Torrey was comparing psychiatrists to primitive shamans and labeling them labelers of behavior. What makes your books more inherently interesting, at least to me, and even perhaps more valuable than those others was the fact that while these psychiatrists explained what they thought about "madnesses" which are situationally appropriate, you illustrated these same basic themes and conclusions—societal madness versus individual sanity; appropriate situational behavior versus apparent psychiatric pathology—which left the meaning not as a reader's agreement with the author, but as a reader's discovery or revelation.

Dick: The only thing I could add to that is a redundant thing: Since I am not satisfied that there is one single reality—I have this feeling we live in a pluraverse rather than a universe—any critique as to which divergent view is correct must be suspended until we can settle certain epistemological questions about the nature of reality. Since we have not settled such questions as Kant brought up—and before him, Spinoza, or the Pre-Socratics—we are not in a position to state categorically that Person A sees reality properly and that Person B does not. The most reputable philosophers have strongly indicted simplistic views of what constitutes reality; I would include among them people like Heinrich Zimmer, and Jung, and David Hume, for example, who doubted causality. *(Laughter)*

Apel: Jung tried that, too, and came up with synchronicity, causality's equal opposite.

Dick: Yeah. He and Pauli. Since it is an actual fact that some of the finest minds of the different cultures, including our own, have not come to an agreement on a.) whether there is a single reality or several, and b.) what that single or those several realities are, I don't see how we can at this point in all fairness to people give guidelines for insanity. I read some Szasz, and he said somebody who talks to God is considered praying, and somebody who has God talk to him is considered schizophrenic.

Apel: They tell you all your life, "God answers your prayers," but as soon as you start to get answers, they lock you up.

Dick: This to me is the crucial question. I'm not satisfied that we know what we are living within. We call it "the cosmos," but what this "cosmos" is we've really not established, to the extent that we can prove what it is. Until that day comes, when we can epistemologically, empirically demonstrate what the nature of this cosmos is, it is not fit or proper that we categorically label Person A's view of reality "rational" and Person B's view "psychotic." Those labels really presume that we know what reality is. This is really the underlying postulate of just about everything I write, I think. I tackle this one over and over again.

The psychiatrist is forever talking about people being in contact with reality... The most charitable thing that you could say about him is that he's incredibly naive. I remember I was in my teens and I saw a psychiatrist—I was having trouble in school—and I told him that I had begun to wonder if our value system—what was right and what was wrong—were absolutely true or whether they were not merely culturally relativistic. And he said, "That's a symptom of your neurosis, that you doubt the values of what is right and what is wrong." So I got hold of a copy of the British scientific journal *Nature*, which is the most reputable scientific journal in the world. And there was an article in which it said virtually all our values are derived essentially from the Bible and cannot be empirically verified, therefore must fall into the category of the untestable and the unprovable. I showed it to him, and he got very angry and said, "I consider this nothing but horseshit.

Horseshit, I say!" Here I was, a teenager in the forties, and here he was, a psychiatrist; now I look back and see that this man was cemented into a simplistic mold. I mean his brain was dead as far as I could determine. Somewhere along his life-track, his brain had ossified. He thought certain things were absolutely right, empirically right. Like I say, "That box over there is blue," and I say, "Balling sheep is bad"...to him, those were similar statements. Thinking of that kind is rarely encountered in such a blatant form; people usually show a little more sophistication. Maybe he thought that since he was talking to a teenager, he was free to "announce." They don't say that to me now. They don't say, "How dare you question these values, these absolute verities." I'm too old for them to say that to me now.

I tackled the reality problem from the standpoint of having read Hume, Kant, Plato and the Pre-Socratics. And that is what bothers me. We have to solve that problem first: What reality is. Or what realities are. And that point may never come. I mentioned my wife, who said the Virgin Mary talked to her... All we can say is that it is unlikely that the Virgin Mary talked to her.

Apel: Right—a low statistical order of probability.

Dick: I've always had a lot of sympathy toward people who saw different realities than we do. Maybe because I'm one of those people.

Apel: In response to the question of reality, I found a quote in the Talmud that I really liked: "We do not see things as they are, we see them as *we* are."

Dick: One of the Pre-Socratics said, "If elephants believed in God, they would assume that God was an elephant." Even before Plato, there at the origins of philosophy, we have this awareness.

So now do you want to proceed to another subject?

Apel: Well, let's just change directions slightly and talk a bit about paranoia, since we've been talking about the nature of reality and psychiatric categories.

Dick: Let me say, before you proceed any further, that I promise I'll take my medication...and I won't mix it with alcohol. *(Laughter)*

Apel: Oh, now, we weren't going to *accuse* you of anything...

Dick: *Oh yes you were!* I know what you were gonna do! *(Laughter)*

Briggs: We were talking about it behind your back.

Dick: You were planning *the whole time*—I *knew* you were working up to this question!

Apel: A great many of the protagonists of your books either are or appear to be—

Dick: It's a *lie*! It's something that's *said* about them by their enemies! *(Laughter)* Really! On behalf of my protagonists, I resent that. They're misunderstood. They're...they're...*ahead of their time!*

Apel: They're the only ones who *really* know what's going on, eh?

Dick: That's right! There was an article on paranoia in *Harper's* a few years ago, and they said that the word "paranoia" has become an essential word in the counter-culture.

Apel: An essential *lifestyle* in the counter-culture.

Briggs: Yeah—how many hundreds of times have friends of ours or yours said, "I'm getting a little paranoid"?

Dick: That was the point of the article...the word has lost its pejorative context. To be really serious about the subject, if there's one thing I don't want to be, it's a paranoid. If I thought I was, I'd really throw in the sponge. All anybody has to do to stop a line of argument I'm pursuing is to say that it's paranoid.

So...what question did you wish to pursue next?

Briggs: One of the things that I'd be interested in is the relationship between you and your readership. One of the obvious differences between science fiction and other genres of literature is that the science fiction people all get together and wear funny clothes at conventions...

Apel: You're slanting the question already! *(General laughter)*

Dick: That is about as slanted as you'll ever hear... Can't improve on that.

Apel: This is the King of the Slanters here... We lived through lean times together, and he leaned so far he's slanted.

Dick: My conception of my readership was primarily entirely that of the editor who would read the story. I was writing for Tony Boucher, or Horace Gold, or John W. Campbell. When I started writing, you know, I was writing stories, not novels, so everything I wrote I really wrote hoping that it would be bought by one of those three. I always wrote for one of the three major magazines. I was in Berkeley, but I didn't have any contact with fans. I went to my first convention in 1954, and I was mainly interested in talking to the writers. I was entranced to meet people like Jack Williamson and A.E. van Vogt. I couldn't believe I was actually meeting these people—they were gods to me. They still are. I was a fan of these giants.

I'm not sure I have a concept of my readership yet. I'm not sure it's ever progressed beyond the idea of an imaginary editor. To me it wasn't the reader who bought it, it was the editor who bought it; it was as simple as that. The big change in my novel writing was when I stopped selling to Ace entirely and began to sell to

Doubleday, where I was not writing for Donald Wollheim, I was writing for Larry Ashmead.

Briggs: What was it like, working for Wollheim?

Dick: My first contact with Donald Wollheim was your typical disastrous contact between a sentient organism and something that grew on a rock on the planet Pluto. To avoid a libel suit, I won't say which was which. *(Immense laughter)* First of all, Donald Wollheim said, "I will buy it if it is exactly 6,000 lines long. I did *not* say 60,000 words, I said *6,000 lines*. I don't really care what's in it, as long as there are not too many characters and it's not too complicated." That was *Solar Lottery*, and he bought it. He would communicate through these harangues... He'd say, "I really think this book is the worst of them all." He really would say things like that. Such a tactful way of handling matters. Like, he said *The Man in the High Castle* was sick, dated, and not science fiction, and a lot of other things like that, which shows it was a good thing I was aiming for the hardcover market by then.

But mostly I wrote for the editor. I have no idea, even today, of who my readers are. If someone comes up to me and says, "I read your books, and all of my friends read your books," that doesn't tell me anything. Unless he's a very unusual person and has 150,000 friends, he's not a sampling I can extrapolate from. I don't want to sound cruel when I say this, but even if I could extrapolate from the people who come up to me, I would prefer not to. This isn't the right sampling. How shall I put this delicately? The worst thing that could happen to me would be to wake up some morning and find myself imprisoned on a planetoid with people who read my books and liked them. So many horrible, ghastly aspects would immediately be evident: First, they'd want to talk to me about my books, which I wouldn't want to do anyway.

Apel: *(to Briggs)* C'mon, let's go.

Dick: Sorry, guys. I make certain exceptions. That asteroid fantasy would be like an infinity of mirrors, reflecting back nothing.

Dick Lupoff put it very well: In 1964 he was at this party, and was discussing with somebody the meaning of the ending of *The Man in the High Castle.* And (he said) there was this guy, smoking a cigar, who kept trying to butt into the conversation and say what the ending meant. Finally, Lupoff turned to the guy and said, "Will you *please* not bother us; we're discussing the ending of *The Man in the High Castle.*" And the guy says, "Well, I'm Philip K. Dick, and I wrote it." *(Laughter)* I can see myself standing at the periphery of a circle of my own fans, and they're all discussing some book of mine, and I'm saying, "Um...um... What I think he meant was..." and they turn to me and say, "Butt out, joker." It would either go that way, or they'd want to know what I thought, and that would be a drag.

Apel: *(to Briggs)* Let's go. *(Laughter)*

Dick: My books don't turn me on all that much. *(Laughter)* The only book I've ever written that I really like is *A Scanner Darkly*. Maybe that's just because it's my most recent book. I don't even like *Man in the High Castle.* I do like *Dr. Bloodmoney*; I reread that recently, and I really thought that part where Bill is swallowed by the owl and the owl barfs him up, and he's shouting, y'know, "Write letters of protest to President Johnson!" was one of the best scenes in science fiction I've ever read. I like the whole book.

So my concept of my readership is that they are my punishment for having written the books. The next worst thing to being stuck on an asteroid with people who read my books would be to be stuck on an asteroid with just the books. I see this scene where I die and when judgment is passed against me—which I hope it isn't—they say: "And your punishment is a very special one, because you've done a very special thing: You are going to have to read your own books for the rest of eternity...especially *Vulcan's Hammer*!" *(Previous great hilarity looks mild in comparison to this.)*

Actually, there is always the theoretical possibility that there are noble minds of high stature whose calm gaze and intelligent eyes are fastened with loving fascination on the deathless prose which I have produced...

Apel: Well, thank you.

Dick: ...but I think every single part of that sentence is wrong. My girlfriend Joan [Simpson] reads my books and remembers them pretty well, and she's cool; she's AOK.

Now there's a perfect example to illustrate my idea of my readership: I get this letter from her boyfriend which says, "My girlfriend has a complete collection of all your books and she would like to meet you," and gives a description. Even though the description was very favorable, I just imagined this... this *thing*, wearing Coke bottle bottoms for glasses, whose knuckles dragged along the ground when she walked. Something with parts falling off...definitely fungoidal. Something that Lanacaine would be appropriate for. *(Laughter)* But, I thought, *Well, y'know, she wants to meet me*. If fans write me and give me their phone number, I always call them up. Once I saw her, though, I was delighted. But how representative of my readership Joan is, I don't know. I'll never know. I have no concept of my readership.

The thing is, I'm going to write the best book I can write under any circumstances, no matter who the audience is. Like when I drive my car, I drive to the best of my ability. And what I write doesn't always come out science fiction, either. No less an authority than Antony Boucher, at first, would not accept *The Man in the High Castle* as science fiction. Really amazing. I was really surprised that a man of his caliber would say something like this. I heard him review it over KPFA, and he said it was really a mainstream novel. Which is what it really was; once you got through the first page, it was really a mainstream novel. Then I talked to him at a party, and he said, "That book was a breakthrough in science fiction." And I thought, Gee, that just goes to show you the hang-up we all have...that if it's good, it's not science fiction, and so on.

Apel: Yeah. And since you and the book both carry the "science fiction" nametag, a fine mainstream novel like *The Man in the High Castle* gets no critical attention, little exposure, and a tenth of the revenue that, say, a Vonnegut book might bring in.

Dick: I was just going to bring that up. If Glenda the Good appeared to me and said, "I have wonderful news for you...You're going to go the route that Vonnegut went," I'd say, "Wait just a minute."

Apel: You'd balk.

Dick: I think if I have to choose, I'll stay with lurid covers... I don't want to end up writing *Breakfast of Champions*. I mean, Jesus Christ! Spare me being crowned Caesar, then becoming like Caligula and making my horse a senator. Nobody knows what the cover on the first edition of *The Rubaiyat* looked like. Or *Moby Dick*. I liked the early Vonnegut so much, and I *loathe* the late Vonnegut. Actually—this is a terrible thing to say, I suppose—but I've gone so far as to feel a personal loathing for Vonnegut, that he has conspired voluntarily and deliberately to do this. This is not something like "he's lost it," like a singer loses her voice and it's a tragedy, but I think he did this with malice aforethought. I hold him personally responsible. He has debased his own talent, and that's what St. Paul called *hubris*. I know what it is and I don't like it. I'd really rather go back to what Spinrad calls the "peeled eyeball" covers and be published by DAW and go my little way, carrying my little light through my little dark corridor and finally come to the end of that little dark corridor and have the light extinguished, rather than inflate myself like that hot air balloon during the Franco-Prussian War that was one hundred miles in diameter. I don't want to be remembered as the world's largest hot air balloon. I'd rather be back on Grub Street, like in the fifties. They're two awful alternatives—stories appearing in *Imagination* magazine, or inflated, sententious, contentless stuff—but then again, I don't have to take one or the other. I've got other alternatives.

Briggs: I was reading an article about John W. Campbell recently, and it included your name in a list of people who couldn't work for him, just because of the way he was, both personally and professionally. Was there some clash between you and Campbell?

Dick: Absolutely. Campbell once wrote in words that I was crazy. He said, "I can't print your stuff, and I'll tell you why: because you don't believe that the psionic talents really exist. Unless you will place them at the core of society, as the master talents ruling society, and not as peripheral, marginal and external to society, I will not print your stuff." And he says, "Psi"—he liked to use that term—"is a necessary premise for science fiction." And I thought, Well, the same to your cat! *(Laughter)* He is going to tell me this is a "necessary premise" for science fiction? He said, not psi where it's somebody who gets stoned, like in *Slan*, but where psi is solemnly regarded as a lofty thing. That did it. After that I knew there was no quarter asked and none given between me and Campbell.

First of all, I didn't really believe at that time that psi talents existed. I honestly thought they were within the realm of the occult. I can't honestly say I've ever believed in psychic talents as real things. I've written about them, but I've never believed them. I'm still not willing to concede that they exist. I'm now willing to concede that they may exist. I certainly have not built, and will not build, my career around what he called a "necessary premise" to the exclusion of all other premises. I'll stick it in when I feel like it. I'll stick time travel in when I feel like it. If he had said, "Time travel is a necessary premise to science fiction," I would have had the same reaction. The man had simply gone mad, as far as I'm concerned. Fortunately, we had Tony Boucher and Horace Gold to turn to, plus the lesser magazines. Some of the lesser magazines may have been disreputable, but at least they didn't tell you that there was one premise for science fiction.

Apel: I know it's impossible to get an objective answer in asking you for an accounting of your best books, so I'm just going to ask you which ones you're proudest of...and which would get you through the least nights on your purgatory asteroid.

Dick: I want to qualify what I've said denouncing my own writing. Whenever I write a book, I really write as well as I can. That even includes *Vulcan's Hammer, Dr. Futurity*, and *The Unteleported Man*. It isn't that I say, "Well, I'm only being paid three cents a word. What the fuck; crummy pay, crummy book." I really try to write a good book, but they don't all come out good. The intent is not sufficient to guarantee a good result. Some of the worst books I've written—like *The Zap Gun*—are books which I've labored over. *Eye in the Sky*, which I think is a much better book, I wrote in two weeks.

Apel: I love that book. I read it about once a year; I think it's the funniest science fiction book ever written. If you can do that well in two weeks, you deserve to be complimented.

Dick: Sometimes it works and sometimes it doesn't. My agent says the harder it is to write a book the worse it is, usually; those that flow well are better.

Apel: It's interesting that Zelazny says just the opposite. He suspects books that are easily written.

Dick: That doesn't always hold true. I really like *A Scanner Darkly*, and I spent years on that. I really like *Ubik*, I really like *Dr. Bloodmoney, The Man in the High Castle, Game Players of Titan, Eye in the Sky*. I love *Clans of the Alphane Moon*, because the entire thing works up to this one funny scene where they call off the attack on the rocket ship and the robot hasn't been told and goes and hammers on the door.

Apel: I really love that book, too, for a number of reasons, not the least of which is the scene near the end where the relations among all the characters get so complex that the main character has to just sit down for about three pages and try to untangle who is on who's side. He finally realizes that it's an impossible equation to solve; there are just too many people doing too many illogical things, some *entirely on their own*!

Dick: That's a funny book in many ways. I like *The Simulacra*; I think it's a very fine book in some ways. It's incredibly complex. There's an incredible number of characters. I don't care for *Martian Time-Slip*.

Apel: That's talked about as one of your major works—

Dick: I know.

Apel: —but I'd have to agree with you. I didn't find it very original.

Dick: I think it's a dull book, too. I rather like *Now Wait for Last Year*. I finally decided that I liked the last part of *Flow My Tears*, but as a whole, I don't like it. I don't think it's totally satisfactory. My appreciation is directed now at *A Scanner Darkly*. One that I vacillate about is *Galactic Pot-Healer*. Sometimes it seems funny to me, sometimes it seems...stupid. Stupid. Nothing can be said for it. Another one I'm not sure of is *A Maze of Death*. I get different reactions when I read different parts. There's a part in there where the same whole conversation is repeated twice. It's long, and everybody's babbling away. But it's different—it's carefully rewoven so that the second time around it's not the same; it has a different meaning.

Apel: Did you ever see the film *Last Year at Marienbad*?

Dick: No. I've been told about it, though.

Apel: It's a beautiful film, and they use that device constantly. There is a whole "party conversation" built of snatches of sentences and ambiguous phrases that are repeated at different times, and as the action of the film progresses, the same words take on new and different significance every time they are repeated.

Dick: Somebody has told me I had to see that him. Anyway... I don't like *Do Androids Dream of Electric Sheep?* at all; I really loathe that book.

[*Note: This was long before the film* Blade Runner, *which Phil admired greatly. One must also keep in mind that, according to Paul Williams and other of Phil's friends, his opinions of his own books tended to change from hour to hour, and seemed to depend in large part on to whom he was talking.*]

Briggs: Oh, good. I have to tell you I detest it.

Dick: Yeah, there are certain books of mine I wish I could shovel under, and that's one of them. An interesting one is *The Three Stigmata of Palmer Eldritch*, as far as I'm concerned. I have read that and had the distinct impression that it was an extraordinary book—so extraordinary that it may have no peer. It may be a unique book in the history of writing. Nothing was ever done like this. And then I've read it over and thought it was completely crazy, just insane; not *about* insanity, it *is* insanity. God, it's a weird book.

Briggs: If I were to pick a favorite from among your books, that would be it.

Apel: Right; same here. It is certainly in a class by itself. That's the book that should probably be pointed to as your major work.

Dick: I think if anything I write is to be retained within the cultural flow that *Three Stigmata* stands a very good chance. Either it will eventually be consigned to oblivion as a bizarre exercise in madness, or it will be considered a breakthrough book. I have a very strong feeling that *Ubik*, too, contains some important ideas.

[*Note: During a break, we talk of the lives of career science fiction writers and how they end up; Heinlein in his cyclone-and-barbed-wire-fence-surrounded acreage, replete with flagpole and fallout shelter is contrasted with Leiber in his one-room, fifth-floor walk-up. Phil shakes his head sadly. "That's what a science fiction writer fears most. You ought to ask me that."*]

Apel and Briggs: *(in unison)* So, tell us, Phil...what does a science fiction writer fear the most?

Dick: I can only speak for myself, but in 1964 I was driving along the MacArthur Freeway in Oakland, and I saw this horrible old, old hotel—"Rooms by the day or week"—and I said, "I'm gonna wind up in a little room in a horrible old, old hotel in the slums of

Oakland. It could be tomorrow, or twenty years from now, but I feel it coming; I feel this horrible destiny."

Then I tried to think why that would be the case. Why would I wind up like that? A lot of it has to do with the financial situation that science fiction writers are in, except for the great ones, like Heinlein. Isolation and loneliness are what's so horrible.

Writing is a solitary occupation. A friend of mine had great ambitions to become a science fiction writer. While he was writing his second novel, his wife left him, and one of the reasons she left him was that he spent all his time writing. Even a year later he was still asking every day, "Is that the price you have to pay to be a science fiction writer?" He was aware of the great similarity with my life. On several occasions, the woman I was living with would leave me when I was right in the middle of the book, and in a very vulnerable position, psychologically. I had all my psychological energy tied up in the book. He said it almost seems like some kind of fate that overtakes science fiction writers. He didn't mention Leiber or Heinlein. Now he's afraid the same thing will happen again if he finds another woman and keeps on writing.

Apel: It takes a lot of personal fortitude to continue in the face of loneliness and low income; to know that day after day you are going to be alone at your typewriter with just your thoughts. But then, in another sense, I suppose that could facilitate the process of writing: if the outer world is so difficult, it's that much more of an incentive to plunge headlong into an inner world and find fantasies good enough to write about. By creating, thereby recreating your own life.

Dick: That's a good point. I was living that way in Santa Ana. It scared me that my first reaction to my current girlfriend moving out was one of relief and happiness. There's a certain attraction in being alone with my thoughts and working materials. For the first time in my life, I was ready to face that fate that in '64 looked so terrible. Actually, I had a good apartment, a car I liked, and so on. For the first time I could see the advantages of solitude to a writer.

When I met Joan, I had a certain fundamental decision I had to make: not, did I want to get involved with her as an individual, but did I want to get involved with *anybody*. I've been involved with so many women, but it always ended badly...at least it always ended, which to me is synonymous. I finally decided that whatever positive effect being alone would have on my writing, I would always be asking myself, "Why are you doing it?" if I was alone.

This brings in a point that I feel very strongly about in my work, which I really would like to say. I hope you use this in the final draft. I feel that when I write a fairly successful book I'm giving something. I'm not just a consumer, who enjoys the products of other people's work and ingenuity and creativity. I feel that I'm giving back something to the world, the universe, the cosmos, my society, other people. I've done a lot of books and stories, and I've given a lot back. And I want something in exchange, in return. What is it I want back, I ask myself, if satisfaction in writing is not sufficient to justify doing it? Well, I don't want admiration. I don't want recognition. Money, no. Well, you always want all those things automatically, because they're connected with the book. But what I want back from the universe is something that has nothing to do with the books. It has to do with my personal life. It's something that every human being is entitled to and every human being wants. And that is someone to love and be loved by, and to be with. Whether I wrote or not, I'd want that. If I think that I have given these books out of me and I'm not getting an affectionate relationship back, I feel it's a gyp. This raises the issue that my writer friend raised. If he's going to lose his wife because he writes, he's lost the very thing that means the most to him.

Briggs: Funny how things almost always seem to work that way.

Apel: Perhaps it appears to work that way in order to make the thing more dear when you get it back. You have to die to be reborn. The one thing Richard Nixon ever said that I agree with, for instance, is that he didn't mind being thrown out of office, because only if you are capable of experiencing the depths can you appreciate the heights attainable.

Dick: Well, I never believed, like my friend did, in a direct connection between the writing and losing a relationship. They would have left anyway; it just happened that way.

This really raises the question of what a writer really gets out of writing, intrinsically, when money, recognition, admiration are stripped away, and you deal directly with the writer's relationship to the book. What does he get out of the book? I don't enjoy reading my writing; I get uncomfortable seeing my books around. I tend to give my books away, because I just don't like seeing them around.

The one thing that I get back from the writing that is really intrinsic to the writing is this: I have seen certain people do or say certain things that I feel should be preserved; that should not be the ephemer of the moment. I have gotten these people down, saying and doing these kind of things. And it's almost always the same kind of thing: it's a meager person, a person who we would normally not regard as exceptional in any particular way, who has momentarily transcended his meagerness—usually unbeknownst to himself—to strike at the heart of humanness; to encapsulate briefly the very core of human thought or feeling; to act in some way that can serve as an illustration to others because of its spontaneity and profundity.

This is why *Scanner* is important to me, I think. There, more than any other book, I was recording what actual people did and said, which would have vanished into the ether otherwise. I was in a position that no one else was in. I was in a position to remember it and recapture it. These were, for the most part, illiterate people, so they'll never know. Some of them aren't even alive to know. The one thing that really means something to me is little braveries, little displays of strength and courage, and something more than competence.

Apel: This seems to harken back to our early conversation about small acts of kindness that separate humans from animals or androids.

Dick: Exactly. Once I saw this junkie, completely out of it, unable to move, who heard the jack slip while a junior high school kid was changing a tire on a car in our garage. The kid was yelling, while this five thousand pound Pontiac started to roll backward onto him. And this poor burned-out junkie, this guy who thought he had bugs all over him, who had almost no brain circuits left, ran out of that living room, out into the garage, and knocked the kid out of the way of the car. At that instant, the jack gave and the car came down right where the kid had been standing. It could have broken his back. This all happened so fast that I was still trying to get the car door open to put on the car brakes when he hit the kid like a linebacker. But he knew that I would be too slow. I said, "Shit. I was too late, wasn't I?" And this burned-out creature—who's now dead—said, "Yeah. If it had been a convertible, I could have leapt in, but I knew there was no time for the brake." This burned-out brain had known what to do. Then he went back and sank into the incredible brain suffocation of heroin, and lived only another year. He not only did the right thing, but he knew *why* it was the right thing. How he did that was an unfathomable mystery to me.

And there was another element here: his caring; his concern for the kid. We're dealing here with the debris of the human race, the people that Shockley would sweep into the incinerator, you know? The heavy metal used to cut the heroin he used—lead or mercury, probably—formed deposits in his neuro-receptors which were irreversible, and eventually killed him. Yet he exhibited at different times tenderness, caring, and appropriate behavior in emergency situations. The falling car incident was not the only time; he saved my life on another occasion when the brakes failed on his car.

I really want you to use this part, to tie in with what we talked about before. In two emergency situations he exhibited appropriate behavior and could rationally explain why he had chosen that behavior. He was fucked up in ways—well, a lot of it is in *Scanner*. His problem was damage, not merely madness. This was damage to a delicate instrument, the human brain. And yet, on some highly important levels, that brain still functioned. He was still a human being, with the finest attributes a human being can display. I say this even though he was stealing everything I had because he was a junkie. I have no animosity towards him...I stand in wonderment. If this person could exhibit these fine human qualities, then what marvelous capabilities all of our brains must have.

It's like this: After having sent my ship of inquiry into the universe to discover the mysteries of the universe, the ship comes back finally, after twenty-six years, and says, "The greatest mystery in the universe is the human brain." And then I say, "And what is the answer to the mystery?" And it responds, "I just said, it's the greatest mystery, didn't I?"

So what I've learned in twenty-six years of thinking and writing about it all is *where* the greatest mystery of the universe is located. It's in between our left and right ears. It's an incredible thing. There are more possible neuronal interconnections in the human brain than there are stars in the universe, and that should tip you off right there.

If somebody asked me "What have you learned by asking 'What is reality?' for twenty-six years?" I'd say, "I've learned that I don't understand the human brain. But, man, do I admire it!"

Apel: Thank you very much, Philip K. Dick.

NOTE: This interview was excerpted from over eight hours of taped conversation with Philip K. Dick. The entire interview can be found in the book, *Philip K. Dick: The Dream Connection* (Impermanent Press, 1986, 1999), edited by D. Scott Apel.

FRITZ LEIBER

Interview conducted at his apartment
San Francisco, CA
February 7, 1977

Fritz Reuter Leiber, Jr., was born on December 24, 1910, in Chicago, Illinois. His parents were Shakespearean actors and he grew up in their footsteps, allegedly able to recite Shakespeare before he could read. Although a member of his father's Shakespearean theatrical company as a teen, he left to study philosophy at the University of Chicago. When he graduated with honors, he rejoined his father's company, then worked for a time as a lay preacher, and (most significantly) began writing during these side-track careers.

He married in 1936, and eventually moved to Los Angeles, where he had a short career as a film actor. He and his wife moved several times, including back to Chicago and to various Southern California locations, following his jobs (including writing entries for an encyclopedia, teaching speech and drama, and working in a Douglas Aircraft plant). When his wife died in 1969, Leiber settled in San Francisco, which he would make his home for the next 33 years.

Leiber's earliest writings were supernatural horror, heavily influenced by the work of H.P. Lovecraft; later writing incorporated the depth psychology of Carl Jung and Joseph Campbell's analysis of mythology. He is also credited with inventing (as well as naming) the "sword and sorcery" genre of heroic fantasy. His life-long interests thread through his work: cats, chess (as a player, he was rated expert), fencing, astronomy, and the theater frequently populated his works, as did unique takes on the cities in which he lived, which often seemed like additional characters in many of his works. He was equally facile with both short fiction and novels and wrote in both forms throughout his life. His mature stories typically display a humanitarian sympathy and empathy for his characters, as well as an emotional depth that connected with readers—not to mention a sly sense of humor.

"Most of us aren't even fit to carry Fritz's pencil case," Harlan Ellison once allegedly remarked, a testimony to the high regard in which he was held by his peers and his literary descendants. Among the 30-plus awards he won were seven Hugos, four Nebulas, the Gandalf Award as Grand Master of Fantasy, the World Fantasy Life Achievement Award, the Nebula Grand Masters Award, and the Horror Writers of America Life Achievement Award. As *Locus* magazine's obituary summarized, "There have been very few writers so extraordinarily honored."

Leiber died in San Francisco on September 5, 1992, at age 81, of "organic brain disease" following a series of small strokes. He is affectionately remembered by all who knew him as one of the finest stylists in the genre, as well as one of its most gracious and charming figures; not only "one of the greatest writers the field has ever produced," his *Locus* obituary read, "but also, perhaps, the kindest."

FRITZ LEIBER

Apel: Today is February 7, 1977, and we're in conversation with Fritz Leiber. It's difficult to know where to start with a man of your accomplishments. But the hook we've been using to open most of these interviews is very basic, and that is the question, How do you function as a writer? I see the "1,000 words a day" sign on your filing cabinet...

Leiber: Well, that's being optimistic, at least for me now. It's a general goal when I'm writing a story, you know. Something to aim at. That's about four typed pages, double spaced. But if I do five hundred words, I'm generally quite happy, and if I happen to do two to three thousand, that would be tops. It generally doesn't happen except when I'm finishing a story, or occasionally when working on a novel, that I hit a rate like that.

Apel: Is there a particular time you like to work best?

Leiber: I write in the mornings, mostly. I used to be a night person, but I find now I like working early in the morning better. I'm not interrupted then, or so apt to be interrupted.

Apel: Same virtue as night writing.

Leiber: Yes, very late night writing. I can remember when that was a good time, too.

Apel: I know it's the worst form of cliché, but do you have any insight into where you get your creative ideas? The reason I ask is that I once read a description by you once about how the writer peers down into the blackness of his unconscious and sees a glimmering green speck, and just notes its size and its form, then a year or two later he goes back and grabs onto it and pulls out a sixty-foot Leviathan.

Leiber: *(Laughs)* Well, I think that's what happens in the first stages, when you have an idea or three or four that seem to be fitting together into a story; you do sort of let it germinate for a matter of days or weeks—or months, even, if you're working on several things at the same time. Yes, it does begin to build up, and when it starts showing signs of growing by itself, it's generally time to try and write it. I sometimes go through a period where I would like to write a story dealing with two or three themes, and then I go through a period when I just take notes as they come to me, until I've accumulated enough to where I can organize the story; plot it out.

Apel: Yeah, I see your volumes of little spiral notebooks there on the bookshelf... What was the most difficult story for you to write?

Leiber: That's hard to say. *The Wanderer* was sort of tough, because I used so many people in it.

Apel: It's quite wide-ranging in character and location as well.

Leiber: Well, it was a series of events that affected the entire world. In fact, you might say I put it up in the appearance of another planet close to Earth—that was something that would affect the entire world, you know, gravitationally, and people would notice it. It seemed to me that to make it real, I had to describe it from a number of localities on Earth, so I really had a multiple plot to start with. I had to have people who were located here and there all over the Earth, ten or fifteen groups of them. If it had been possible to relate all those people in some sort of personal plot—well, I doubt if I could have done it realistically. And so I had to accept that the plots would be separate and the only thing that would tie them together was the other planet, The Wanderer, and its tidal effect on the Earth.

Apel: And the symbolic meaning of the wanderer that each of the characters read out of it.

Leiber: Yeah, well, they would. I had a planet that would have obvious features that would look like certain familiar symbols to the different people. The moon is the only object in the heavens, really, that when viewed without a telescope has parts—the only object that is more than just a point of light. I wanted to get that feeling very strongly.

I had all these characters, and that was quite a deal to write about; quite ambitious. And at that time, too, around sixty to seventy thousand words was as big as most science fiction novels ever were. I had to contemplate from the start something that would be two or three times as long as that. I knew there was going to be trouble getting it published

I remember at one time, after I'd started it, I contemplated just cutting out most of those different groups of people and simplifying the story a lot; writing it almost entirely from the point of view of the one group of people in California. And I really tried to do that for a few months. But then I realized that that was really just a retreat on my part: I was sacrificing the very effect that had made me want to write the novel in the first place. It took about two and a half years to complete, although I was working on other things during that period as well.

I was really lucky to get it published. I had an advance from Ballantine Books, but it wasn't a large enough advance; it was just the ordinary sort of advance I'd have gotten on a short novel, so it really wasn't enough to finance me during the writing period. I wasn't in the position where I could tell them, "Well, it's getting longer; you'd better advance me some more money."

Apel: That's not what they want to hear.

Leiber: No, they don't want to hear that. I'm happy about it, though. They had the courage at least to go ahead and publish it, which was something, in those days. Because of the structure of the novel, because of the multiple plot, I couldn't get serialized in any of the magazines. Naturally, my agent and I tried for that, but no dice. I can understand why. It was like a six-part serial, and none of them could take on anything of that magnitude.

Apel: Just the synopsis for Part Six would take up half the magazine.

Leiber: Well, a serial, generally speaking, has to have some kind of climax at the end of each installment. In a novel like *The Wanderer*, there are no good points at which to break it. Also, the reader has to carry so much in his memory from chapter to chapter. It would have been far too much if you'd had to break off for a month between parts. Even as it is, there are an awful lot of people who won't read a serial until the last installment is in. They're not used to the serial idea. I think toward the beginning of the century they were. That's the way Dickens wrote...

Apel: And Twain...

Briggs: And Thackery...

Leiber: ...and many others. That way a novel would keep you going for months. It probably had its own special excitement, and gave people something to talk about for days or weeks.

Briggs: Do you think that might be why science fiction is about the only art form that uses the serial semi-intact today? Because science fiction is such a social literature, with people constantly getting together to talk about what they're reading?

Leiber: It's possible. But judging from the people I talk to, about half don't like serials.

Apel: How do you get along with the different social aspects of the "science fiction subculture"? I understand that you're extremely gracious toward fans, and publishers and editors, and anyone who comes to you...

Briggs: You've certainly been gracious with us.

Apel: Yes, certainly. Do you get along well with people who consider themselves fans?

Leiber: Oh, yes, I certainly do. It's odd, in a way, because when I was reading science fiction as a youth and as a young man, I wasn't much conscious of fandom. You know, there have been a number of books coming out recently—*The Early Pohl, The Early Williamson*, and so on—and reading their accounts of their early lives, while they were writing their earliest stories, I found that most of them were very much in touch with other science fiction fans and would-be writers. They were working along together, whereas I was pretty much on the outside, I always felt. I had one or two friends who read science fiction, but they were generally people with whom I was only in touch with by correspondence. So in the early days, I just wasn't very aware of fandom. It was only in 1949, when I was—gee, almost forty years old—that I went to my first science fiction convention, in Cincinnati—the Cinvention—and met a bunch of science fiction writers, and editors, and editors, and enthusiasts. Before that I had literally only known about five or six writers. And I had not seen too much of them.

Apel: Writers within the field?

Leiber: Yes. The earliest were Henry Kuttner and Robert Bloch, and I corresponded with Lovecraft, of course...

Briggs: Didn't you correspond with Kuttner and Bloch because you first knew Lovecraft?

Leiber: That's right. Lovecraft was responsible. My wife wrote to Lovecraft, in care of *Astounding*. We had been reading *The Shadow Out of Time*, and wanted to know where we could get ahold of copies of his earlier writings, you see. He wrote back very graciously and explained that they only existed in old pulp magazines, but graciously offered to lend them to us. My wife told him that I did some writing—I hadn't sold anything at that time, of course—and he solicited me to send him anything I had written. He set a very gracious example to me as to how to behave with young enthusiasts, fans, and would-be writers. So I sent him the first Fahfrd-Mouser story, "Adept's Gambit." After asking my permission, he circulated it to Robert Bloch and Henry Kuttner and August Derleth.

Apel: Lovecraft was, as I understand it, a major influence on your writing. I remember something you said about Shakespeare and Lovecraft being the two big influences on you.

Leiber: I'd say so, in retrospect. It didn't seem that way at one time. A good half of my writing has been science fiction, and Lovecraft really didn't have a great influence on me there. He did influence me in the supernatural-horror story, though I never got into the business of writing Cthulhu mythos stories. But yes, in retrospect, I can see that he was a great influence on me.

Briggs: One of the things that I think is really interesting about science fiction is the relationship between the tightly-organized science fiction fandom and science fiction writers. Everyone we talk to seems to have a strong opinion about fans. Of all the writers we've talked to so far, you are the person who's been most honored by fans—I can count six Hugos on your bookshelf there. So I'm curious about what you think about fandom as a phenomenon in general. Did you ever believe, for instance, that the fact that there is a science fiction fandom at all has caused you as an artist to reach fewer people?

Leiber: No, I don't believe that. Well, I'm aware of a tendency to take certain things for granted that I know fans or readers in the field will know about. I have to watch myself so I don't introduce too much of this stuff into my stories, and write in such a way that there are things in my writing that wouldn't be immediately understood by someone who had no connection with science fiction fandom and who had read very little science fiction. I think all of us have to watch out for that. But no, I think it's helpful that fandom exists. If any sort of writing is successful, there are going to be people enthusiastic about it.

The thing about science fiction seems to me to be that there is a core of these people in science fiction who are very vocal and who communicate with each other. It's essentially just being aware of a more organized, highly aware readership than if you were writing detective, or love stories, or Westerns, or whatever.

Briggs: Another thing we've been talking with writers about is their relationship with their publishers. Do you think you've been well-treated by the publishing establishment?

Leiber: Yes, on the whole, I think so. I think some of the big publishers who do science fiction perhaps don't seem to devote energy and money enough to promoting science fiction. They look on it as a kind of trade that will take care of itself, where they depend on this rather small but steady readership. There isn't much you can do to promote the stories in a general way. But I think all writers are hoping that their publishers will devote as much money and time as possible to promoting their kind of story. There's always a certain amount of competition for the publisher's attention.

Apel: How about your relationship with editors? John Campbell printed your first story, isn't that right?

Leiber: Yeah, that's right. My first story was sold to the magazine *Unknown*, which Campbell edited for about four years. Campbell had a lot of influence on me. In the case of two novels, *Conjure Wife* and *Gather, Darkness!* I sent him the opening three or four chapters, and he commented on those and made suggestions of a general sort. He helped me a good deal in learning how to put stories together and how to plot them.

Apel: We've been talking with a few people about the artificial but financially real distinction between what's generally referred to as "mainstream" literature and that ghetto subculture that publishers with money refer to as "science fiction." Has this split caused you any concern?

Leiber: Kipling, in his day, published a number of science fiction stories that were just run along with his other stories, and no one talked about Kipling writing in some special genre. There was at that time no tendency to isolate his science fiction stories from his historical stories, his soldier stories, his sea stories, and God knows what others. I think that aspect of science fiction being ghetto really relates to the fact that for the first twenty years in this country science fiction was limited mostly to pulp magazines. It was a form of magazine fiction, and book publishers weren't very interested in it. There just weren't many science fiction books published in those days. And there was nobody in this country who came out as strong as either Verne in France or Wells in England. So the distinction was rather natural then. But I think it's been disappearing ever since.

Briggs: Do you think that the fact that your books are labeled "science fiction" keeps them from selling to a wider audience?

Leiber: No, I don't believe that. I think that label is helpful nowadays. The audience is somewhat limited. Every once in a while some fan, or even a publisher, seems to get the idea that there ought to be a sudden, big expansion in readership; that there ought to be something the writers could do that would suddenly double or quadruple the audience. That just hasn't happened. The way science fiction has developed has been through a slowly-growing body of readers. And they are people who are interested in science and receptive to science, and to plots involving invention and technology. I think that this readership really is a minority of the reading public. In many fields I just read for fun and relaxation, and I don't want to have to do a lot of thinking. Science fiction asks me to do more thinking than most other kinds of writing. So I think the audience is limited but growing. Just as more and more of us are becoming aware of the degree to which science and technology are shaping our world, to that degree we become receptive to science fiction.

Apel: I've always been fascinated by the connections between your experience and your imagination. I have a quote from a biographical sketch you wrote entitled "Fafhrd and Me" which says, "Fantasy must be fertilized—yes, watered and manured—from the real world." I wondered if the many different jobs you've had over your life—actor, lay preacher, teacher, and so on—each added something to your writing, to your styles and to your ideas.

Leiber: Oh, I'm sure they did. Everything a person does can be of use someday. I suppose that all the time you're rehearsing what's happened to you, and trying to fit it into a story somewhere. All we can work with is our own experience: things we've actually handled, and touched, and seen, and smelled, and tasted, and that sort of thing. They're the only things we can describe with convincing vividness. Then, of course, that's supplemented by everything you get from secondary sources, from reading about life. Some of that, especially the work of great writers, can be very vivid, too. It's all material that you may draw on sometime or other. I went to the University of Chicago, for instance, and that location turns up in a story called "The Reward."

Apel: You used a university background for *Conjure Wife* as well. Was that drawn from any specific source?

Leiber: Yeah. Specifically, *Conjure Wife* comes from Hempnell, from Occidental College. I taught for a year— '41-42, the year of Pearl Harbor—at Occidental College in Los Angeles. I taught speech and drama. It was there that I began *Conjure Wife*, and it certainly gave me the immediate experience of being a member of a small college faculty. That stuff I used very soon afterwards; *Conjure Wife* owes a lot to that. Of course, I shifted the college to New England, and made it a different sort of college, but there are a lot of similarities. Some of the characteristics of two or three of the faculty at Hempnell are in *Conjure Wife*. So there's no end to the way you do that.

Briggs: Do you ever find yourself in situations when the line sort of breaks down; when you're living something and thinking at the same time, "What a great story this would make!"?

Apel: That's exactly what I was going to get at, that the end to this process might be something a character in *Our Lady of Darkness* said: "I live firmly in the world of art, where fantasy and reality are one."

Leiber: *(Laughs)* Yeah. Usually, there's a time-lapse, generally speaking. It's seldom that what's happening to you right now will turn up in your stories. It's more apt to wait a year or two. Or ten or twenty years.

Apel: That distance can be beneficial, I suppose.

Leiber: I think so. While things are happening, it's harder to tell what details are important, and what aren't. In recollection, you see things a little more clearly and in balance, and can more easily make use of them. There's no rule. It's just that this happens so often it makes authors tend to say the question, "Where do you get your ideas?" is just ridiculous. I remember Harlan Ellison saying in New York last Halloween at the second Fantasy Convention that "Where do you get your ideas?" is the stupidest question anyone can ask a writer. You can explain it, but it's a matter of saying, "Well, all my life I'm looking for ideas. I can use anything that's happened to me. But there are no rules that I've heard about." And so on. There isn't a formula for how you get your ideas.

Apel: I suppose you could develop a stock answer, like, "The space brothers send me all my material."

Leiber: That would be about like it. And that notion has turned up in my stories; somebody makes that remark in one of the cat stories...you know, "All science fiction writers get their ideas from the space people."

Apel: "Our Saucer Vacation" was a little like that as well—humans being programmed by both sides of the "space brothers"—the good people and the bad.

Leiber: Yeah, that's true.

Apel: Another thing that really intrigues me about your career is that you seem to have alternated periods of great activity with periods of relative inactivity. In the forties you brought out *Conjure Wife* and *Gather, Darkness!*. Then there was a lapse of several years, until the fifties, when you came out with some of your best science fantasy stories, all clustered around 1955 or so—a tremendous output of top-flight science fantasy stories. And then again there was another lull period, until the early sixties, when you published *The Big Time*, *The Wanderer*, *A Spectre is Haunting Texas*...

Leiber: Then there was another lapse, and now I've just come out with *Our Lady of Darkness*, and I'm going to have a new Fafhrd and Mouser book coming along.

Apel: And in this latest period we could also list the Nebula you won for "Catch That Zeppelin!" It appears to me as if you have had three or four different careers in writing. You'd break back into print again in a new form, after silences of years. Do you have any explanation for this? Were there specific incidents that stopped you from writing, or specific incidents that started you writing again?

Leiber: There have only been about three or four of these cycles. It's hard to generalize from so few instances

I got started writing slowly, like most people do. And I'd say that first burst built up to writing the novels *Conjure Wife* and *Gather, Darkness!,* and the short novel *Destiny Times Three*. And then, it is true—there were three or four years when I turned out hardly anything. What was happening then was that I got a new job. I went to *Science Digest* magazine and I moved back to Chicago, and my wife and I bought a house, and we had our child, Justin. So those things were going on, and my writing did indeed fall off. The first three years I worked at *Science Digest*... It was funny, I wrote almost no science fiction. I was just concentrating on the work. I was just written out.

World War II brought a sense of danger, of crisis, and the feeling, well, if I was going to write anything, I'd better get it written, because who knew what was going to happen. I mean, I might get drafted, and that would really be it, you know. Either for a few years, or permanently. So there was that feeling: "Better do it now!" It was the threat of death, basically.

Then after the war, there wasn't that pressure anymore, so I sort of relaxed and didn't do much writing. I'd have liked to—I'd always like to be writing. But somehow it seems to take a little more than that. So for about three or four years I really completed very little. The Second World War kind of left me up in the air. I'd been completely opposed to it inwardly—not to the extent of becoming a dedicated or declared pacifist; that was too much. I wasn't about to do that; that sounded as if it would simply be too much trouble, require too much boldness, and might involve me in too much discomfort. But I was opposed to World War II. But by the end of it, especially with the discovery of the concentration camps, which finally proved that yes, the Germans and Hitler were special threats at that time, you couldn't help but feel that the war had been justified, that it was an unavoidable war. For instance: Bertrand Russell, whom I admire greatly, was against World War I, but not against World War II. There were other signs like that. This left me at the end of the war in a rather mixed-up state of mind. At any rate, the result was that I didn't write any major stuff for about three or four years.

I'd always found it easier to write fantasy and supernatural horror than science fiction, so to get started again, I wrote a few stories for *Weird Tales*. Then, gradually, I came back to science fiction. I think, this second time, it was partly due to the discovery of the science fiction community. I went to the '49 Cinvention; about this time Frederick Pohl had become the first agent I ever had. Meeting these new people stimulated me to write more science fiction. I'd gotten over being depressed by the war.

The second time I quit writing was around 1954. That was the result of various personal problems. Chiefly it was that alcohol had become a big problem to me, and I had to get away from that. Also, at the time, it was necessary for me to give up my job at *Science Digest* and try to write full time. This worked out after a few years.

In retrospect it seems a sort of silly decision; I should have been able to keep up my work at *Science Digest* and write at the same time. There are people who have kept on writing a good amount of science fiction while holding down other jobs. Clifford Simak, to take a seemingly comparable case, was a newspaper editor all through his working life, and he was able to write a sizable amount of science fiction on the side.

Apel: Roger Zelazny, too, was working for several years for the Social Security Department while doing his early writing.

Leiber: Sure. James Blish, too, always had another job, up until the last three or four years of his life. But with me, it seemed that I finally had to give up other work, which I did around 1956. Then I got to writing again. I'd say that period peaked around the mid-sixties, with *The Big Time*, going through the production of *The Wanderer*, then later, *Spectre*. I guess it was my wife's death, among other things, that sort of brought that to a halt in 1969. And it was 1973 before I was writing a great deal again.

Apel: How much of an influence do you think that your experiences in the theater have made on your work?

Leiber: Considerable. Coming from a theatrical background has made me tend to visualize stories, to see them in terms of scenes and acts, and set them as you would on a stage. But my earliest stories—say the first twenty years or so—I don't think contained a very conscious autobiographical element. Later on I did some stories about the stage, like the weird story "Four Ghosts in Hamlet." I acted a couple of seasons in my father's Shakespeare company back in the 1930s, and I used the general background of a Shakespeare touring company in "Four Ghosts in Hamlet" quite consciously, so that, in a way, did make use of scenes I knew very well.

Apel: "No Great Magic," your sequel to *The Big Time*, was one that was built completely around the theatrical theme of a traveling Shakespeare company.

Leiber: Yeah, that too. Right, right.

Apel: And *The Big Time* itself is written as if it were a play.

Leiber: Yeah, well, *The Big Time* is written as if it were a play, but the autobiography is slight, minimal.

Apel: You seem to have a rather unique perspective when it comes to autobiographical material. Sometimes it's there, sometimes it's not, and sometimes it's imaginary. In several of your works—"The Lotus Eaters," for instance, and "Myths My Great-Granddaughter Taught Me" and "Catch That Zeppelin!"—that's such a great story!—you are the main character, or some parallel universe version of you is the main character.

Leiber: Well, in "Catch That Zeppelin!" at any rate, it's more the way I told that story, making the writer a man of about my own age, and having the parallel universe brought in as if it might have been just a daydream of the narrator. It does make it seem more autobiographical.

Briggs: There are a number of little things that appear in your works that I know you know something about, or a great deal about. Fencing, for instance, which is why the Fahfrd and Grey Mouser stories have always been instantly more interesting than a lot of swords and sorcery. The details about it are always so precise and correct.

Leiber: There are more people getting into that, and especially the actual fighting with what amounts to broadswords and shields. The Society for Creative Anachronism, for instance. They're working at a sort of swordplay that is more characteristic of the kind of combat you'd have in sword and sorcery worlds than swordplay based on experience with fencing with foils and épée and saber and the like.

Briggs: Still, your stories are so subtle that it sort of fits in that that's the way they fence; even in Lankhmar, the combat form is esoteric and artful.

Leiber: Oh, sure, sure. Yes, that's true. *(Laughs)* Take the rapier—that was a much heavier weapon than the dueling sword, the épée, that represents it in fencing today. You needed a heavier weapon for street fighting, I imagine. The épée simply would have been too light for that sort of thing. The blade wouldn't have been strong enough to survive in the street and alley fighting that the rapier of *The Three Musketeers* was used in. That was a fairly heavy weapon, though they did do thrusting with the point, and so on. Then later on, in the 18th and 19th centuries, by that time they were using a rather light court sword.

Briggs: Chess is another theme used your works a great deal—"64 Square Madhouse" and "The Dreams of Albert Moreland" both had chess backgrounds, for instance.

Leiber: Sort of superchess—he plays during his dreams.

Yes, well, I've probably devoted about ten percent of my "waking intellectual life" to chess, playing chess and reading about it, so it's natural enough that it comes into my stories. And yes, I do try to use the things that I know about. It's just the easiest way. And it's fun to write about things you've had some experience with.

Apel: It's the theatrical background that impresses me as being the big influence on your work.

Leiber: Yeah, you'd think I'd get into playwriting and such, but I haven't done that as yet. I've written short stories in the form of one-act plays, though. Three or four of them.

Apel: Your influences seem a bit different than many of the writers we've talked to. Most novelists point to other novelists as primary influences, but I'd bet you'd say that playwrights were just as significant for you.

Leiber: I've tended to rate plays slightly higher than many writers, simply because I grew up in the theatre. Some of my earliest serious reading was plays rather than novels. So, yes, between Shakespeare and Ibsen, for whom I have a great weakness, and a number of others—I can remember reading Shaw and Galsworthy and Barrie when I was in high school and being very much taken with them, for instance—I would certainly count playwrights among my primary influences.

Apel: I notice, as well, a distinct O'Neill influence. In *The Big Time*, for instance, the drunken doctor bears a striking resemblance to the drunken doctor of *The Iceman Cometh*, as does the theme of gathering a few people together in a small space and a desperate situation.

Leiber: I've always been very conscious of O'Neill, I'll say that.

Apel: I know it's almost ridiculous to ask you if you've been influenced by many people within the science fiction field, since you are the person who has influenced almost everyone else. And yet I detect a strong note of Heinlein influence on your own work. Heinlein is mentioned by one character in *The Wanderer* as another's "god," for instance, and you dedicated "Our Saucer Vacation" to Heinlein as well...

Leiber: Yeah, that's true. I've gotten a lot of my science from Heinlein, to tell the truth, especially in the area of space flight. The same goes, to a lesser degree, for Arthur Clarke and Isaac Asimov and James Blish. They've certainly all influenced me. The writers who have influenced me the most have probably been the ones like those mentioned who do the most conscious popularizing of science and who use actual scientific themes in their writing, as opposed to just the general science fiction background that you can pick up from any writer in the field.

Apel: Something that struck me very forcefully when I read *A Specter is Haunting Texas* is how that book could easily have been your reply to Heinlein's *Stranger in a Strange Land*. Both books were masterful satires, and you used several of the same themes as Heinlein, yet approached them from a completely opposite point of view than as they appeared in *Stranger*. Your Scully was pure theatre, for instance, while Heinlein's Val Smith was pure sincerity, except for the theatricalness forced upon him. Scully came to earth from an alien culture in order to foment a revolution, while Val Smith came from an alien culture in order to ferment *revelation.* Where one of Scully's main problems was personal sexual jealousy, the thing that causes problems for Val is the issue of social sexual freedom. And so on. I really think the two books stand as two opposite sides of the same coin: a symbiotic pair, in much the same way as Blake's "innocence and experience"—Val, the innocent; Scully, the experienced.

Leiber: Well, I'm glad you think that way about them. Come to think of it, there is a certain element of similarity. I've always felt very close to, been very conscious of, Heinlein. The main element of difference is that my characters are more apt to be "little people," rather haphazard in their operations. They don't get so close to the central government and all that as some of his do.

Apel: Speaking of the government—and to tie this into your biography—did your "internal pacifism" cause you any discomfort or affect your work during the Vietnam war?

Leiber: That was an altogether different sort of case than my feelings about World War II. The Vietnam war didn't take any great degree of independence or courage to oppose. The science fiction community was split on that question.

Briggs: I remember there being back-to-back monthly ads in *Fantasy and Science Fiction* at that time. One was a petition listing the names of all those who wished to publicly state they were in favor of the war; the other was a list of those opposed to the war.

Leiber: Even there, neither of the positions was very extreme. I think the ones you might say were "in favor" of the war were saying they thought the United States should honor its commitments to the Republic of South Vietnam. And the others said they were "not in favor" of U.S. involvement in Vietnam. Incidentally, we came in with our opinions rather late. And that was pretty much the extent of our involvement. But no, it certainly didn't present any problems for me.

Briggs: Around that same time, science fiction started dividing into two separate factions that people called... well, everything: the New Wave and Old Wave, the Vanguard and the Old Pros, the Young Turks and Old Turks—and all that sort of thing. Even though you'd been writing science fiction for a long time, nobody ever accused you of being anything but right on the cutting edge of the field. When looking around for old fuddy-duddies to point at, nobody ever looked around and pointed at you. I was wondering if there was some particular reason for that; your cycles of writing, for instance, keeping you fresh.

Leiber: Well, probably that starting and stopping business has kept me out of step with everybody else for the most part. Another reason might be that I've never been terribly close to other writers in the field.

Briggs: Do you think it's because you weren't in touch with other writers that you were never grouped with either side in this latest division?

Leiber: That's part of it. And yet the funny thing was I did come to know that whole group that started in New York in the thirties: Wollheim, Pohl, Kornbluth, Knight, Blish. I went to the first Milford writer's convention in 1956, I think, and afterwards I had close contact with those people. So I always had a sympathy for their kind of writing. I knew and sympathized with some of the more conservative writers at the same time. I managed to play both sides, so I never felt very keenly this opposition between the "old, hard science fiction" or "old style" writers and the "New Wave"; I didn't see any struggle there. Certainly I liked writers on both "sides" of the fence.

Apel: You saw perhaps that this was just another generation of writers coming along, as you had seen it happen before?

Leiber: Partly, yes.

Apel: I've got a couple quotes culled from your works that I thought might be nice to illustrate a few points. Let's try this one:

"And what are man's gods but his imaginings of a more advanced race?" Does that character's statement echo your own sentiments—that what perhaps we are striving for, through such literatures as science fiction, is to contact a more advanced race, or become one? Is that what our mythology is all about at this time?

Leiber: I would say so, yes. Certainly science fiction has been friendly to the idea of the superman, and so on. And when we try to picture the future, if we assume there will be progress, we do have the problem of trying to envisage what the life and concerns of a more advanced race would be. Of course, for a modern person to do that is like trying to lift yourself by your own bootstraps, but that is the concern there.

I would say that one of the inspirations of a great many science fiction writers has simply been the desire to see science have a greater influence in the shaping of men's lives. The search for knowledge, and so on, making people more apt to accept change in an intelligent way, and to envisage the possibility of changing and shaping human life. In the past the idea has often seemed to be stability, the idea that whatever the present culture is, it can somehow be maintained unchanged, and that that's the desirable thing.

Apel: And stability turns into paralysis.

Leiber: Yes. I think that adaptability has become an obvious necessity of life in our time. The need is for people who can distinguish among different kinds of change. Obviously there are some things that have to be changed, some things we'd like to change, and other things that we'd like to maintain to a degree. I think writing about this, giving form to imagination, makes it more possible to do these things. Imagination allows us to explore different possibilities without having to live them all out in actual fact. And this is one of the things that science fiction tries to do.

Apel: I've discovered that that "possibility trying" is an actual physical principle in the universe. In atomic reactions, an atom being smashed will send out several different subatomic particles in different directions, with different speeds and different radiation qualities, to try out any number of survival possibilities. There are even theories that some particles travel backwards in time for a very short period, to try even that possibility of survival. Eventually a number of smaller particles will survive for a certain time, but not until the "pulverized" atom has sent out "feelers" to try many potential avenues of safety. Maybe we can draw an analogy between these so-called "virtual processes" and imaginative literature.

Leiber: Yes, yes. That sounds very attractive. I would agree with you.

Briggs: I think people who read science fiction have an easier time accepting the rapidity of change, and the science-fiction-like changes going on in the modern world.

Leiber: Yes. When the Russians put up the first Sputnik, I remember reading the reports of that and running across the business that it took a little over two hours for this satellite to revolve around the earth just outside the atmosphere. And I remember my reaction was, "That's right! It *would* be about two hours." Not because I'm a great physicist or mathematician, but simply because I'd run into that in science fiction stories and articles. So what seemed strange about it superficially was really what confirmed it for me.

Apel: That's one of the many reasons I see science fiction as the modern mythology. Even its name suggests a fusion of two equal and opposite points of view: The search for truth through science and its expression in the imaginative lies of fiction.

Leiber: Yes.

Briggs: That and the fact that there are certain mythic themes that run all through science fiction. The Prometheus theme, for example, constantly turns up, in many variations. *Slan* is a good example of the tormented Superman aspect, as is *More Than Human*. The "lightbringer" aspect shines through in works like

Childhood's End. Even the destructive effects, the great changes due to the new powers, comes out over and over again: about every third science fiction story ever written has been about someone deliberately disrupting a given set of cultural norms because he finds out that they're not true. *Gather, Darkness!, A Specter is Haunting Texas, Stranger in a Strange Land*, all make me think of that—people who single-handedly bring down a society because they know the truth.

Leiber: There's also the point that the science fiction authors have been following what the scientists have actually been thinking and doing, and then putting this into popular language in the form of fictions. So the science fiction writer is introducing people to the real world they live in, in terms of what the scientist and technicians are thinking and doing. I'm sure you've all run into some of the "flying saucer" people, like we talked about earlier; people who believe—at least they tell me—that I'm getting my plots from people out in space; members of some superior race who are trying to soften up the earth for the first social contacts with these aliens from other planets and more advanced cultures...

Briggs: *(with mock incredulity) You're doing that? (General laughter)*

Leiber: What I am doing, I feel, is helping to introduce the majority of people to the world the scientific minority are exploring right now.

Apel: The frontiers of physics and parapsychology?

Leiber: Yes, things of that sort. Between the two World Wars, one of the greatest preoccupations of science fiction writers was atomic energy; the other was space flight. Even so, the number of scientists who were working on those very problems was very small, it was from them that the science fiction writers got their cues. The majority of scientists at the time weren't any too well aware of this sort of work. The tendency of many of them was to think that these weren't developments that were coming soon. I'd say the average scientist before World War II thought of atomic energy as a possibility, but something that would be developed perhaps several hundred years in the future. They knew enough to know that this sort of thing was possible, but the tendency with those big things like atomic energy and actually getting to the moon has always been to put it off further into the future; thinking of it as, "Well, not in our lifetime." This is where we've gotten so many surprises in the past half-century.

Well—Have you got another question in your notebook?

Apel: Oh, I could think of one, if you'd like.

Leiber: Sure.

Briggs: He has an almost bottomless notebook.

Apel: There are two or three topics we could talk about, actually. You can take your pick, if you want to do it that way. We were discussing the different minor themes that run through your stories—pacifism and chess, for instance. But there is also a "Big Theme" and that is the "Love-Death" theme. This is constantly appearing in your works, and is represented in your works probably in its most overt form in *A Specter is Haunting Texas*, where you have two women representing these two necessary compliments: one, a sexy blonde, representing life; the other, a fiery-tempered dark revolutionary, representing death.

Leiber: The Love-Death theme was the one Damon Knight chose in *In Search of Wonder* as representing the theme of any serious writing. So it would be natural I should hit that. I brought the pacifism stories together in my book *The Hour of the Wolf...*

Apel: *The Night of the Wolf*?

Leiber: That's right. *Hour of the Wolf* was a Bergman film.

Apel: Well, even that could take us onto another tangent. One of the finest pieces of symbolic fantasy I've ever read—one which reminded me very strongly of Bergman, and was something I'm sure he would be proud to have done—was your story "The Winter Flies." I think that's a perfect example of what science fiction can be at its peak as symbolic literature. The interconnections among the characters and the images you chose were perfectly archetypal, and in easily readable and enjoyable contemporary form.

Leiber: That's essentially a psychology story, based on the thesis that there's nothing stranger than the life of the average man the thoughts in his head at any one time. You have three people—mother, father, and child—just spending a quiet evening at home. All we do is see what goes through their minds during that time.

Apel: They spend a quiet evening at home with their local household gods and demons, their machines that talk and read minds, and their fantasy vehicles that explore the cosmos.

Leiber: And yet at the same time you realize—the kick of the story is—that none of this is visible. You could have a camera on them, and it wouldn't record any unusual movements at all.

Apel: Another one in that same vein that I really enjoyed was "The Secret Songs."

Leiber: Yes, that's very much the same sort of thing. One of the influences that led me to write these stories, certainly, was an anthology that Judith Merrill was putting together called *The Thin Edge*. It was never published.

Apel: Speaking of those two stories specifically gives us a chance to talk about mythology. You were a student, in a certain sense, of Lovecraft, who was consciously trying to establish a mythology within the science fiction/fantasy realm with his Cthulhu mythos, which people are still writing nowadays.

Leiber: I don't think Lovecraft had a very conscious feeling of trying to set up a new mythology that would be significant in some way. I think he was trying to find something that would give the reader a thrill of supernatural terror without bringing in the standard themes from religion. Lovecraft was trying to find some way to embody the strangeness of the vast cosmos that was being revealed to man by his sciences, especially astronomy. He felt that he didn't want to invoke the traditional horrors of the vampire, the werewolf, the various types of ghosts and demons, and the devil; he felt that this really was outmoded and no longer frightened people. He wanted to have entities that were still more unknown, and so he invented these names; he was looking for names that wouldn't fit into ordinary language patterns. Suppose you heard the name of some deity or monster or power in an alien language, spoken perhaps by non-human creatures. If a human being tried to pronounce this name, how would he do it? How would he write it down?

Apel: Scientists now are having the same problem with dolphin research—how do you translate grunts, clicks, and whistles into human speech?

Leiber: That's it exactly. That was the sort of thing that Lovecraft was trying to do with the names of these beings. You get to "The Shadow Out of Time" and "At the Mountains of Madness," and he's pretty well broken away completely from the black magic feeling that you get in "The Dunwich Horror" and the earlier stories. The beings are more or less what today you would consider as science fiction beings. Time-travel, mentally, in various ways, beings that come to the earth from outer space, and so on.

Apel: It seems to me that this is something that you have done in many of your stories as well. The two examples that spring to mind are "Smoke Ghost," which you wrote years ago, and *Our Lady of Darkness*, which you wrote just recently. I think "Smoke Ghost" is a good example of creating a contemporary mythology. If you have to have ghosts in an urban setting, this is what they'll look like—thick and powerful, and so on. The same unknown forces, but in new clothes. So in these stories you have consciously been adding to the mythology of the twentieth century.

Leiber: Yes, I'd say so. I've been trying to do that. Of course, for my purposes, it hasn't been necessary to give them names; I haven't personified them to that degree. They've remained sort of forces that are apparently conscious in some way or other, but we're not close enough to them as yet to know anything about their language. That would make them too human and intelligent for my purposes. But yes, that certainly is true.

Apel: Thank you, Fritz Leiber.

ROGER ZELAZNY

Interview conducted at the home of Kevin Briggs
Santa Clara, California
June 1977

Roger Joseph Zelazny was born on May 13, 1937, in Euclid, Ohio, a suburb of Cleveland. In high school, he became editor of his school newspaper and a member of the Creative Writing Club, and in 1959 he graduated with a BA from Western Reserve University in Cleveland. In 1962 he was awarded an MA in English from New York's Columbia University, where he specialized in Elizabethan and Jacobean drama. Many of the themes that define these dramatic periods would eventually find their way into his fiction.

Between 1962 and 1969 he worked as a claims representative for the U.S. Social Security Administration in Cleveland and then in Baltimore, Maryland. He spent his evenings writing science fiction; short stories at first, then longer works, and eventually novels. He first published professionally in August 1962, and the following year he won critical acclaim for his story "A Rose for Ecclesiastes," which also brought him his first Hugo nomination. In 1965 he won a Nebula award for his novella "He Who Shapes" (which he later expanded into the novel *The Dream Master*) and a second for his novelette, "The Doors of His Face, the Lamps of His Mouth." In 1966, he won a Hugo for best novel for *This Immortal*, and a second in 1968 for his novel *Lord of Light*.

In 1969, Zelazny quit his day job to write full time; in the following decades, he proved to be a prolific and popular author, not only of science fiction but also of poetry. The critical appreciation afforded his works is indicated by his three Nebula awards (and 11 additional nominations), while his popularity can be noted by his six Hugo awards (and eight additional nominations).

The Encyclopedia of Science Fiction (Ed. by Clute & Nicholls, St. Martin's Griffin, 1993) notes: "His arrival in the sf [sic] world in 1962 ... marked that year as a milestone in what seemed at the time to be the inevitable maturing of sf into a complex and sophisticated literature, whose language might finally match its intermittent hubris."

This language ("corrosively playful," as Clute & Nicholls describe it) was as much a hallmark of his style as his themes. His dialog consisted of sharp wisecracking and banter, reminiscent of the hard-boiled detective genre epitomized by Raymond Chandler. Stylistically, Zelazny was experimental, often writing an entire novel to test a theory of characterization or plot. His "other life" as a poet contributed significantly to his elegant prose style.

Many of Zelazny's plots revolve around technology and magic and their interactions, blurring the line between sci-fi and heroic fantasy. By regularly incorporating elements of world mythology (Greek, Norse, Hindu, Egyptian, Christian, Japanese, Native American, Irish) in contemporary settings in his work, he virtually demolished the artificial line separating these genres.

Roger Zelazny died in Santa Fe at age 58 on June 14, 1995, of kidney failure, a side effect of colorectal cancer. In an appreciation published in *Locus* magazine (August 1995), his friend and collaborator Robert Sheckley praised him as "one of the greatest talents our field has produced, a unique and compelling voice. He was an original, a one of a kind."

ROGER ZELAZNY

Apel: Let's start out with the most basic of questions, which is: How do you work? Do you have any regular, established working habits?

Zelazny: Well, over the years I've tried a number of different techniques. There was a time when I'd set myself a word-quota, for instance. Back in those days I'd do a flat thousand words per day. I wasn't always satisfied with the results, though, and I decided to try a time schedule. That was not totally satisfying either. Eventually I came up with a system whereby I would sit before the typewriter at four different occasions during the day and force myself to write a minimum of three sentences. Hopefully, on one of these occasions something takes fire and I keep going, so that at the end of the day I've probably accomplished at least the same thing I would have if I'd been observing the word-quota or time schedule. But it gives me more of an illusion of freedom, and if at that moment I just don't feel like doing any more, I can leave the typewriter without any sense of guilt, having produced something. And if nothing special happens, I at least have a dozen sentences to show for the day. This procedure will get me 1.9 books per year. *(Laughter)*

Apel: How do you plot a book?

Zelazny: Normally, what I start with is a chapter or two. First, I figure out the sort of person I want to write a book about, and once I've come up with something of a character, I let things gel in my mind for a few days, trying, every now and then, to take up the character and look at him in terms of some situation or other which might bring out something I'd like to show about him. When I've done this long enough and I feel I've sufficient understanding of the character to make a beginning, I sit down and begin writing. I don't really have an elaborate plot. But in the course of moving my character from the first sequence to the second, things happen. Secondary characters who are introduced to help advance the action take on characteristics of their own and often become interesting to me. So, I might go off on a tangent and turn a minor character into a major character, or there could be some element which crops up in the background of a minor character that grows into a plot element. So the first thirty or forty pages go slowly for me, as I set all these things up and feel my way ahead. By the time I've recorded that much I get a feeling for the general action and rhythm of the book, and the pace of the writing picks up.

Apel: By that time your characters are pretty well established...

Zelazny: ...and once they come alive and have been through a few events, something happens to the book. I don't know what it is, but there is a point—and it's not anything quantifiable; I can't tell you page such-and-such, or after so many words—but there comes a point in various books, a point where everything suddenly falls together, and you see where the entire thing is heading. From that point on, the writing is extremely easy. Almost a matter of transcribing something.

Briggs: You've worked in collaboration with several people. Do you enjoy this?

Zelazny: Oh, not particularly. It's sort of the same reason I'm not particularly interested in working for TV—the fact that the final product is not mine. Anything I'd write in the way of a script I just know would be changed at various points along the line and wouldn't come out exactly to my liking. I feel somewhat the same about collaboration. I normally don't like to do it just because I like to do my own thing. The reason I was turned on by *Deus Irae* [written in collaboration with Philip K. Dick] is simply that I liked that particular story. It wasn't the sort of story I'd normally do myself, but once the situation had been created, it was one I could enter into and enjoy working with. And I have long been an admirer of Phil Dick.

Briggs: Did you like working with Ellison?

Zelazny: Yes. That, of course, was a much shorter story—though we did it in pretty much the same way, through the mails. I'd write a section and send it to him; he'd write a section and send it back. Harlan and Phil both have a very professional approach to things like this. There was really very little discussion. Near the end of *Deus Irae*, when Phil and I were taking a look at the final form, there was a brief exchange, but it was almost the proverbial meeting of the minds.

Briggs: Your work seems to fall into two categories; novelettes for magazines or novels that are often serialized in magazines. Was there any point where you decided that you were tired of the novelette form, or that you were tired of the restrictions of magazines, and decided to write novels?

Zelazny: Actually, I think the novelette is ideal for science fiction, for me. That is about my favorite form. It was primarily the exigencies of working on a full-time basis that led me to try to work up to novels. There is a peculiar psychological factor at work here, and I'm not alone in being influenced this way. When one is writing a novel it is quite difficult to shift mental gears and switch over to a short story or a novelette, and then go back to the novel. If for some reason I have to do such a switch-over it takes at least a day—generally several days—to get myself into a proper state of mind to go over to the other form. So what I've been doing in recent years is almost exclusively novels. I feel a bit badly about this because I started out as a short story writer, and I still tend to think of myself as one, even though I haven't been doing much in that area. I'll get back to it eventually. It was mainly a matter of necessity—going full time—that led me into doing as many novels as I have.

Apel: Let's talk a little about some of the themes that run throughout your novels and stories. One of the major themes that forms the backbone of a lot of your work is the idea of *power*. The Amber series in particular is a good example of this; every one of the major characters in that series is involved in powerplays and the jockeying for position. The same is true of *Isle of the Dead, Lord of Light, Creatures of Light and Darkness*, and, to a lesser extent, most of your other books as well. The common thread is that lust for power, and its uses and abuses. Are the opinions of your characters on this topic necessarily your own?

Zelazny: No. I normally try to keep my own feelings apart from my characters' simply because I like to create different characters. And I've always attempted to avoid the tendency to moralize in my books.

Apel: That seems pretty generally true. Your heroes are basically amoral survival artists who will draw their own code of ethics if they have to, and only if they have to. I think the one key line to all this is in *Creatures of Light and Darkness*: "Whatever I do with my newfound power, I do for one person: Me!"

Zelazny: I'm not saying this isn't my personal opinion—*(laughter)*—I'm just saying that I try to create realistic characters; I try to keep myself apart from them.

Briggs: I'm interested in you saying that you try to keep yourself out of your characters, because so many of your characters have so many things in common. There seems to be—in the same sense that there is a Raymond Chandler "character," or an Ernest Hemingway "character"—there seems to have developed a Roger Zelazny "character"...

Zelazny: Right.

Briggs: You seem to have this one sort of person who tends to be a hero in your stories....a man who is very facile with words, who's extremely competent, but underneath that competence is an underlying strata of existential doubt. You made a comment in one of your Amber books where you mentioned the writer John D. MacDonald, and I wondered if you think there's any comparison between his kind of hero and your kind of hero.

Zelazny: Yes. Let me recast something I said earlier before I get to that. I said that I try to keep myself apart from my characters. I did not say that I succeed. There are certain tendencies... Well, you just can't keep yourself out completely. Writing has a certain autobiographical character to it, no matter how hard you attempt to divorce yourself from it. I am aware that I handle certain sorts of characters better than others. I try to avoid falling into the habit of taking an easy way out and using a person who is too similar in too many books. But one is limited in extent by one's own psychological makeup.

Apel: Let me see if I understand you correctly. What you're saying is that there are certain things you couldn't write about accurately or validly, not feeling them in yourself, or not having had an experience yourself such as you wanted to write about. Something like that?

Zelazny: That's neatly put, yes. To get back to MacDonald, then, I have read all his Travis McGee books and a number of his other things. There is a certain attraction there. The whole "free spirit" setup. I identify with this. As a writer I feel rather free myself and I like the feeling. Also, I admire a person who is capable of many things but refrains from exercising some of the power he possesses.

And yes, my characters do tend to be somewhat literate. I should say this is because I've read a lot and this sort of thing creeps into my vocabulary when it's slowed to a writing pace.

And I do like dealing with characters in any science fiction setting who are in the prime of life yet older than a person in the prime of life would be in that society. Some means of extending life is necessary, because I like to deal with a complex character and most people in the prime of life are not quite as complex yet as I would like them to be. What I'm getting at is that I like a man capable not only of action but also of some thought. One needs to be in relatively good physical condition just to carry out some of the actions my characters are required to engage in. And have had the time for some of the reflection that they need. I found the easiest solution is often simply to make them a century old.

Apel: That's an interesting theme in your work, as well—that virtual immortality that so many of your characters possess. What they've learned in their extended life-spans seems mainly to be how to survive. Would you characterize that as, say, the wisdom of age, combined with the bodily strength of youth, so they are able to actually put into effect what they see as the wise course of action?

Zelazny: Yes.

Briggs: It occurred to me recently that—aside from stylistic considerations—you are a very traditional writer. The things you deal with are for the most part traditional science fiction themes just handled from different viewpoints and different stylistic bases. There's a lot of very traditional elements in your fiction, and yet you're constantly being categorized as a member of the "New Wave," or someone who's changing science fiction. On which side of this debate would you place yourself?

Zelazny: I think of myself as being basically traditional. Places where I've attempted to innovate a bit would be in the general structure of the book and in stylistic endeavors.

Apel: My impression is that quite a bit of what you write could have been written by, say, Robert Heinlein, or vice versa. *Glory Road*, for instance, is one that might have been written by you very easily. There seems to be a long line of traditional science fiction in your own background, and you fit very well into that tradition. To whom are you indebted in the field for your background, would you say? Who is it you admired—or still admire—and what part did they play in your own development?

Zelazny: Well, the ones that impressed me the most when I started reading science fiction at a tender age were Stanley Weinbaum and Henry Kuttner. They were basically traditional storytellers. Kuttner was a very versatile man in switching styles, and could write anything from fantasy in the A. Merritt vein to hard-boiled first-person narratives. I admired that versatility. Weinbaum, while he may not seem so to a modern reader, was very innovative when compared with his contemporaries.

Apel: It's apparent from your fiction that your reading extends far beyond of science fiction. I don't think I've ever read a book of yours that didn't include a quote or two from Shakespeare, for instance. And your characters are always quoting or referring to literary figures like Rilke, Gide, Hemingway...

Briggs: Yeah. I've never read a science fiction story, until yours, that quoted from Rilke. Is that tendency to quote very literate and very esoteric just automatic, because you're widely read, or are you doing it deliberately?

Zelazny: It's just that that sort of thing becomes second nature. In the making of comparisons, in the creation of metaphors, I automatically reach for this kind of thing. It's not so much a conscious maneuver. It is a kind of reflex action.

Apel: So you can't help but call up trains of associations that lead you into intellectual realms.

Zelazny: I've always had a pretty good memory. Things tend to linger.

Apel: Who is it that you would point to from the so-called mainstream as being an inspiration?

Zelazny: Well, gee... The first major mainstream figure who made a strong impression on me was Thomas Wolfe—and that was at a very early age. I don't know that I tried to emulate him in anything I did, but he's the only one that comes to mind. I think there is an influence there; I don't know just what it is. You reach a certain point eventually, once you've begun writing, where your thought processes and feelings sort of...*harden*, and then take off on their own track, so that you no longer seem open to influences in ways you were before you started working as a writer.

Apel: That happens when you've developed some kind of style that you could call your own?

Zelazny: Yes. Once you've got it, it seems you also acquire antibodies of some sort, to protect it.

Apel: How about poets? Any particular inspirations? Again, we could cite Shakespeare, Rilke, Kipling...

Zelazny: I did my Master's thesis in the area of Elizabethan drama and theatre, so I was immersed in that for a time. And I wrote primarily poetry myself in college.

Briggs: In the Amber books, and in a lot of your other books, you use dramatic conventions similar to those used in Elizabethan and Jacobean drama—the machinations, the constant jockeying for position, and so on, in plays like *The Jew of Malta, The Duchess of Malfi.* Do you feel some kind of natural affinity for that sort of plot?

Zelazny: Yes. One of the reasons I elected to do my thesis in that area is that I felt a certain attraction for the tragedies of blood and revenge.

Briggs: Of that series of drama, which ones do you find yourself coming back to? Which are your favorites?

Zelazny: As you mentioned, there's always Shakespeare, because of the beauties of his language...

Briggs: I suppose what I'm asking is not so much Shakespeare, but specifically the writers of tragedy and blood...Marlowe, for instance.

Zelazny: The subject of my thesis was Cyril Tourneur, actually, and his *Revenger's Tragedy*, which is a beautifully constructed piece with intricate plots feeding back into the main direction. It's very well contrived. There was a time when I did a lot of thinking about that play, just considering the way that it worked.

Apel: Most of your heroes have a streak of existentialism in them as well—if they don't suffer from actual despair, like Render, then they seem to have adopted the other answer to the existential dilemma, which is "Why *not* go on?" A character like Sandow is a good example—he's pretty much reached the peak of where he can get, yet he continues to go on living after that point. Were the existentialist writers a conscious influence on your thought and work, or is this philosophy something you've developed on your own?

Zelazny: The ones I've read were an influence, but a kind of negative influence.

Briggs: I seem to recall that after several years of writing for *Amazing* and *Fantastic* you published a number of stories, starting with "A Rose for Ecclesiastes" and "The Doors of His Face," in *The Magazine of Fantasy and Science Fiction*, and got sort of instant acclaim. Did you think you were like Byron; did you wake up one morning and find yourself famous?

Zelazny: I don't think so. When I began writing, I felt there was an apprenticeship I had to serve in the way of short stories before I attempted anything of greater length—with one exception, to which I'll return. What I did was simply write short stories, trying something a little different in each one, to gain some facility with characters and situations. And of course it occurred to me that I'd been selling all these stories to a single editor, and I said, "Well, let's see if anyone else likes my things." And that's why I began submitting to *The Magazine of Fantasy and Science Fiction*.

It was sort of peculiar, because of the first story I had written before I made the attempt to break into writing in February of 1962. At that time I hadn't read any science fiction in about six and a half years. I went out at that time to try to familiarize myself again with the market; I read all the magazines and picked a handful of paperbacks at random and read them. But I had written one science fiction story the previous fall. I'd simply put it aside, and then started in '62 trying to catch up on the area and also trying to write. And I succeeded in March of '62 in selling and I went on that year and sold sixteen more. From March through June I was selling them to *Amazing* and *Fantastic*.

Apel: Were you still writing three a week then?

Zelazny: Yes. Very close to that. I wanted to have ten stories out at all times, but I fell behind. I didn't have ten, I had seven out, and I didn't have an idea for a new story, so I decided to haul out the old story I had written in '61 and send it to a different market; I wanted to see if I could sell it to someone else. And that story was "A Rose for Ecclesiastes." So I typed it up and sent it to *F&SF*. After I did, it occurred to me that it would be nice to try something else of that length again, because it was about three times as long as anything else I'd sold. I also had a thing, a certain feeling of...*sentimentality* is the word, for the stories on which I'd grown up; the old pulp stories from the thirties and so on.

Apel: Do you see yourself in the role today of a *Planet Stories*-type science fiction writer? A lot of the work you do seems to be *Planet Stories* type material, in the very best sense of the phrase: "A Rose for Ecclesiastes" and "Doors of His Face" in particular.

Zelazny: I had always wanted to write something like that when I was much younger, and time was rapidly passing when one could write that sort of story, of a princess of Mars, or great oceans on Venus. We already had some pretty good information that the planets were not the way they were conceived in the thirties. But I did "A Rose for Ecclesiastes" anyway, because if I didn't do a story like that right then, I could never do it again. It was a form of tribute, in a way, to the stories I'd read of Mars. After it sold I decided, well, I ought to try something else of this length, and if I'm ever going to do one on Venus, I'd better do it in a hurry, too, because it appears to be a bit hotter than we expected. So I wrote "The Doors of His Face, the Lamps of His Mouth," and sold it to *F&SF*, and then I said to myself "That's it; I won't be able to use the solar system this way anymore. But I've paid my tribute to the stories I grew up on."

Briggs: The story is told of Henry Kuttner that people used to come up to him and say, "Henry, the best thing you ever wrote was 'The Graveyard Rats'," and he'd get livid, because that was the first story he ever wrote. Does it bother you that people still bring up those two stories of yours? Did you think when you wrote them that they'd make as big an impression on people as they did?

Zelazny: No, I didn't think that, really. In fact, one of the reasons I refrained from submitting "Rose" to a magazine was that I felt I had overdone it, that I'd thrown in everything but the Martian kitchen sink, that I'd overwritten it, and that I'd made the character too introspective to be sympathetic. I wasn't really sure of that as a story, but I was prompted to submit it because I wanted another story to send in that week. So for a time I did feel rather peculiar that that particular story should be so well-received. That phase too has passed, though. It had to be written when it was written, but that's really about all I can say.

At any rate, after I did these two, it occurred to me that I might have offended an editor I liked very much because they did get some acclaim, and "Rose" was nominated for a Hugo that year. Cele Goldsmith was the editor; she was very nice to me, buying all my early short stories and such. So I decided to make it up to her by doing something at greater length other than those novelettes, and putting a lot of thought and effort into it, and I wrote "He Who Shapes," and sent it to her. Then her tenure as editor was up, and I didn't feel any emotional obligation to the magazine after that, so I attempted to switch over to better-paying markets.

Briggs: I suppose what prompted me to ask the question about if you suddenly woke up and found yourself famous is the fact that in 1965, when the Nebula awards came into being, you were awarded two—not only the first awards in this category, but a first in the fact that you won in two categories. That must have been some kind of affirmation; that must have had some effect.

Zelazny: Well, it did make me feel awfully good, yes. It was about that time that I began trying to think ahead to the time when I'd be going full-time. When I received those awards, it reinforced the thought that this might be possible in the sixties. And it was that same year that I received the Hugo for *And Call Me Conrad*. When that came along I pretty much decided that I was going to be a full-time writer as soon as I could. It took about two more years...

Apel: This is when you were working for the Social Security Administration?

Zelazny: Yes. I quit my job to write full-time in May of '69.

Apel: ...And the rest is history, as they say. Or mythology. Speaking of which, you got involved in science fiction through mythology, did you not? How did this happen?

Zelazny: I had a rather peculiar childhood, in the sense that my parents didn't particularly like me to read fairy tales, or books of that sort. They thought it would encourage me to be too imaginative. So when I got to reading myself, and I found literature of this sort on the shelves of the school library, I took to it quite readily, because I was not familiar with that sort of thing and it fascinated me. At the time, I didn't know what science fiction was, but I did like fantastic literature, so I began reading all the books on mythology and that sort of thing

It wasn't really until I was eleven years old that I came across science fiction. And it was love at first sight. I began to read all the books in the school library. There weren't that many there in those days. In the following year, at a different school, a fellow told me there were also science fiction magazines. This opened a whole new area for me, and I began reading the magazines. I had, in the meantime—even before I discovered science fiction—decided that I wanted to write. It was the thing I enjoyed doing most. And once I began reading science fiction, I started writing science fiction stories. In my early teens I submitted some stories to magazines without particular success. So I made a decision when I was about sixteen that I wouldn't try to sell any more stories for a while; I'd wait until I finished college, get some more experience, and not worry about writing. But I promised myself that the first chance I got, I would write. Not science fiction, necessarily; just the general idea of writing. When I did get the chance, I decided that science fiction was right for me.

Briggs: Are you involved in fandom much at all?

Zelazny: I attend conventions, read fanzines, and speak to fan groups on occasion.

Briggs: How do you feel about fandom? Does it annoy you that such a thing exists, or does it please you? Do you think it hurts your progress or helps your progress as an artist? Or do you even have any strong emotions about it?

Zelazny: Well, first, I consider myself a fan, still. I was a fan back in those early days in this field when I was trying to write. In fact, I was assistant editor of a fanzine in the fifties. It only lasted a couple of issues. But I enjoy fandom quite a bit—going to conventions, meeting people I know only through their writing... I think it has its benefits. A number of good science fiction writers were fans before they turned professional. It's a good place to meet other people with knowledge of the area, to meet editors and learn some requirements and also hopefully to have them know who you are so you might get a better reading—that sort of thing.

I didn't go this route when I started writing. As I said, I had been away from science fiction for a number of years. Not just the reading of it. I had had nothing to do with it. But I got back into attending conventions after I began writing. I feel it does have its virtues.

Briggs: Do you think being considered a science fiction writer affects the sales of your books one way or another?

Zelazny: I don't know. That question has been kicked around over the years, whether the fact that it is a genre limits the sales. People point to mainstream general fiction books which are essentially science fiction novels but aren't classified that way.

Apel: Yeah, Theodore Sturgeon was talking about that in the introduction to your book of stories *Four for Tomorrow*, and listed about a half-dozen. *1984*...

Zelazny: ...*On the Beach.* In France now, where my books have been selling pretty well, they don't publish them as science fiction. The thing is, I have no standard of comparison. Maybe if they published them with a science fiction label they'd sell exactly the same way. I just don't know enough about the nature of their reading habits.

Briggs: While we're on this subject, I'd like to ask your opinion of a few people who write under the banner of mainstream fiction but who are still working essentially with the science fiction idiom. Vonnegut, Pynchon, Fowles, Barthelme, Borges... Those kind of people who use science fiction idioms, yet are avoiding the pariah aspects of being labeled a genre writer. Do you read those people?

Zelazny: Yes. I think we're going through a sort of phase now where science fiction is becoming more popular. I think it might be partly because of the fact that it's "made the scene" on campuses. It's become academically respectable. But—and this is just a feeling, personally—I don't feel that the label "science fiction" is as deleterious as it was ten years ago, even. We've got a different reading public now that is perhaps a little more sophisticated in the sense that they've been through a decade in which there have been a lot of space efforts, and that there have been a lot of breakthroughs scientifically, and so on. A man with a transplanted heart could sit in front of a wall-sized television set and watch people walk on the moon. That's bound to influence thinking in science to some degree.

Briggs: There's a long tradition in your work of people who, for all intents and purposes, are immortal. Did you get interested in various methods of immortality only because you were interested in its goals and had to make it sound plausible, or is this something that personally interests you?

Zelazny: Well, it's interesting to speculate on the effects of extended life span on the individual and future society. And yes, it is something in which I'm interested that happened to combine very nicely with my ideas of design for my books.

Apel: With that thought in mind, and considering also the artificial types of life-extension in your books—cryonics in "Graveyard Heart," or the preprogrammed reincarnation of *Lord of Light*—what do you conceive for yourself as an afterlife?

Zelazny: To tell the truth, I'd rather just remain here. *(Laughter)*

Apel: Live forever or die trying, eh wot?

Zelazny: Exactly. In the books themselves, after a while, it became something of a game to find as many different mechanisms as I could for extending life. At first it was simply... Well, with "Conrad," it was somewhat unexplained; he could be a mutant, he could be something else, and I wanted it that way. In that same book, they talked about the drug treatments they also had to extend life and the very unusual way Hasan reacted to this; mostly it just preserved people at whatever age they were when they took the treatment, but Hasan actually appeared to grow younger. In *Lord of Light* it was the body-changing mechanism; with Sandow it was a combination of extending his life through freezing until he reached a point in society where there were drugs which would extend it. You have to keep finding different things.

Briggs: It seems that you use the exact opposite of that same device quite a bit as well. Many of your protagonists suddenly start to exist without much memory of what they were before. Conrad in "And Call Me Conrad" has been alive longer than he can even remember, so he occasionally forgets whether such-and-such a story is even about him. Corwin in the Amber books is the classic example of this point: he begins his story as an amnesiac who's suddenly brought back to his own present. In *Jack of Shadows* the protagonist has two schizophrenic lives; he's an anthropology professor on the day side, and Jack of Shadows on the night side, and there are times where he gets into a situation where he wakes up with a set of memories and doesn't know where they come from.

Zelazny: I think it's a good mechanism. I'm afraid it's almost *too* good; you could get trapped into using it constantly because it automatically provides an element of mystery, which is one of the main things an author tries to do—get the reader's attention quickly and maintain it. It works if it's handled properly. It's easy to produce a good story by just drawing out that element of mystery and gradual discovery. But I think it could also be a trap. I'm a sucker for that sort of story myself. I found it easy to do the few times I've done it, and now I'm trying to avoid it. I don't want to be bound to any particular approach.

Apel: Does that opinion guide your use of the immortality theme, too? Have you found more ways of writing about how a person can be immortal, or is that a device that's outlived its usefulness?

Zelazny: Well, lately, I haven't been thinking about it, just because I've been working on another Amber book and the problem's already been handled there. Now, with Fred Cassidy in *Doorways in the Sand* I looked for an alternate way of getting the sort of character I wanted. In him I didn't have to have him immortal because his mind was in the shape it was just by the fact that he'd had an awful lot of schooling.

Apel: You mentioned the other night that you've written nineteen books and *Doorways in the Sand* was one of your favorites because it came out exactly the way that you intended. How would you rank your other books? What would you say would be the top three or four? Are there any you would rather not have written?

Zelazny: My favorite is *Lord of Light*, because I put more work into it than anything else, and it did come out the way I wanted it to. "And Call Me Conrad"/*This Immortal* is a favorite...because it was my first book, for one reason. I was also happy with the way it turned out. Two more recent books which I enjoyed doing and felt were effective were *Today We Choose Faces* and *Doorways in the Sand.*

Briggs: I would really be interested in hearing what your least favorite four books were; the ones which you thought were least successful. Because at least one of those that you've mentioned before, *Damnation Alley*, I have a mild disagreement with you. I sort of liked that.

Apel: Yeah, me too. Very tight little story; the tone and characterizations never faltered.

Zelazny: Well, let me put it this way: The books that I'd put at the other end of the list are not necessarily things I consider bad. It's hard to say you hate a particular book, or anything like that; I don't actively dislike any of my books. But I tend to be suspicious of anything that I write too easily. Maybe it's a carry-over of the old work ethic or something. But the books that I did the fastest jobs on are the ones that are lower on my list. *Damnation Alley* was written quite quickly. So was *Nine Princes in Amber*, actually. For a long time I didn't have a really high opinion of that book, just because I wrote it so quickly.

Apel: You were writing that mainly for your own amusement, correct?

Zelazny: Yes. And I do like it. I went back recently and looked through it. I have to go back and look through the Amber series periodically.

To Die in Italbar was another quickly-written book. I'm still not sure whether I played fair with my intentions at all in that book. I don't know that bringing in Sandow as a *deus ex machina* was the best thing to do. I still sort of think that if I had it to do over again I would've continued and worked out a disease mechanism. It's better than a goddess. *(Laughter)*

Actually, I'll tell you what I had in mind on that book. It was an experiment, in that I had just been reading about Max Brand, a very prolific man. He said that he had one basic formula he used in writing a novel, and he just used it over and over again. It was fine for his purposes. He said he started out with two characters, a good man and a bad man. And during the course of the story the good man turned into a bad man, and the bad man turned into a good man. So you had something in the book for everybody; for the people who liked redemption stories and for the people who like something a little more sordid. The characters passed each other on the way up and down. So I was toying with the notion of doing something like that and I was going to do that with my two characters, Malacar and H., the disease carrier. Partway through the book, though, the novelty of that finally wore off and I got more interested in the characters and I just abandoned the whole notion. I just wanted to finish the book. *(Laughter)*

Briggs: I've noticed that you and Samuel Delany seem to write about similar themes and in similar idioms in your short fiction. "Driftglass," for instance, appears to me to be a story that you could have written, or "Time Considered As a Helix of Semi-Precious Stones." Do you see any similarity between your work and his in the novelette form?

Zelazny: This is a good question. Chip and I have talked about this on a number of occasions. We agree that we don't feel we are like one another—he doesn't consider his work like mine; I don't consider mine like his—and we pretty much came to the conclusion at that time that it was partly due to the fact that we arrived on the scene at about the same time, and partly the fact that we were innovative and occasionally using the same sorts of materials, like mythology, and partly an optical effect that our names look somewhat alike when seen in print.

Briggs: They do in fact.

Apel: Yeah, just the other day someone asked me when "Roger Zelany" was coming to town. I hope he reads your books more carefully than your name.

Zelazny: And that's pretty much where we left it. I feel I use myth differently than Chip does. I use different sorts of settings.

Apel: Yes! Mythology! I did want to talk to you about mythology! You've used the established myths of so many cultures in your works... Is there any one set that appeals to you more than the others?

Zelazny: Not really. I'm democratic about the whole thing.

Apel: Do you in any way think of yourself as a mythmaker—someone who's consciously creating mythology?

Zelazny: Well, I'm not consciously trying to create a new mythology. There's a tendency, if you write anything of any length, to automatically have them approach some logical construct. I never really set out to form one exactly. Letting things fall where they would is my usual method.

Apel: Do you consciously try to present archetypal images to the reader—or to encourage these images to rise from the unconscious of the reader?

Zelazny: No, not really. I can see it happening sometimes while I'm writing—things falling into patterns like this—and if I do, I will exploit it. But I don't normally plot ahead to achieve such effects. I'm kind of a myth and symbol opportunist rather than a plotter or designer.

Apel: Do you see science fiction in general as a modern form of mythology? The modern cloak that the monomyth is wearing in the twentieth century?

Zelazny: Do I consider science fiction modern mythology? I've thought about this question on and off for some time. I think it has similarities, in that science fiction is the only form of modern writing which uses characters of the sort that appear in mythology. Northrop Frye's categorization of characters into modes is illuminating. He divides them into the following types: The mythic, the high mimetic, the low pathetic, and the ironic. Most modern fiction is dominated by the low pathetic and the ironic. The figures in the high mimetic would be the people who are generally feared...bigger than life figures. And the mythic figures themselves usually are used in very few other places than science fiction and a few modern poets who work with them in concentrated form. But science fiction seems the only place where you're consistently using characters who are mythological figures. So in that sense, there is some mythologizing process at work.

Apel: So characterization could serve as one area to justify a case for science fiction as a modern mythology. Another one that I see is the idea that science and science fiction give a rational grounding for a wide range of imaginative ideas or conceptions, just as previous mythologies were attempts to explain the workings of the world. You can build an artificial pathway to virtually anything that can be imagined starting with a basis of scientific research combined with some science fiction extrapolation. A minotaur, for example, is not something that can be considered a completely fantastic or impossible animal, because we can say, "Well, look at genetic engineering. A few decades from now we could build one of these. At least we see that it's possible to build one of these." That kind of thing. Even the mythic and impossible become possible through this vehicle. Just like ancient mythologies: You start with what you know, and extrapolate an explanation for what you don't know, based on the state of your knowledge at the time.

Zelazny: Yes. I do agree with that—finding a way to justify almost any situation.

Briggs: On that point, do you think *Creatures of Light and Darkness* is essentially a work of fantasy or a work of science fiction?

Zelazny: I never thought about it until now. I suppose I would have to classify it as fantasy. I do this through habit; I normally don't think in terms of whether the work is fantasy or science fiction when I'm writing or reading—it's a kind of artificial breakdown. But if I am pinned down and have to make that sort of distinction, I usually give the nod to science fiction if everything is explained or explainable in terms of extensions of what we know now, or what may be possible; whereas, in fantasy, there are large gaps in the explanations. They may be of a supernatural nature, or they may simply be omitted, leaving the reasons to the imagination. When you get into that sort of situation, I feel it deserves the label fantasy rather than science fiction—just because the element of rationality isn't exercised as fully.

Apel: That's why I point out science fiction as a possible vehicle for mythology, because the rational explanation is there. We're taking a mythic situation, an archetypal pattern, and explaining it in terms of genetic predispositions, or some other extrapolation of current scientific knowledge, while at the same time using these patterns to support an interesting story. Science fiction stretches the mind into the unknown and makes more of the unconscious conscious, like mythology does; science fiction is often about the immense power of individuals, just as one definition of mythology is "stories of the gods of a people," and so on. The main point is that just as mythology was once used to rationally explain the unknown, so now is science fiction. See what I mean?

Zelazny: I think so, yes. In my first book, *This Immortal*, when talking about mythological and semi-mythological creatures running around the world at that time, I provided two explanations and let the reader make up his own mind. And one other time I did try to create the distinction—or to destroy it, in a way. In *Lord of Light,* I felt that I wanted to explain the body-changing mechanisms, the justifications for the rulers reviving Hinduism, and I came up with logical explanations for everything. If I'd written the book exclusively in that fashion it would be a science fiction novel. And on the other hand, I wanted to write it in a style normally characteristic of fantasy writing, because there is, in my mind, a certain higher tone taken in a lot of fantasy. More descriptive. You're hauling in more similes and metaphors, and also perhaps indulging in slightly longer, more complex sentences, and slightly more formal speech patterns. I wanted to take what could be just a science fiction story and write it in a more elaborate fashion, to see how it would come out. I figured—if nothing else—that fantasy fans might like it for the one reason, and science fiction fans for the other. And I was curious.

Apel: *Lord of Light* is a perfect example of science fiction as mythology. You've got both magical and scientific explanations; you've got that principle of complimentary working, where no single explanation is ultimately correct, but two equal and opposite answers complementing each other do come closer to the truth. A union of opposites, symbolizing psychic wholeness. This, in addition to the great themes you're working with, indicate to me that what you're writing approaches myth.

Zelazny: I see what you're getting at. In that sense, and in the sense I spoke of in terms of the sort of characters that science fiction uses as being closer to those in myth. Between what you say and that, I feel you have a good case.

Briggs: What interests you for the future? What do you burn to do?

Zelazny: It doesn't usually work that way. I don't know too far in advance what I'm going to do next. I like to keep it that way, just so I'm ready to move when the time comes. I don't know what the next book will be, and I don't really care to think about it until I finish the Amber book. I'm just going to take a couple weeks and turn over everything in my mind, then go from there. I don't like to plan too far in advance, because times change, and I change.

Briggs: Do you think of yourself as being prolific?

Zelazny: Oh, not really, no. Compared to so many science fiction writers: Poul Anderson, Andre Norton, Isaac Asimov, Robert Silverberg...

Briggs: Still, you've produced better than a book a year, if you assume you've been writing for fourteen years, seven as a part-time writer and seven full-time. You've written nineteen books. You don't think of that as being prolific?

Zelazny: Well, again...by comparison, I don't. I mean there are people who turn out three or four books a year quite regularly, with no strain, and if I do two books in a year, I consider that a good year's work. But I don't know that that's considered a good number of books. I've never written a novel over 100,000 words in length. If I were to do all my books on the order of *Lord of Light*, I'm pretty sure I'd be down to under a book a year—point eight b.p.y.

Apel: Robert Anton Wilson confessed that the main character in *Illuminatus!* was a man he hoped to become. What do you hope to become in the future?

Zelazny: I hope to increase my versatility as a writer. I'd like to be able to do bigger themes and a greater range of characters. There was a time when I was working on style, and there was a time when just the structure of the book interested me. I found I kept shifting focus back to expanding the number and sorts of characters I do, and so forth; bring in some new ideas. If I succeed in doing that, I can become something I'd like to become in the next few years.

Apel: Rich and famous?

Zelazny: Well, that too.

Apel: Is there anything you'd like to talk about that we haven't asked?

Zelazny: I can't think of anything. I don't even have any books coming up to plug. *(Laughter)*

Briggs: This'd be the chance, y'know.

Apel: And I'll be appearing at Tahoe next week, Johnny... *(Laughter)* Thank you very much, Roger Zelazny.

NORMAN SPINRAD

Interview conducted at The Westercon
San Francisco, California
July 1973

Norman Richard Spinrad was born on September 15, 1940, in New York. He attended the Bronx High School of Science and graduated from City College of New York in 1961 with a B.S. degree.

In the late 1960s and early '70s, Spinrad became one of the primary voices of the New Wave movement, a younger generation of science fiction writers who tackled controversial topics such as violence, sex and drugs in an attempt to write mature SF, mirror the changing society, and elevate the genre stylistically. Spinrad's particularly controversial writing often made it difficult for him to find a publisher. And yet throughout his writing one can easily also discern a utopian streak, where he posits worlds, societies and governments that work better than our current systems.

Spinrad's wide knowledge and deep understanding of such institutions as politics, business (particularly publishing and media), psychology and technology, combined with an imagination the equal of any of his peers, has resulted in 23 novels, five short story collections and a classic *Star Trek* episode, as well as numerous reviews and columns in his lifelong role as an outspoken and opinionated media and social critic.

As of this writing (March 2014), Norman Spinrad is alive and well at 73, living in New York, and continues to write powerful fiction. He is active online in virtually every major form of social media and is currently involved in a massive effort by publisher Orion to reissue all of his fiction in ebook form.

Included are a pair of interviews with Spinrad, separated by 16 years. The first was conducted in July 1973, at the Westercon in

San Francisco; the second in July of 1989, by phone, literally hours before Spinrad left the U.S. to live in Paris.

As of our publication date (April 2014), Spinrad is the last of the authors in this book to be alive. We wish him many more years of literary production, good health, and world-class hell-raising.

NORMAN SPINRAD

Apel: Since we're interviewing you here at the Westercon, it's probably appropriate to start by discussing the scene. There seems to be a real dichotomy, for instance, between people who seriously read science fiction and people who come to the conventions. Do you see this, too?

Spinrad: Yes. The conventions started and are put on by the hardcore science fiction fans. Science fiction is their whole life. It's a subculture. And they're more interested in the subculture than they are at this point in science fiction. So they're very "in-groupy," and they're the people who are running the conventions, basically for the benefit of the fans. And I say "fans" in that restrictive sense; in terms of the hardcore groupies. So they look down on the people who are coming here to hear writers talk, or look at artwork, things like that. They're making money off them.

Briggs: Science fiction is unique in having that kind of hardcore fandom. Do you think that's particularly good for the genre?

Spinrad: No, I consider it very bad. The writers lose perspective on reality. A great many writers in science fiction either started out as fans, or after they've started out they came to a few conventions, where they're surrounded by people who have this love/hate relationship with them, and they end up writing for this audience, which consists of three to four thousand people all over the world. Now, the average science fiction book sells fifty thousand copies, so you see, even if you sell a copy of your book to each one of these fans, it's still a very small proportion of the readership.

Apel: How much of a voice do these fans have?

Spinrad: Very large. When publishers, for instance, try to judge what they should publish, they see a large phenomena. They see two thousand fans in a hotel, and they figure, "Oh, these must be the people who are into it, and this is what we're editing for; this is who we've got to aim our literature at." And it's really disproportionate. Also, when a major publishing house—this is a little bit less now than it used to be—wants to start a science fiction line and wants to get a science fiction editor from somewhere for this who's supposed to know something about science fiction, well, they go get a big-name fan, like Donald Wollheim, who started out as a fan. Or Forry Ackerman. And these are people with no literary taste. But the fact that someone is a well-known fan is no guarantee of good or bad taste. The two things don't correlate. A guy like Donald Wollheim has no taste at all...no literary taste.

Briggs: It would seem to me that conventions like this would be kind of dangerous from the standpoint of building an ego that would be impossible to deal with.

Spinrad: Well, building the ego isn't the worst part, although it does happen. You also get your ego deflated. People come up to you and say, "Oh, you're Norman Spinrad." "Yes." "Well, your stuff stinks." You get that, too. You get almost as much attack as you get ego-boo. *["Ego-boo": a primitive seventies psychological term; a diminution of the term "ego boost."]* What's really bad about it for a writer is both. You're getting negative criticism and positive criticism from this universe of people that surround you, none of it valid, or much of it invalid either way. Somebody may tell you that they love a book of yours that's really bad; very often for some pathological reason. Or they may tell you that they liked something that was good, for an equally pathological reason. Writers are particularly vulnerable to this. Writers aren't sophisticated. They have very little experience in the outside world. In the alleys.

Briggs: Do you feel this way about all criticism, or just fandom criticism?

Spinrad: An ignorant favorable review is a useless review, no matter where it appears. But in the fan press, particularly, you get attacked. There was a guy, for instance—I won't give his name because I don't want to give him publicity—who for two years in these fanzines wrote scathing reviews of everything I wrote. When reviewing other people's books, he used me as a horrible example. Never met him; he had never met me. But what he was trying to do was to get me to attack him publicly so that he would get some reflected glory by being noticed by someone bigger than he was. A lot of that goes on in the fanzines. Of course, I knew what he was doing and I never paid any attention to him. So a lot of the so-called "reviews" you get in fanzines have very little to do with any literary qualities or literary reasons. There are these personal things.

Apel: Like, this is the in-season to be against Norman Spinrad?

Spinrad: No, not even that. It's like, "Norman Spinrad is someone who doesn't sit still to be attacked, so if I attack him he'll notice it and therefore I will be noticed." Early in my science fiction career I fell into that trap, where I would respond to stuff. But I don't do that anymore.

Briggs: Another dichotomy that's appeared during the past few years concerns the science fiction writer's approach to his craft. It seems like writers are being divided into two camps, the "Old Guard," who started in the thirties and forties and are proud of having cranked out millions of words of pulp fiction, and the "New Wave"—the "young Turks," who have more artistic aspirations...or pretensions. Why has this happened?

Spinrad: Well, there's always been an American tradition in anti-intellectualism. We all know this—you know this, don't you? Great tradition in America—anti-intellectualism. It explains Norman Mailer and Ernest Hemingway, for instance. Why Hemingway had to go shooting things in Africa and incessant bullfights, and Mailer has to go around stabbing wives and getting into fights. It's because, somehow, being a writer in America, being an intellectual, is somehow considered effete, often even by the people who are doing it, and so you have to prove how hairy-chested you are in some other manner. Similarly, in science fiction, the same mystique is, "Well, I'm just a story-teller." What I'm trying to get at in terms of the SFWA is that Mailer and

Hemingway have that kind of macho image; in science fiction it becomes, "Well, we're not really artists, we're entertainers; we're commercial writers; we're professionals." They always say professionals; professionals, meaning, "I can turn out a book in three months, sixty thousand words, and it'll be exactly sixty thousand words long."

Briggs: There does seem to be an obsession with the mechanics of writing rather than the content. The panel discussion that I was sitting in on this morning just amazed me, because the people are, you assume, serious writers, and they're saying things like, "The most important thing is to know your publisher."

Spinrad: You see, science fiction writers have always starved.

Apel: That must be changing, though. You're dressed very nicely.

Spinrad: I am writing a mainstream novel. I'm an atypical case; I have always done other things too. I've written a little television, I write political columns, I do articles and whatever else I can do. Somehow I've always managed. Also, for some reason, I'm very popular in Europe, so I get a lot of European sales. I'm not terribly wealthy even now. This is not an expensive suit; I just have good taste. But science fiction writers have always been on the ragged edge economically. So that's why they're obsessive about money. And it's not just science fiction writers; it's writers in general. Mark Twain was always involved in some scheme or another to make more money from publishers and always ended up losing his shirt. Writers are always broke.

Briggs: What I was getting at is that there seems to be less concern with the aesthetics of the craft and more concern with the salesmanship mentality.

Spinrad: That's true. This is such a hard, hard thing to explain. First of all, I'll give you a philosophical base, all right? I believe that there's no such thing as pure writing. All writers—because they're human beings—have their work affected by their lives. You can't be unaffected by this situation of your life. So if you're always broke, and if publishers have an economic whip hand on you—and in science fiction they always do, because you're being paid so little—they can warp your mentality. Especially since science fiction is a very easy field in which to break into print. You know, you're nineteen, twenty years old, you get a story published, and before you have any maturity, you're being influenced by these commercial things, because you're surrounded by them. And most of the editors and publishers of science fiction don't really conceive of science fiction as literature. So the formative influence that they exert on young writers who aren't mature is very negative. It's, "Don't make waves"; it's "Give me sixty thousand words of something we can sell to libraries," and so forth. It's the job of the editor to get better books written, to find and publish them, and to help writers develop; to give them advice. But not just advice, you know. They've got to give them *good* advice. And there are very few editors like that. There are a few. Michael Moorcock, of course. Best editor in his field today. But that's in England, not here, so it's a different situation.

Young writers really don't have a chance. You have to mature on your own. You have to mature despite the influences around you, as a writer in science fiction. That's why you find so many science fiction writers who are burnt out by the time they're thirty-five. The majority of science fiction writers do their best work in their twenties, early thirties. By the time they're forty, they're hacks. There are exceptions, of course. But you think of... All right, even Zelazny. Now Zelazny was somebody who I thought was a really fine short story writer. Outstanding, in the beginning. And his first couple of novels were really good. And then he got involved with dealing with mythological things. At one point his agent—his crazy agent—got him a contract to do *eight books* like that. One right after the other. And you can't grow as a writer in a situation like that. That's why I never contract for more than one book at a time. I decide, "This is the book I want to do now," and I go out and get a contract for it. When that's finished I decide what I want to do next, and then I do that. A lot of science fiction writers, because of the economic situation, want to get as many book contracts as they can, ahead on into the year 2001, you know. At one point Robert Silverberg was booked up for five years. He knew what he was going to write for the next five years, and that's death. He used to, but he stopped doing that. He determined to be rich before he was thirty-five, and he indeed got rich before he was thirty-five, and then he retired.

Apel: What's your opinion of the mainstream writers like Vonnegut, Pynchon, Barth—the ones who write science fiction, but say, "I'm not gonna call it science fiction, because science fiction doesn't sell."

Spinrad: I understand Kurt Vonnegut completely because I feel the same way. Vonnegut started out as a straightforward science fiction writer. His first couple books were published as paperbacks by the usual places; he was appearing in *Fantasy and Science Fiction*, and so forth. And one day it dawned on him that he wasn't getting read by as wide an audience as he wanted, and he wasn't making any money. So he said, "Well. Why do I have to have this label on my book? Why do I have to have peeled eyeballs and bug-eyed monsters on my book? Why should I do that?"

Apel: Do you think that he's made a serious contribution toward elevating science fiction then?

Spinrad: No. He's made a serious contribution towards elevating Kurt Vonnegut. A lot of people within science fiction put Vonnegut down for doing this. I don't. Why shouldn't he? He should cut his income to one-quarter of what it is, and cut his audience to one-tenth of what it is? He's reaching his natural audience, which is what a writer wants to do, and he's done it by disassociating himself with science fiction while continuing to write it.

Briggs: Do you think the label "science fiction" even has any validity anymore?

Spinrad: Science fiction needs two things. A lot of people try to introduce the label "speculative fiction." I use that too, but I use it in a little different way. What I consider "speculative fiction" is anything that is literally science fiction, that has an inherent quality of being science fiction, in other words, that's about the "could-be-but-isn't"; that's about the *possible*. That includes *1984*, it includes Pynchon, it includes Vonnegut. You understand what I mean. Whereas science fiction is also a genre, like nurse novels, or mysteries, or spy novels: a commercial genre of literature; a publishing category. The perfect example is Philip K. Dick. Now Philip K. Dick is a better writer than Kurt Vonnegut, in my opinion. The body of his work is far more impressive than the body of Kurt Vonnegut's work. I think perhaps when the literary history of the twentieth century is written, that Phil Dick will be regarded as one of the important writers of the century, probably. I think he'll be remembered and read long after Vonnegut. Maybe not. I think Vonnegut will last, too. But I think the relationship that Dick is considered a minor writer and Vonnegut is considered a major writer will reverse itself in time, simply because the body of Phil Dick's work far outweighs the body of Vonnegut's work if you really look at it. In my opinion. There's an example, though—Philip Dick is stuck with the label, so he's obscure, and his works come out with peeled eyeballs on the cover, and don't get reviewed in serious places, and he isn't regarded seriously by serious critics. In Europe, it's different. In Europe, Dick is probably more highly regarded than Vonnegut. In France, also in Britain—I don't know about Germany—Dick is regarded more highly than Vonnegut. And rightly so.

Apel: That could be a cultural emphasis, since Vonnegut is writing middle-class American—

Spinrad: Dick is very American, too. But Dick has more depth of understanding of what it is to be an American. He can explain it. Philip K. Dick really has his finger on the pulsebeat of America. He writes about the American condition, he understands it, and he can generalize from that condition; whereas Vonnegut describes, Dick transcends. Anyway, there's a very good distinction. Dick is a science fiction writer; Vonnegut isn't, so the limitations of that label confine Dick to a smaller audience, which means he has to write more books to stay alive, and means he writes too fast sometimes, and means he writes some books he shouldn't write, and means he doesn't have as much time to spend on some books as he should, and means all of the unfortunate things that go along with that. So in that sense, I think that the label is very bad. On the other hand, the majority of science fiction being written and published doesn't deserve to be reviewed in important places; it doesn't deserve to be regarded seriously. The latest Lin Carter novel, or the latest Marion Zimmer Bradley novel, if looked at with any kind of absolute critical standards, are ridiculous.

Apel: "Ninety percent of everything is crap."

Spinrad: *(nodding in agreement)* "Ninety percent of everything is crap." Unfortunately, Sturgeon's Law has too often in science fiction been used as an excuse for continuing to turn out the ninety percent. It's like saying, "I'm only an entertainer, a poor minstrel; it's perfectly all right for me to write crap, because that's all I can do." And again, there's a validity to that. There are people who want to read *Thongor at the Mound of Venus*, and there are people that want to go to porno movies, and there are people who want to watch John Wayne movies. I'm not suggesting that they shouldn't have their product. But I would like to see the serious stuff dissociated from it. That *Camp Concentration* should be treated the same as *Dragonquest*...and it is, when you think about it. In terms of the *New York Review of Books, Time* magazine, the way the book looks in the store, what does *Camp Concentration* have in common with *Dragonquest*, or the latest Retief novel? Except for the kind of speculative subject matter.

Briggs: I guess what I'm getting at is if there's such a divergence between the classy stuff and the dreck, why even try to have one label that defines it? Why not just say, "This is all part of the mainstream anyway"?

Spinrad: The answer is complicated. That's what I'm trying to do. I'm trying to dissociate myself from that kind of packaging. I'm writing a book that's a mainstream novel now, probably after that my science fiction will come out as novels, I hope. Again, it's the kind of thing that each individual writer has to do for himself. You can't do it as a field; then you're involved in a situation like SFWA trying to upgrade the thing as a whole, saying, "Yes, this is serious literature; it should be treated as serious literature," and then somebody gives you a pile of books, and there's a bunch of Lin Carter novels in there, and Anne McCaffery books, and so on and so forth, and one Philip Dick novel, and *Camp Concentration*, and *Bug Jack Barron*, and a ream of space opera. You give that to a critic and say, "Here, this is serious literature, review it seriously," and what do they say? "God, what're these people talking about?" Most of it is not suitable for general readership.

Briggs: I was interested in your remarks on Zelazny, and there's another one I'd like to ask you about, and that's Samuel Delany, who seems to me to be one of the more consistently interesting authors.

Spinrad: He's one of the more consistently interesting authors; he's consistently screwed by publishers. He writes unusual books. They're long books, and he's been getting into longer and longer books, less and less science fictiony—and harder and harder to get published. Again, with a few exceptions, the editors in this field, and the publishers, do not really feel they have a literary responsibility to this literature. They feel it's product, so when they get a book they think isn't going to sell, or they think has to be handled individually, they're leery of it. They'd rather turn out ten space operas than one *Camp Concentration*. So the only way out for the individual writer is to pursue his individual career. I feel very badly about this, because I think there's a great deal of vitality in science fiction, and I think in many ways, more vitality in good science fiction, especially, than there is in so-called mainstream. You can see that a lot of so-called mainstream stuff is the same thing as science fiction—like Vonnegut. The difference, I think, is that science fiction has never been afraid to tackle the great themes, but they're usually tackled in a trivial, surface way. Whereas modern mainstream literature deals with very small things in great depth.

Briggs: Some elements of science fiction seem to be incredibly naive—

Spinrad: Oh, yeah.

Briggs: —like the whole field of sex has very seldom, as far as I know, been used well.

Spinrad: Try it, then try and get it published.

Briggs: Didn't you run into that problem with *Bug Jack Barron*?

Spinrad: *(resignedly)* Oh, yeah.

Briggs: I've often wondered why a genre that's at the forefront of other kinds of ideas has trouble with sex.

Spinrad: Very, very, very simple. The things that are usually paid most attention to in any literature get published in hardcover, right? Those are supposedly the "serious" books. Hardcover science fiction has always been aimed at libraries by the publishers. They count on selling eighty percent of the books to libraries. In libraries, science fiction gets put in the "young adult" collection. There's a censorship operating in hardcover science fiction, namely, the crazy censorship that it has to meet the librarian's conceptions of what young people should be reading, which is pretty rarified. Not even what young people *want* to read, but what librarians *think* they should read. So that's the simple reason for the fact that there has never been much sex. But that's changing, too. *Bug Jack Barron* was a watershed book in that way, because it was published. You see a little bit more free treatment of sex in science fiction in the past six, seven years than previously. Farmer, for instance. But Farmer is always running into trouble. Sturgeon.

Briggs: It seems that all the people who wanted to deal with this theme, though, not only had problems publishing it, but also had problems with certain science fiction readers who would say, "Why are you doing this to our genre?"

Spinrad: I have a book out now called *Men in the Jungle*, and I got a letter, literally from a little old lady in Pasadena. The letter came from Pasadena; you wouldn't believe a letter like this until you've seen it. Too much of a cartoon. And it said, "The sex in this is all terrible. This is wrong; this is not what it should be. Help keep science fiction sterile." *(Laughter) Literally.* I saved that letter. I have that letter, if anybody wants to verify it. It's the classical "little old lady from Pasadena" letter.

Apel: Are there any women writers in the field you'd consider top-flight?

Spinrad: The conventional one to say is Ursula LeGuin. Ursula's work is interesting, but I'm not a great fan of hers, particularly. I think Kate Wilhelm is a very fine writer. Not well known in the field. She's written a lot of books and short stories. A really fine writer.

Apel: The fact that you can only come up with a couple is a good indication that this is a very male-dominated field.

Spinrad: That's true. Ursula sold a story to *Playboy* and *Playboy* insisted on publishing the story with the by-line "U. K. LeGuin." They did not want their readers to know it was a woman. Ursula's a good writer, but she could just as easily be a man. Her novel *The Lathe of Heaven* had a male main character. This seems to be a fairly common conceit among women science fiction writers. Kate Wilhelm and Catherine Moore are possibly the two foremost writers who are not only female but are attempting to explore the female sensibility; female viewpoints. I would say those are the writers to watch. One of the reasons for that is that this has been a very male-oriented field, and in rather unwholesome ways. I have a book, *The Iron Dream*—it's about Nazis; it's about a lot of things—but one of the things the book is about is the traditional kind of formula science fiction novel, which has always involved this repressed homosexual phallic fetishist hero, the point being that when women came into writing commercial science fiction they had to do the same thing. They had to write male machismo stuff. Leigh Brackett is a good example. Even some of Catherine Moore's stories had to be written through a character like Northwest Smith. She couldn't write from the point of view of Shambleau, because that wouldn't be published. Women had to distort themselves to write this stuff. This is the kind of criticism I write when I write criticism. You can't understand science fiction unless you look at it in these kind of psychological/sociological terms. A great deal of what affects this literature is psychopathology. It is. Because science fiction is the literature of *anything*. It's the literature of fantasy; of fantasy made real. And fantasy is the kind of literature you read and you're aware of the fact that you're reading something that's unreal. It requires a suspension of disbelief. Science fiction creates a suspension of disbelief. So what it does is, it takes fantasies and makes them real; gives them verisimilitude. That's how Charlie Manson got involved with *Stranger in a Strange Land*, and crazy things happened. That's why there is a science fiction fandom. If you look at the basic "fan" personality, it's an immature adolescent male.

Apel: Is that still true? We're trying to get the other side of the story. The head of the present convention was telling us how the modern fan is college educated—

Spinrad: That's exactly right. Usually an intelligent, highly educated, psychosexually immature arrested adolescent. Of course there are exceptions; I'm not saying that every fan is like that. But if you're looking for a basic personality type, that's what you've got. A lot of transference from ordinary sexuality into militarism and fetishism.

Apel: Would you be referring to something like the Trekkies?

Spinrad: The Trekkies are different. The Trekkies are atypical because they're mostly young girls who are hung up on Spock as a kind of safe, satanic sexual figure.

Briggs: You're talking, I assume, about the people you see running around here. Leather clothes seem to be real popular.

Spinrad: Leather gear, the Society for Creative Anachronism, swords, quarter-staffs. You're affected by lots of that. Science fiction is the literature of Jungian archetypes in many ways. So when you're putting a lot of heavy Jungian archetypal elements into your fiction, you're going to attract people—not really on a literary level, but on a deep psychological level. People will read the literature, not for literary reasons, but for psychosexual reasons. Look at this interesting progression: Van Vogt wrote *Slan*—about a Nietzschean superman—and at the same time he was involved with L. Ron Hubbard and Scientology, which is an attempt to create the Nietzschean superman. Then another branch of it is Robert Heinlein and the authoritarian personality, leading to Charlie Manson. About the same time Van Vogt is getting into the Nietzschean superman, Adolph Hitler is very deep into it in an entirely different way. That's also what *The Iron Dream* is about. So you see how this manipulating Jungian archetypes creates an extra-literary effect.

That's another uniqueness of science fiction. It's not merely literature. Sometimes not *even* literature. It's also a social, psychosexual phenomenon that cuts across literary bounds. That's why some incredible crap is published, on a literary level. It's moron stuff; it's terrible. Heinlein. How can anybody take Heinlein seriously? He's an abominable writer. His characters have no depth; his prose is wooden; he can't write at all. In conventional literary terms, Heinlein is a terrible writer. But Heinlein is right in there with the Jungian archetypes and he knows how to manipulate Jungian archetypes. That's what Van Vogt does, and what cheap sword and sorcery does. Moorcock, who is a very good writer, and writes sword and sorcery for money, understands exactly what he's doing. He knows how to manipulate. He says, "I started writing sword and sorcery stuff and it wasn't doing very well. What can I do? Well, this seems silly, but I'll experiment. I'll throw in straightforward Freudian and Jungian imagery all the way through." And sure enough, it worked. In a way, that's a valid thing to do. If you do that and work it successfully on a literary level as well, it's very powerful fiction. It gets people not merely on the surface of their life, but it gets them deep inside. That's why a lot of bad science fiction is more interesting than a lot of good literature—interesting in the sense that it holds the reader. It's got you literally by the balls, not by the brain.

There's a very powerful manipulation of Jungian archetypes in science fiction. It doesn't have to be logical. It does have to have verisimilitude, which is not the same thing. Verisimilitude is the illusion of being real, however you create it. It isn't real. As Vonnegut puts it, "All art is lies." None of it is the truth. It's all lies. People say, "This fiction is realistic and this fiction is unrealistic." Well, what does that mean? It's all lies. What they really mean is, "This fiction gives the illusion of being real, and this doesn't." What's a good example? If there had been no Nazi Germany, and somebody wrote a science fiction novel about a place like that, people would say, "That's unrealistic. That couldn't happen." And yet it did. You never know what's going to be realistic. You know what *feels* realistic. It's an illusion.

All fiction is effect. Some fiction doesn't intend to give an illusion of reality. Fantasy, real fantasy, doesn't intend to be real. The question is, "What is the effect that this particular work is designed to create? Does it do so well, or does it do so poorly?" If you're trying to give the illusion of reality, you have to succeed in giving the illusion of reality.

Apel: How would you judge the success of a piece then?

Spinrad: I don't know. Who can say? Success is judged partly by whether it works. Like it or not, Heinlein is a successful writer, in that he achieves what he sets out to achieve. He doesn't achieve what somebody else sets out to achieve, or what somebody else thinks he should achieve. In his own terms, he's a successful writer. He's the master of his material, and he knows how to create the effects he wants to create. So that is successful in his terms. You may say, "But his prose is very wooden, and his characters are very simplistic." It's true. So from your point of view, then, he's not successful. There's no absolute criteria, really. There's stuff that anybody recognizes as being bad, because it's boring and it's dull, and it's written by somebody who seems to have a tin ear for language; it's just bad. Like Tolkien. *Lord of the Rings* is a *terrible* book, in literary terms. The characters are shallow, the prose is self-consciously archaic; on a literary level, it's a bad book. And yet on another level, it's a successful book, because it creates this alternative reality and transports the reader into it. That's another thing that science fiction can do that other literature usually doesn't do.

A good definition in literary terms is "Science fiction is a literature in which each work sets its own parameters." You can talk about writing a romantic novel, or writing a historical novel, or writing haiku...each one of these art forms has a set of parameters that defines it. You know, that's what it means to write a historical novel, that's what's supposed to be in there, and that's how the effects are achieved, and this is haiku, and you have to use so many syllables, so many lines. Science fiction has a formula which is another set of parameters, a very rigid set. But in literary terms, what science fiction really is, is a literature that says, "There aren't any parameters; there's nothing but blank paper." And therefore, wherever you can put the mind of the reader, that's legitimate.

Apel: You're dealing with the future, or with alternate realities, so you can set up your own parameters. Consensus time and space are transcended and can be manipulated.

Spinrad: That's right. Not merely setting up your own parameters for what you're writing about, but setting up the parameters for how you do it. *Bug Jack Barron* is a book like that. Something I did very deliberately. The story is a conventional science fiction story. It's got the strong hero, et cetera. That's a set of parameters I chose to use. But then I said, "Instead of dealing with these parameters in the surface kind of way that they're usually dealt with, I'll impose a different set of parameters on how I tell it." The result is a story where the prose is not exactly realistic, and yet it's very realistic. *The Iron Dream* is another example. That whole book exists because of the intricate set of twisted parameters that become the form of the book. *Camp Concentration* is an example. First person narrative of a guy slowly becoming a genius then going crazy. Brian Aldiss' book *Barefoot in the Head*, where the basic premise is that Kuwait has bombed Europe with acid bombs, so that everybody is stoned on LSD all the time, is another example. The book just starts there, and does some very strange things. Brian has never taken acid in his life. It's a good idea; it's a very dense, difficult book to read. A very Joycean-type book. That's the best example of a book that sets its own parameters, and that's why you can't define science fiction in literary terms. It's not a genre, it's not a form, it's not a school, it's not a single viewpoint, it's not a single philosophy, it's not a single technique; it's none of these things. It's the absence of all of these things as a formula.

The creative parameters of speculative fiction—as opposed to the genre thing—are unlimited. The only definition is that there are no definitions, that it's completely open. Of course, the genre thing, that's another story in itself. They keep talking about, "You have to have a strong hero that the reader can identify with. This hero isn't strong enough; he does a bad thing here." You can't have your hero punch a woman or kick a baby. If he does, then he's not a hero.

Apel: Didn't anyone ever show them *Yojimbo*? Or *Clockwork Orange*?

Spinrad: Well, you see, Anthony Burgess did a very nasty thing with *Clockwork Orange*; the kind of thing I did with *Iron Dream*, really. He gave you somebody who you identified with as a hero, because he used all the psychological tricks to make you identify with him as a hero, but he was a reprehensible creep. And so you find yourself identifying with this guy as a hero, because you've been tricked into doing that, yet you step back and look at what you're identifying with and you see terrible things. But he's really doing the things that heroes always do. What do heroes do? They hit people on the head, they kill... They don't do very nice things.

Apel: But heroes can get away with that sort of behavior because they're doing these things in the service of an important goal or an enlightened point of view.

Spinrad: Right. That's what *Men in the Jungle*, another book of mine, was all about. I did that trip there too, deliberately. I had a guy who you identified with as a strong hero, and he's doing just terrible things. Finally he gets to the point where he sees what he's doing to some degree, but at the end, he really hasn't seen; doesn't understand. Science fiction readers got a very uncomfortable feeling reading a book like that. The same is true with *Iron Dream*. They're getting the same identification with the hero that they get off on, then they see he's doing these awful things and enjoying it. The idea behind writing that kind of book is to try to break that brain-freeze, to give people some kind of self-consciousness of what they're identifying with. Like where Burroughs got the title for *Naked Lunch*: to take a good look at what's really on the end of the fork.

Apel: You read a lot of Burroughs?

Spinrad: I like Burroughs stuff a lot—that's William Burroughs, not Edgar Rice. *(Laughter)* There's a marvelous story by Philip Jose Farmer. ["The Jungle Rot Kid on the Nod."] It's Edgar Rice Burroughs as rewritten by William Burroughs. Farmer knows both writers really well, and can really write like William Burroughs. But he's also a Tarzan fanatic, and can write like ERB, too. And here he combines them, and you really believe you're reading William Burroughs writing about Tarzan. And it's so weird! And very good; very funny.

Apel: Why don't we get in one last question then get you back into the world again. Since we've been talking about science fiction creating its own future as it goes along, how does that lapse over into reality? How much is science fiction defining the future right now?

Spinrad: Once I was involved with a panel on this very subject, in which people started getting up and saying, "Science fiction should take over and transform the world!" and I got up, in a bad mood, I suppose, after having listened to this, and I said two good examples of science fiction transforming reality are Charlie Manson and Scientology. I think it's a very dangerous thing for people who are involved with literature to confuse metaphor with reality. Michael Butor, a French critic, once seriously suggested that all science fiction writers should get together and agree on what the future should be like, and write all their stories in that future, so that they could bring that future into being. He's really crazy when it comes to science fiction. What he seriously believes is socialist realism with a vengeance—socialist surrealism, really. Get together, decide how you want the world to be, write all your stories in that way, and call that world into being. That's very dangerous.

Apel: That seems to defeat the whole purpose of the freedom of science fiction; the numerous possible alternate worlds.

Spinrad: Science fiction is multiple-reality fiction. What's generally called "mainstream" fiction is something that evolved in the nineteenth century along with the Victorian mind, which is an attitude, like, "Life is real; life is earnest; and we know exactly what reality is." A single viewpoint. Science fiction gives you many viewpoints, multiple viewpoints of reality. The style of consciousness which science fiction has in part created—which is the modern consciousness, I think—is this multiple reality viewpoint, rather than the single reality.

Apel: So you'd say perhaps that modern science fiction is less concerned with describing the future than with mirroring the mindset of the present?

Spinrad: Right. You see many different realities, and the total reality of the total universe is in some way a compilation of many realities. Each person is his own reality, and your consciousness is involved in all these changes.

We live in a great many realities. Science fiction is the literature of multiple realities, and it's simultaneously been a product of this new change in consciousness, and one of the shapers of it, which is why, more and more, it's becoming the literature of the culture. The culture is more and more becoming a multiple reality culture. The older, more traditional fiction can't cope with that, because it's a single reality fiction. In other works, in the nineteenth century, writers were in effect doing what Butor suggested science fiction writers do: agreeing on what reality is, and writing in that reality. The whole world was like that, up until post-1945. And now the notion of multiplex realities is a more modern consciousness, and that's where science fiction is really at. That's why—despite the fact that a lot of it is crap, despite the fact that no one's publishing it correctly, despite fans, despite all the negative aspects—it is becoming, slowly but inexorably, the literature of the civilization. It's the only literature that is in tune with and can express modern consciousness. The only literature that's realistic has to be unrealistic, because reality is unrealistic.

Apel: Allen Ginsberg said several years ago that we're living in science fiction now.

Spinrad: We're living in science fiction times, yeah.

Apel: Thank you very much.

NORMAN SPINRAD, Part 2

Conducted by phone July 18, 1989

In preparation for an (aborted) attempt to publish this book in 1989, I contacted Norman Spinrad at his home in Los Angeles and set up this phone interview, which was conducted literally hours before he left L.A. to move in Paris, where he has resided since.

Apel: First of all, thank you for taking time out from your move to participate in this interview. I appreciate it no end.

Spinrad: Not a problem. Where would you like to start?

Apel: Can you tell me a little about your working habits?

Spinrad: It all depends. If I'm writing a novel, I write five days a week, or something like that. My habits are pretty regular. If I'm not writing a book, then I'm not writing a book, and my habits are not all that regular. I do four columns a year for *Asimov's*. I was doing a monthly column for *Locus* at the same time, but that got to be too much. That's sixteen columns a year. You can't really write books like that.

Apel: Do you actually go out and do research about the places you write about?

Spinrad: It depends on the book. Obviously, I didn't do that for *Child of Fortune* or *Void Captain. (Laughter)* Most often the things that seem heavily researched are really that I've gotten into something one way or another and then written about it later. I very rarely go out and do research for a book. In some cases I'll do some journalism, say, that gets me into an area which I'll later write a novel about. What I'm doing now is sort of research. I'm going to Europe to write *Russian Spring*, and I'm going to have to go to the Soviet Union because I've never been there. That's the kind of research that I do. But most often I don't work that way. What looks researched is really a lot of stuff that I've done for other reasons, which later on becomes material for a book.

Apel: Do you still contract for just one book at a time, to keep fresh?

Spinrad: Well, I now have two contracts. One is for a novel; one is to turn the *Asimov's* columns into a critical book, from the Southern Illinois University Press, which is an academic press.

Apel: I really enjoyed *Staying Alive*, your collection of columns—

Spinrad: Yeah, from *Locus*. Thanks.

Apel: Let's move on then. Who were some of your major literary influences while you were developing as a writer.

Spinrad: Early on? Well, I suppose Bradbury, really early on. Then Sturgeon, Bester...

Apel: How about outside the field?

Spinrad: William Burroughs. Mailer. Kerouac. Some of them were; some of them weren't.

Apel: Was there ever a moment when you read one of their books and knew that's what you wanted to do? Or that you could do it better?

Spinrad: Why copy someone else's book? I really can't remember exactly when that happened. I do remember when I read Mailer's novel, *American Dream*—as a matter of fact, I read that when I was working at Scott Meredith; I was an agent there—I really liked it, but there were things about it that bothered me. At some point I thought, "I could do this sort of thing better. I can see things that he did wrong here." Even though I liked the book a lot. I still do. And that sort of had something to do with *Bug Jack*

Barron, in a way. I've always thought that Mailer should try some science fiction. That *American Dream* would have been a stronger book if he'd had that option open to him in his own head. It's hard to explain why I believe that. But he's writing about a talk show guy who's involved in presidential politics, like in *Bug Jack Barron*. But Mailer did not feel he could extrapolate things. So he dealt with the myth of the Kennedys. I always felt that book would have been better if he had been able to be looser. So perhaps years later that contributed to *Bug Jack Barron*.

Apel: Do you consider Mailer's Egyptian novel [*Ancient Evenings*] to be science fiction?

Spinrad: Well, yeah. Of course. I covered that in one of my columns. I thought that was a very good book. A lot of people hated that book.

Apel: Do you still see a schism between science fiction and what's called "literature" in the *New York Times Review of Books*?

Spinrad: This is really complicated. That schism between "literary establishment approved fiction" and science fiction still exists. And I still feel that. On the other hand, that schism also exists, and has existed, between what's considered the accepted canon and a whole other tradition of American writers, which has nothing to do with science fiction, which is a tradition in another way I consider myself part of. It's a tradition which starts with Walt Whitman, Ralph Waldo Emerson, and goes up through Henry Miller into William Burroughs...

Apel: The mainstream versus the "underground."

Spinrad: Well, it's a little more elusive than that. Whitman wasn't exactly underground. Or Emerson. Miller was. Call it a "second stream" of American literature, which is *gone* now!

Apel: Yeah. Kesey was about the last one of that breed.

Spinrad: *I'm* the last one! I consider myself that, too, in a way. I'm conscious of that tradition as much as I'm conscious of the science fiction tradition. And I think that to the extent that anyone is carrying that forward anymore it is within science fiction. It's Tom Robbins, in a kind of pale way. It's, in a weird kind of way, William Gibson. Sam Delaney is actually a very self-conscious member of that tradition. I've always felt very strongly influenced by both those traditions—the science fiction and the, the...I don't even know what to call it. In the fifties and sixties, they called it...

Apel: Bohemians? Beats?

Spinrad: Yeah, the Beats. But the Beat stuff, too, had some other history behind it too. Whitman and Emerson. So I consider myself a part of that, too, not that there's much of that left.

Apel: Where do you see that "second stream" going over, say, the next decade? Are there others coming up to fill that stream, or is it drying up?

Spinrad: I think science fiction of a certain kind is carrying the tradition. And nowhere else. I'm conscious of that myself. Look at a novel like *The Dream Years*, by Lisa Goldstein, which directly connects science fiction with Surrealism, which was also part of that "second stream," on the European end. So in a way, there's more connectivity between science fiction and that "outsider" stuff, that "second stream" stuff—whatever you want to call it—than there is between it and mainstream literature. If that tradition is being carried on anywhere, it's being carried on mainly in science fiction. I can't think of anyone outside of science fiction that is doing that.

Apel: Maybe Paul Auster.

Spinrad: Or William Kotzwinkle. Vonnegut, up to a certain point, was doing that. Pynchon, of course, is the guy who bridges the whole thing.

Apel: It seems that these lines between mainstream and science fiction are blurring during the last decade. You've got Heinlein and Clarke on the bestseller lists every year...

Spinrad: Oh, yeah. Those lines are quite blurry. And that's all about money. I mean, if Kerouac wrote *On The Road* today—which was a bestseller then—I don't know if he could sell it now. The stylistic weirdness of it... I mean, how many books have you seen on the bestseller lists that are even remotely that stylistically inventive? It's almost impossible to do, except in science fiction. *Child of Fortune* does that, but that wasn't a bestseller, either.

Apel: Well, it was too difficult. *(Laughter)*

Spinrad: Y'know, some people—people who were more savvy about it in retrospect—said to me, "You've cut out a large portion of your potential readership for this thing as a bestseller, because people have to be too literate to read it." And I think that's probably true!

Apel: It taxed my limited knowledge of several different languages—

Spinrad: Well, you don't need to know those languages.

Apel: No, you're right. And you could pick up the meaning of the phrases in context. And, God forbid, you might actually learn something by reading it. But it accomplished what I think you wanted it to accomplish—that polyglot, future, melting-pot Earth language. But it's not a beach book.

Spinrad: I think it would make a great beach book. There's a lot of surface in there.

Apel: Well, I think what your friends were trying to tell you is that it's just too damned intelligent. People want vampires and you gave them mythology.

Spinrad: I don't think it was mythology that made that not a bestseller. I think it's more that it's non-standard prose. How many big books do you see that are written in non-standard prose?

Apel: Let's transfer this same concern from literature to film, and carry on the debate. The last decade has seen an explosion of science fiction in the public awareness mainly through films, from *Star Trek* to *Star Wars*. Do you think that this rise in science fiction in the movies jeopardizes your "second stream," or your literary experimentation, by further standardizing or homogenizing the ideas of science fiction?

Spinrad: No, I don't think so. I suppose I'm a little responsible for that awareness myself. *(Laughter)*. There's a lot of shit out there, but there's a lot of all kinds of shit out there. I think that what it all did, particularly starting with *Star Trek*, is that it made the imagery and symbol systems of science fiction accessible to the mass general audience. A great service! You don't have to explain everything now. It was *Star Trek* that really did it, so that when Lucas starts *Star Wars* with "Once upon a time in a galaxy far, far away..." — Well, if the same thing had been done in the fifties, it would take twenty-five minutes of set-up to get you from here to there. Now those background explanations are part of the general culture. People accept it. And that's all to the good.

Apel: Artists are notorious for being poor businessmen, yet you've managed to combine a very successful career as an artist with a deep understanding of the business of publishing—enough to write books like *Staying Alive*. How do reconcile those traditionally mutually exclusive character traits—the artist and the businessman?

Spinrad: Well, I think any artist who has a bad attitude toward business is being self-defeating and stupid. I have never hacked out anything for money... Unless you want to consider that *Star Trek* script *(Laughter)*. Well, OK, once in a while. But basically, in terms of fiction, I've never written anything I didn't want to write. And I've been able to do that all these years, without having any big best-sellers or anything, by taking care of business. My aphorism for this is: "The price of liberty is taking care of business." You *have* to take care of business. I think the kind of mentality that makes you a science fiction writer—a *real* science fiction writer, whatever that means *(laughter)*—is that you're the kind of person that has to know how the engine in your car works. If you've got a computer, you end up learning a little programming, taking the thing apart. Well, maybe not taking it apart...

Apel: Yeah, you'll void the warranty.

Spinrad: Yeah, I take that back. I've never taken my computer apart. I will not get into the hardware much. But I'll fuck around with the software! And it's the same thing with business. In order to write science fiction—"real" science fiction—you have to know about a lot of things. You have to have that kind of pack rat curiosity about how things work anyway—including business. Business is a big part of life!

Apel: So it's a native curiosity about everything that enables you to do both?

Spinrad: That's part of it. But this is not just some idle curiosity about how business works. This is how my *life* works! Also, if you're writing about America, if you're writing about peoples' lives, and you *don't* take into account work and business... I mean, that's two-thirds of reality! That's one of the things I admired about Phil Dick. One of the few science fiction writers, one of the few contemporary writers, who really deal with peoples' jobs. Think about it: in how many science fiction novels...in how many novels—does the main character have an actual job? How much of that do you see? Phil's characters always had jobs. Most of mine do.

Apel: Do you find the same thing that Phil did as a writer-slash-businessman; that you're making money cumulatively by regularly selling your old novels again as reprints?

Spinrad: Yeah. Also like Phil, on European sales.

Apel: France best?

Spinrad: France best. Germany doing real well right now. England used to be good, but not as good as it was.

Apel: I understand you have a book on the "blacklist" in Germany right now.

Spinrad: I had two books, actually, on the Index. One was *The Iron Dream...*

Apel: Had to be! *(Laughter)*

Spinrad: But I have to give them credit. They fought this for five years, all the way up to the German equivalent of the Supreme Court, and finally won. And created a different impression on a really pernicious law they had. So *The Iron Dream* is no longer on the Index in Germany.

Apel: How's it doing?

Spinrad: Well, it went into its third printing while it was still on the blacklist... *(Laughter)*

Apel: Another thing that intrigues me about your dual personality—the artist and the businessman—is that your science fiction shines with optimism—but your books about the industry, like *Stayin' Alive* and *Children of Hamlin*, are certainly pessimistic—almost bitter in parts. How do you maintain this positive outlook in your fiction feeling as you do about the realities of the industry?

Spinrad: Well, the industry isn't everything. I'm right here in the middle of a Writer's Guild strike, which is becoming a huge exercise in assholery. *(Laughter, followed by a long pause.)* That's a very complicated question.

Apel: Sorry.

Spinrad: You mentioned *Children of Hamlin*—Well, that's about one aspect of the industry. The lowest aspect of the industry. *Stayin' Alive*...that's just reportage. That's the way it is; that's the way it is. That book tells you this is the way it is; this is the reality you have to deal with. On the other hand, that's not all negative either.

Apel: No, you give a lot of helpful suggestions.

Spinrad: I think my novels are optimistic. But they're not optimistic in the way that Herbert Gold—the guy who used to write all that shit for *Playboy*—used to tell a story about having his fiction come back with a rejection slip that said, "No, no, Mr. Gold. We want happy stories about happy people with happy problems." *(Laughter)* So I don't think the optimism in my fiction is like that. It's not the optimism of saying the world is set up so great. It's the optimism of the human spirit and coping with it. To be realistic about things without being cynical.

Apel: Most of your recent books seem to me to be attempts to achieve some kind of synthesis between science and technology, and human feeling—the emotional valuation that makes us human. Do you think this might be called your Grand Theme?

Spinrad: Well, it's one theme. It's a theme of *Songs From the Stars*, and, in a different kind of way, I suppose, of *Child of Fortune*. But in *Child of Fortune* it's not the theme, *per se*; it's not about working this out; it's about a society that's figured this out already. It's a story set in that system.

Apel: It's the theme of *Songs From the Stars*, in that you've got the people who've evolved a natural technology facing the dilemma of the necessity of accepting space age hi-tech in order to submit to their destiny—

Spinrad: Yeah.

Apel: In *A World Between*, it's the masculine Transcendental Scientists versus the Femocrats with a softer view of technology—

Spinrad: Well, that's in there. But to me, the theme of *A World Between* is kind of a Jeffersonian thing. How do you maintain a democracy in the face of an attack by forces who are not playing by your rules and admit they're not? If you exclude them, how do you maintain your democracy; and if you don't, how do you maintain your democracy the other way? It's essentially the problem that any kind of democratic society faces when it's confronted with something totalitarian.

Apel: It's a Catch-22. You used a variation of that in *The Mind Game*: If you submit to this fascist religion, we'll set you free.

Spinrad: Yeah. What did the Beatles say? "Come together over me." *(A horrid duet and great laughter follow.)* That describes certain people that I don't want to follow around. Messiahs bother me.

Apel: Let's move on to *Child of Fortune*. Now, maybe I'm stupid, but it took me about half the book to realize it was an allegory of the late sixties. After I caught on, though, I enjoyed it even more, at an even deeper level.

Spinrad: Well, it is and it isn't. It is what the introduction says it is. What happened in the late sixties was not something without historical precedent. All of that came out of something that's inherent in the human spirit, that has come out at different times in different ways, and has always existed in a sense.

Apel: That's something I greatly admire about that book—the continuity of consciousness. You're writing future mythology, but you don't overlook past and present mythologies; you string them all together in an unbroken chain. There are no missing links. You didn't take the easy way out, like postulating an atomic war that wiped out all traces of the past.

Spinrad: I was very conscious of that when I wrote it. If you think of how replicated all our records are, unless there's a complete and utter cataclysm—and maybe even then—the people of the future will know a hell of a lot more about us than we know about the Greeks. I really believe that is really true. The "great discontinuity" is a convenient fictional device.

Apel: It's a lazy way out.

Spinrad: Yeah. It's a lazy way out.

Apel: And you refused to take that lazy way out. You had to be educated in history and aware of the present to postulate your fictional future. So in a sense what was the Grail Quest in the Middle Ages becomes the Yellow Brick Road in the twentieth century and transforms into the Wanderjahr in your future society. And you've even taken this a step further. These are not just events or intellectual ideas, but are all understood as metaphors for self-discovery.

Spinrad: Every culture has a version of it. It's cross-cultural.

Apel: And cross-temporal as well. It's the Hero's Journey. I think you had your heroine Wendy say something about "the eternal tale in all its time-bound incarnations." It's archetypal. Now here's my question about this: Do you think that by writing about a society like this—one deeply in touch with its mythical and archetypal roots—that you're helping create that kind of society...and possibly even helping elevate recent cultural events to the status of mythology?

Spinrad: That's happening already. There are new Jungian archetypes developing. The atom bomb, for instance. The atom bomb is the crown of creation. It's Mankind, being given for the first time, in mythological terms, what Prometheus had, and then some. The fire of the gods doesn't belong to the gods anymore.

Think of the power we have over our own DNA. I happen to have in my room here—I'm looking at it now—something I carved a long time ago...on an acid trip *(Laughter)*. A wooden cane with a strange knot on its head. Under acid, I carved the head of this cane into a symbol: an eagle rising out of a double helix.

Apel: That sounds like the caduceus; the wings on the medical staff, flying above two entwined snakes.

Spinrad: Yeah, which represents the DNA double helix. And the eagle represents consciousness. What this means to me is consciousness transcending the evolutionary process. And I think that we've done that. We're there, for better or worse. For better *and* worse. We have the power of life and death over the planet; we have the ability to fuck with our own genes. We've got it in our hands, whether we like it or not. We have transcended the deterministic level of the evolutionary process. We are no longer controlled by the physical world. The physical world is as much influenced by us as we are by it. I mean, look around! Look what we're doing—for better or for worse. Look at the Greenhouse Effect business that's going on. We're doing this! We are changing the nature of the planet.

Apel: This brings up what we were talking about a few minutes ago: the perception I get from your novels that they're an attempt to achieve some kind of synthesis between technology and human emotion—which could be seen on a grander scale as an attempt to achieve a synthesis between the material and the spiritual, or in this case, the DNA of our material bodies and the consciousness that guides it. This seems to be one of your key images.

Spinrad: Yes, it is. It's really a very complicated subject. I believe in the continuity of knowledge. What I have against things like Scientology, or the Roman Catholic church, or the Cabalistic tradition, is the idea that knowledge is something to be held in secret. I have a very democratic attitude toward knowledge. I believe that the poorest person today—if you look at it in a certain way—is far richer than the kings of the Middle Ages. A king of that time would acknowledge this. The riches are *knowledge*. Anybody who wants it has access to it now. It's something the kings couldn't have gotten their mitts on. You want to know the secrets of the universe? [Stephen] Hawking has just published his book [*A Brief History of Time*]; go out and buy it, or check it out of the library.

Apel: Your books seem to exhibit that "Aquarian Age" attitude that the days of occult knowledge is past; now it's time to reveal all knowledge.

Spinrad: I don't believe in the supernatural. At all. I believe there are some natural phenomena that have yet to be adequately explained—some relationships that have yet to be elucidated. I think you ought to apply the test of science to anything. Sometimes it's bullshit and sometimes it isn't. For example—I used to think Linus Pauling was a weirdo. Then I had serious medical conditions, and I read his book [*Vitamin C and the Common Cold*], which was rigorous biochemistry. Molecular biology. There it was: a good piece of science. What convinced me—and this is the test I apply to all this stuff—is, don't tell me *what* it does, tell me *how*. And his book does.

Apel: Didn't I read somewhere that you saved somebody's life with vitamins?

Spinrad: Oh, Harlan Ellison claims I cured him of a virus—which of course I haven't done. You can't cure yourself of a virus. All you can do is keep your immune system up.

Apel: I want to talk more about *Child of Fortune*. I love that book. And it dovetails really well with one of the themes of this interview book, which is the idea that science fiction is remythologizing the twentieth century. Do you consider science fiction the modern version mythology?

Spinrad: Well, that's one of the functions of science fiction. It's not the same thing, though.

Apel: We're dealing with manipulation of the archetypes—

Spinrad: I think science fiction *creates* archetypes. With the mass media of the twentieth century—with television, with radio, with telephones, with everything like that—there is the ability to create archetypes and implant them in the mass consciousness at a speed which would have taken generations before these media existed. The atom bomb is a good example. Everybody who grew up in the fifties or later probably has dreams about The Bomb. The Bomb is as strong an archetype as anything. The Rock Star! There's something about that one, too. And I've done this; I've made some records. I sang on one record; I did some demos from *Little Heroes*. There's something about that. No matter what you are, you'd rather be that. The Rock Star: that has archetypal echoes. Things change; things mutate. I think that science fiction does not remythologize the twentieth century in the sense of remythologizing it with the old mythic structures, but it extracts from the ongoing stream of history the new myths. *Neuromancer* [by William Gibson]; there's a good example. Cyberpunk.

Apel: Perhaps we've transcended the old myths?

Spinrad: Well, we haven't transcended all of them, but we add to them things that are just as deep, even though they're not as old. Just as we have the ability to screw around with our own DNA, we have—through science and technology—the same ability to screw around with our own mythic substructure, as profoundly as we can with our genetics.

Apel: And if this screwing around comes out badly, and the wrong people fuck with it?

Spinrad: Well, if it comes out badly, you've got Ronald Reagan.

Apel: And if it comes out correctly, you've got *Child of Fortune*?

Spinrad: You have *Child of Fortune*, you have... Well, who really knows what "correctly" ends up being?

Apel: Once again, thank you very much for your time.

ROBERT ANTON WILSON

Interview conducted at his home
Berkeley, CA
January 12, 1977

Robert Anton Wilson was born Robert Edward Wilson in Brooklyn, New York, on January 18, 1932. He attended Catholic grammar school and Brooklyn Technical High School, then studied Engineering at New York University. A childhood bout with polio and its cure by the controversial Sister Kenny method informed much of his personality and attitude throughout his life.

Like so many budding writers, Wilson worked a number of jobs early in his career, including ambulance driver, engineering aide, salesman, and copywriter. Early in his writing career, he integrated his maternal grandfather's name, Anton, into his own as his *nom de plume*. In 1965, he became an associate editor at *Playboy* magazine, where he met Robert Shea. Together they began work on the epic picaresque comic sci-fi novel (and "fairy tale for paranoids"), *Illuminatus!*, which was published in 1975.

In 1958, Wilson married Arlen Riley, a poet and writer (who had worked with Orson Welles, one of Wilson's cult heroes) and adopted her three children from a previous marriage. Throughout their forty-year marriage they moved frequently, including residences in Ohio, Chicago, Berkeley, San Francisco, Dublin, and Los Angeles before finally settling in Capitola-by-the-Sea, California, on the Monterey Bay.

Although perhaps best known as the co-author of *The Illuminatus Trilogy*, "RAW" (as he was known among his devotees) developed a worldwide cult following mainly for his non-fiction books. During the '80s and '90s, he was a frequent lecturer and public speaker in numerous US and European cities. By 2005, he had published 35 books, including several novels, plays, screenplays, and numerous nonfiction volumes of what he eventually referred to as "quantum psychology," his synergetic synthesis of General Semantics, Neuro Linguistic Programming, Jungian depth psychology, occult research (as documented by Aleister Crowley, among others), and mental reprogramming as detailed by John Lilly and RAW's close friend, Dr. Timothy Leary. Quantum psychology was an attempt to assist readers in expanding their consciousness by breaking out of their "reality tunnels" defined by language and preconceived beliefs, and to develop critical observation and independent thought. Other significant influences on Wilson include James Joyce, Ezra Pound, Beethoven, and Orson Welles, all of whose works are referenced frequently in his writing.

Given his wide range of interests, it is difficult to pigeonhole a writer like Wilson. Among the many labels that have been applied to him, we could include stand-up philosopher, psychologist, futurist, essayist, cult figure, editor, playwright, poet, civil libertarian, Promethean, Discordian saint, and (as he described himself) "agnostic mystic." As a popularizer and synthesizer of bleeding edge discoveries in psychology and physics, Wilson developed a large cult following among alternative intelligentsia and great respect among the foremost figures of the consciousness expansion movement. As a satirist, Wilson's aggressive humor was engineered to offend the closed-minded and challenged readers to question authority and examine their unconscious ("programmed") beliefs. He was a well-known expert on conspiracy theories—documenting the reality of some and debunking others—and in his later years he founded the "Guns and Dope" political party and publically promoted the use of medical marijuana, which he found effective in treating the symptoms of the Post-Polio Syndrome that plagued him during the final decade of his life.

Post-Polio Syndrome reduced Wilson's mobility in the early 2000s, confining him to a wheelchair and eventually to his bed. He died on January 11, 2007—a week shy of his 75th birthday—at his home in Capitola. Readers interested in more biographical details of the man who was "either a genius or Jesus" (*Sounds* magazine, London) are encouraged to seek out the documentary film *Maybe*

Logic or Wilson's own semi-autobiographical works, *Cosmic Trigger* Vols. 1, 2, and 3.

ROBERT ANTON WILSON

Apel: Professional Showtime, with Robert Anton Wilson, Take One! I'd like to start out by turning the tables on you, and applying one of your own tricks to you. I'd like you to do the Theravada Buddhist exercise "What brought me here tonight?" on yourself—two or three paragraphs of biographical information describing how you find yourself in this particular space-time nexus.

Wilson: I had polio when I was a year and a half old, and I had it again when I was two and a half years old. I think that gave me a basic imprint that the universe was a mean mother, and that you have to fight like hell to make it, to survive. Also, I was born right in the middle of the Depression into a working-class family. I think between polio and the Great Depression of the 1930s I developed a Faustian spirit which escalated over the years until the point where I was taking on the whole universe. You know, "Yea, though I walk through the Valley of the Shadow of Death, I will fear no evil, for I am the meanest son-of-a-bitch in the Valley." At that point, the only choices were to go mad or become a science fiction writer.

I'm definitely an anti-theist rather than an atheist, and I've often wondered how I got that way. I think the polio and the Depression are a big explanation. Thanks for making me think about this.

Apel: You worked as an associate editor at *Playboy* for five years, and you were writing long before that. How many articles have you published?

Wilson: I don't know. Over a thousand, let's say.

Apel: What are your working habits, now that you freelance for a living? Do you have set times or amounts to produce, or do you just work when inspiration strikes?

Wilson: I think I average around ten pages a day. I often get bursts of twenty or thirty pages... The biggest burst I can remember was one where I did seventy pages in a day and a half. Without cocaine, if you'll believe that. It was an article for a magazine called *Cheetah*, and they published it in three parts.

Briggs: *Illuminatus!* was done in collaboration with Robert Shea, and you and Timothy Leary have also produced some collaborative efforts. Do you enjoy collaborative efforts?

Wilson: Yeah. Very much so...with the right people. Shea was very good to collaborate with. Leary is also very good to collaborate with. We listen to each other. We don't argue.

Apel: Would you say that you had the major hand in writing *Illuminatus!*?

Wilson: I think so. But the basic plot is Shea's: the yellow submarine, the rock festival, and things like that.

Apel: Could you give us a quick breakdown of what parts were his and which were yours?

Wilson: Oh, Christ, it's awfully hard to disentangle it. The libertarian, mind-your-own-business politics is both of us. I would say that the actual words are about seventy percent me and thirty percent Shea. That's a guess; somewhere around there. It gets complicated, because some of the incidents we both wrote. We wrote them over several times, taking turns rewriting. The book went through several drafts. So it's hard to say on some pages whether this is me or Shea. There are some pages where it's just pure Shea and some pages where it's pure me. Atlantis is all by Shea; Simon Moon, Markoff Chaney, the Dealy Lama, and Robert Putney Drake are all by me. But otherwise there are a lot of pages that are very ambiguous. A page that's otherwise all me may have had a single word changed because Shea kept insisting, "That doesn't look right," and I'd finally realize, "I guess you're right, Bob." And on pages that are almost pure Shea you'll find a word that I put in; I'd say "Your word isn't right there," and he'd agree.

Apel: Are your relationships with publishers generally favorable?

Wilson: Well, by and large, I am not madly in love with publishers. Publishers are businessmen, and businessmen are really not my favorite type of human beings. James Joyce went into business briefly, and after a while he said to Italo Svevo, "You know, I think my partners are cheating me." Svevo said, "You only *think* they're cheating you? Joyce, you *are* an artist!"

I worked for seven years for an engineering corporation that had nothing to do with publishing. The rest of my working career was all in books and magazines—the whole publishing field—and I wrote advertising for brief periods. From what I've seen of businessmen, I would say that they have no more morals than a scorpion.

There are two types of predators. There are predators who just go out and grab what they want and take their chances on getting caught. If they spend a little time in jail, that's all part of the game. They lose a few points. As soon as they get out they try to win again, at the same primitive level. And then there is the second type of predator, the type who has figured out that you can do all that grabbing without risking jail. There's a great novel about this: *JR*, by William Gaddis. It's one of my favorite books. JR keeps saying that anybody who steals is a fool; you can get as rich as you want in this country by using the laws creatively. Businessmen are people who know that. They've got the same mentality as pirates. When they think they can get away with it, they break the law as boldly as thieves.

As Gene Fowler once said, "Every publisher should have a pimp as an older brother, so he'd have somebody to look up to." At this point, nothing a publisher does would amaze me. If a publisher came in the door and shit on the table and said, "You've got to accept that because I'm a publisher and you're a writer," I'd be awed, but I wouldn't be surprised. Nothing they could do would startle me at this point. If a publisher was caught the way Nixon was caught it wouldn't surprise me. In fact, I wonder why none of them *have* been caught yet. Sometimes I puzzle about things like the Clifford Irving case. I don't know how guilty Irving was, but certainly the whole ambiance of the publishing business is to incite people to behave that way. It wouldn't surprise me at all if the publishers were ten times guiltier than Irving himself.

I guess I sound uncharitable or unforgiving... *(raucous laughter)* but as you go around interviewing writers, you'll hear this from all of them. This is what writers always talk about when they get together. I'm not really bitter, because I realize the way things are is the order of nature. You can't get yourself too emotionally wrought up over it; that's the kind of primitive planet we're living on. These mammalian types, the alpha-baboons, are still running the herd. Stupidity and rapacity have been around for so long they must have an evolutionary function. Far be it from me to challenge evolutionarily stable behavior that dates from the Permian Era.

Briggs: The other side of the publisher coin would be to talk about your relationship with your fans.

Wilson: I love them. I adore them. I worship them.

Briggs: Even when they cluster around you at conventions?

Wilson: I think conventions are vitally important in the science fiction world. It's just about the only gratification most writers in that disadvantaged neighborhood of Literaturopolis ever get. I do lots of different kinds of writing; I'm not limited to the science fiction ghetto. But I think the conventions are necessary, or the full-time science fiction writers would all give up. They never make much money; they're all poor. I think without the conventions they'd all throw away their typewriters and become shoe salesmen or something. But at the conventions, the writers are allowed periodically to see these adoring faces of their fans, and that gives them the incentive to go on and write some more, even though they're getting paid less than a sewer cleaner.

Briggs: It's interesting to hear you claim that you're not limited to science fiction. When Dell published *Illuminatus!* they published it as "science fiction." Do you think that limited your audience?

Wilson: Does a bear shit in the woods? I think if *Illuminatus!* had been published in hardcover, and promoted as a major American satire—which several critics now claim it is—it would have gotten reviewed in the *New York Times*, and the *New York Times Review of Books*, and it would have been an intellectual "must." Everybody claiming to be an intellectual would have had to read it. Bookstores would have featured it. But putting it out in paperback as a science fiction pulp limited the audience. Bookstores buried it in the back shelves. I think it definitely harmed the book. I think that the twelve-hour stage version of *Illuminatus!* at the National Theatre in London being such a whopping success has begun to reverse all that.

Apel: Why did Dell take five years to publish it?

Wilson: Dell cursed the book every way they could. Not through malice, just through brutal ignorance. I have several reviews in the files where the reviewer has commented, "It looks like Dell doesn't know what they have here." They're businessmen, and businessmen can't tell literature from sausages. They said, "Cut out five hundred pages." They have no concept that a work of literature, like a painting or a symphony, has a structure; that there are integral rhythms, and so on. They buy it by the pound, like potatoes or something. "We want five hundred potatoes less."

Apel: Why did you put up with that?

Wilson: Why did I put up with that? Why did I do it? Well, by that point, after five years of struggle and having gotten to the point where we were living on Welfare with four kids and all that, I just collapsed. I couldn't struggle anymore. I said, "OK, I'll give up on this battle; I'll win the next battle." Basically, I decided I'd rather have a mutilated *Illuminatus!* published in 1975 than no *Illuminatus!* published in 1975. I just couldn't wait another year. You see, even if we got another publisher right away, the next month, (which wasn't likely), it would still take another year before the goddam book would come out. And it wasn't possible we'd get another publisher within a month, y'know? New York publishing moves no faster than the Great Canadian Glacier. I was just defeated; I was ground down. The eight missing appendices were among the five hundred pages that were cut. There were eight more appendices on various subjects, such as the Illuminati interpretation of the Tarot, and the Discordian interpretation of the Tarot, and a lot of other things like that.

Apel: Will those ever be published?

Wilson: Yeah, I think so.

[*Note: This prediction turned out to be accurate; in 1980, Berkeley's And/Or Press published* The Illuminati Papers, *which included much of the 500 pages of material cut from the original manuscript of the* Illuminatus! *trilogy*.]

Apel: What's your opinion of people like Vonnegut and Pynchon, who write what is easily recognizable as science fiction and yet claim that it's not science fiction, it's mainstream?

Wilson: Well, Vonnegut had a long, uphill fight to establish that. He kept getting classified as science fiction, and the *New York Times* kept ignoring his books. He went through decades of poverty, because of the "sci-fi" label and its dire financial consequences. I don't know how Pynchon escaped it; he got around them somehow. He had the good luck that his publishers didn't promote his first book as science fiction, and so it was recognized as a work of literature. I don't mind the label, aside from its monetary disadvantages. Some of my favorite books are science fiction.

Briggs: Do you read much science fiction? If so, who do you like?

Wilson: Well, in the first place, I don't read as much as I used to. I was an omnivorous reader in my youth, a monster of erudition, but I find I'm reading less and less. When you become a full-time writer, you're using your eyes so mucking fuch that you look for something else instead of reading as relaxation. You want to rest your eyes. So I'm reading less every year, and walking in the woods more. I've got an agreement with myself that when I have a hundred thousand dollars in the bank, I'm going to stop writing for six months and just catch up on my reading. Aside from that, my favorite science fiction writers have long been Stapledon, Heinlein, Clarke, and Sturgeon.

Apel: That's easy to understand, I think. They're all very imaginative writers, and all idealists, in their own peculiar ways. What else about them that appeals to you?

Wilson: I agree with the Oriental teachers who say it's very important to be careful what you feed into your nervous system. I prefer to feed my nervous system on images of heroic things that human beings have accomplished, or could accomplish. I like to read biographies of people of great courage and people of wisdom and so on. I would much rather program myself with things that give me an idea that we can all be sublime creatures, which I think we can, rather than with the programming that we are merely the most vicious beasts loose on the planet. Mark Twain, by the way, said the same thing as I've just said. He said, "Don't associate with people who have a low view of humanity; it'll give you a low view of yourself." Associate only with people who are heroic and striving. I agree with that.

Apel: I'd add to "heroic" and "striving" people with a good sense of humor.

Wilson: Yeah. Ezra Pound in the later Cantos keeps repeating over and over phrases about the virtue of *hilaritas*. Scotus Erigena counted *hilaritas* as one of the supreme virtues: the ability to have a hearty sense of humor. I think cheerfulness is one of the most important and least appreciated virtues in the world. Anybody can bring the room down by sitting around bitching and griping, but it takes real creativity to bring the whole room up.

Briggs: Is that why your books have such a strong comic sense? Are you consciously being comic?

Wilson: Yes and no. I'm consciously being comic part of the time now, since my long-time fans expect it of me. But also it's my basic nature to see the humorous aspect in things. The Cosmic Giggle Factor, the SNAFU principle, Murphy's Law, and so on.

Briggs: The thing that springs to my mind is one of the great comic devices of *Illuminatus!*, the Stan Laurel-Oliver Hardy analogy of human relationships: "*Now* look what you made me do!"

Wilson: That's part of my assault on class snobbery in literature. I am deliberately trying to elevate Laurel and Hardy to the level of metaphysics. I think anybody with basic Zen savvy can see what I'm doing there, but most of the literary intelligentsia still believe in those great dichotomies between the serious and the trivial, high art and low art, and all that bullshit.

Apel: Who influenced you as a writer? In *Illuminatus!* you mentioned Faulkner, Lovecraft, Chandler, as well as strong tribute to James Joyce. Who else would you add to that list as being a significant influence?

Wilson: First of all, I think everybody you read influences you. Every writer I've ever read has left some trace on me. And I think that's true of every reader, since what you feed your nervous system today becomes your reality tomorrow. Every time a writer is reading, he's always thinking, "What can I rip off here?" That's not original with me, that was Shakespeare's attitude. What was Virgil's response to *The Odyssey*? His response was "How much of this can I rip off?" and then he wrote an imitation *Odyssey*.

You're always looking for what you can learn from everybody. I've learned something from every writer I've ever read. The strongest influences are certainly Joyce, the blind man who saw, and Ezra Pound, the crazy man who understood. And Raymond Chandler, and H. L. Mencken, and Faulkner, and Mailer... Well, you see, I could go on and on; after you get past the first three, you could just keep adding on and on. The major influences are definitely Pound, Joyce and William Burroughs. Burroughs definitely comes in third, after Pound and Joyce. I'm much more influenced by people in this century than in previous centuries. There's no doubt whatsoever that I've stolen a hell of a lot from Shakespeare. But what I purloined from Shakespeare really comes through a filter, so to speak.

Apel: A twentieth-century filter?

Wilson: Right. People like Pound and Joyce are practically my contemporaries. Pound died only a couple years ago, actually; Joyce died in 1940. But he's still the central twentieth-century novelist. Nobody has found a way yet to surpass Joyce in cosmic, mythic, epic scope, or in sheer crazy humor.

Apel: You do something which I've rarely seen in another work, which is not only imitate the style of other writers, but indicate that you're imitating their style. You'll say, "Here comes a nice run of Joycean prose," and then do a nice run of Joycean prose.

Wilson: I don't do that all the time. There are a lot of people in *Illuminatus!*, for instance, who aren't directly acknowledged. There's a lot of Chandler in the style, but nobody says, "Here comes another Chandler metaphor."

Briggs: I thought it was interesting that you added a review of *Illuminatus!* within the body of the book itself. I was wondering if that was done to respond to criticisms people might level against the book before they had a chance.

Wilson: No, it was a groping attempt at something I'm doing much better in my new book—

Apel and Briggs *(in unison)*: You mean *Schrödinger's Cat*? *(Laughter)*

Wilson: —which is incorporating self-reflexiveness into the novel.

Briggs: What kind of reviews did you get for *Illuminatus!*?

Wilson: They were delightful.

Briggs: I loved the review in *Playboy*; it said *Illuminatus!* would do for paranoids what *Lord of the Rings* did for schizophrenics. I thought that was a good analogy.

Wilson: Most of the reviews were extremely heartwarming. There were a lot of very nice things said about the book. Out of around thirty reviews so far, there were only two negative reviews. And I was delighted to see—just like I had predicted in the book—that the two negative reviews were by people who admitted they hadn't read the whole book. Both said they quit around page fifty.

Apel: Dell, when they published *Illuminatus!*, called it science fiction. Hagbard Celine, the main character, says the events they're living through, when put in the form of a novel, are a tragedy. Joe Malik, another character, looks at what's going on and says, "We're characters in a book, and it's low camp." What is your view of the book, looking at it from your universe?

Wilson: Well, one of the main points is that all those views are simultaneously correct. Actually, the book is doing all sorts of things, but in one dimension I am continuing something that Joyce started, which is breaking down this artificial distinction between high art and low art, between great literature and folk literature. I can't emphasize too strongly how much I despise class distinctions in literature. One of the things *Illuminatus!* is trying to do is be all things at once. Detective story, allegory, science fiction, satire, porno, fairy tale, novel of ideas, adventure story and the literary equivalent of pop art in a sense.

There's no scientific instrument that you can point at a work of art that will give you an objective reading of how many mega-Michelangelos of genius it contains, or how many kilo-Homers of genuine poetry it has in it. These are all subjective judgments, and it's pre-scientific to pretend that you're talking objectively when you're arguing about how good a book is. All you're really talking about is how your own nervous system responds to it. I write criticism myself, but I always try to make it clear that my opinion is the way my nervous system is perceiving this thing. I don't think there are any absolute judgments about what's better or worse in literature. And I don't think this semantic confusion is a minor symptom. That state of mind that believes in those class distinctions in literature is the state of mind of the willfully stupid. Such people have decided to be narrow, have decided to remain Medieval, have decided to ignore three hundred years of science and post-Cartesian philosophy. It's the philosophical equivalent of Fundamentalism in religion.

Apel: How does the Robert Anton Wilson nervous system perceive *Illuminatus!* ?

Wilson: Nobody can judge his or her own work. T. S. Eliot said, "That's not our business; that's not our affair." It's up to the future to decide whether a thing is going to last or not. If people go on liking it, it'll go on for centuries, or millennia, like Homer. Or it may be a flash in the pan. I don't know. I'm one of the two people in the world least able to form an objective judgment about *Illuminatus!* My private personal feeling at times has been that this is the greatest mock-epic since *Don Quixote*. And then I figure that's just my own artistic ego massaging itself.

Apel: Hagbard speaks of Orwell's *1984* as "not a fantasy of the future, but a parable of the present." Does that sum up how we could characterize *Illuminatus!* ?

Wilson: Exactly. Everybody on the planet has been brainwashed. That's the real joke that the book revolves around. Everybody has been brainwashed, but the attempt to find the brainwashers is rather fruitless, because everybody is in on the conspiracy, the victims most of all.

Briggs: Sort of a negative *Parliament of Birds*—everybody gets together and they discover "Ah! Collectively, *we're* the brainwasher!"

Wilson: Absolutely. As Emerson said, "Every society is a conspiracy against the manhood of each of its members." Or the womanhood. Every society is a tacit conspiracy to prevent the intelligence of the next generation from functioning freely—to condition, train, limit, and castrate the intelligence so that it repeats the patterns of the past generation. That's known in anthropology as acculturation.

Apel: Let's talk a bit about your style. You are probably the only person writing science fiction who uses scientific principles as part of the *structure* of a novel, in addition to the scientific content. Your books integrate many of the findings of modern physics into the very structure of the plot, into the rhythms and harmonies of the book itself. You were talking about quantum wobble in *Schrödinger's Cat*, in the form of alternate beginnings, middles, and endings, so that the reader can put them together in many ways, for instance. A good example of quantum wobble illustrated in *Illuminatus!* is Hagbard and Malik at the Ingolstadt concert, where there are two specific, yet diametrically opposed scenes of Joe confronting Hagbard. In one potential reality, Joe shoots him dead; in one other, he doesn't shoot him at all.

I also noticed your using relativity as well: Adam Weishaupt's concept of the "Tomorrow-today-yesterday world," for instance. And the people in your book are constantly traveling through time; continually popping in and out of scenes they won't live through for months or years. There's a scene in Chicago, for example, where the characters start remembering the event before it happens.

Another physics principle I picked out was the principle of complementarity, where no single answer will explain the whole truth. You need two equal and opposite answers, at least. That was used as an old occult principle—"opposites are equal"—and it was used within the book as a major and pervasive part of the structure.

Wilson: Well, Bohr, of course, saw that symbolized in the yin/yang. He had the yin/yang put into his coat of arms when the Swedish court granted him a knighthood. In *Illuminatus!* it appears as the Sacred Chao, with the Pentagon in the yang and the apple in the yin, which is Greg Hill's emblem of Bohr's principle of complementarity.

Apel: Within the structure of the novel it appears again as the Illuminati seem both good and bad; the two opposite viewpoints integrating into a third thing.

Wilson: I decided it had to have some kind of resolution, so basically, they are the bad guys. But in *The Sex Magicians*, a little-known novel I did that was published before *Illuminatus!* (although written after) the Illuminati are definitely the good guys. Very few people have realized that aspect of *Illuminatus!*, and I'm delighted that you recognize it. I've found people who were vaguely aware of something like that, but they haven't caught it as precisely as you did. I figure that's because I didn't make it explicit enough. Nothing in *Illuminatus!* is merely bizarre. It's a precise rendering of findings in quantum physics and neurology. The scientific thing that's most integral to *Illuminatus!* is the multi-model approach.

Apel: Right—the interpenetration of universes.

Wilson: That's a little bit more than Bohr's complementarity. It's the idea that not only is there no one "correct" model, but that we can learn a lot by using several models. Bohr was talking about two opposite models, but the idea of using several different models weighs very heavily in *Illuminatus!*. That idea comes out of Marshall McLuhan, and Korzybski, and Benjamin Lee Whorf, and the Physics/Consciousness Research Group. And Joyce.

Apel: Yeah. If you consider an entire universe as a model, I can see that happening in *Illuminatus!*, since the events in that book demonstrably do *not* take place in our universe. Nixon, Agnew, and Jane Fonda have all been assassinated; Lovecraft's Miskatonic

University is an actual location where characters go to look up books, and so on. It's not our universe.

Wilson: There are other clues. The road from Dayton to New Lebanon in Ohio is going in the wrong direction, for instance.

Briggs: And cigarette commercials appear on television years after they've been banned here.

Wilson: That one was a happy accident, in the Zen tradition. Shea wrote the cigarette commercial and I pointed out to him that this novel was set after they were made illegal. He said, "Oh, I'll change it," and I said, "No, don't. I've got an idea—that's one more clue that we're in a parallel universe."

Apel: If that's the case, then when Joe Malik discovers that he's nothing but a character in a book he would be correct if he were living in our universe. But since he's not, he's hopelessly insane about his conclusion.

Wilson: No, Joe is right, actually. They *are* all in a book, and the proof is just pick up a copy and you'll find them all in there.

Apel: Discussing your book and your influences leads us right into something else, a quote that I'd like to read from *Illuminatus!* During the process where Hagbard is creating the Eris figure, there are two men who come in daily and discuss opposing sides of great social issues or meaningless absurdities, like the merits of socialism versus capitalism, or, if you wear shoes are you a foot fetishist. This constant debate ends with the sentence: "All categories collapsed, including the all-important distinction, which they had never argued, between science fiction and serious literature." Would you like to argue this all-important distinction?

Wilson: That's a lucky accident again. I had no idea *Illuminatus!* was going to be published as science fiction when I wrote that. It sounds like we're defending ourselves in advance, but I have no idea why I wrote that sentence. I can't remember my state of mind when I put that in. I guess I had just read a science fiction novel that I liked a lot, and I got an illumination that the distinction between science fiction and serious literature was as illusory as all those other great oppositions which all mystical schools try to transcend.

Apel: I wondered if that might be another illustration of your desire to break down class distinctions.

Wilson: You betta you ass, amigo. I'm very definitely an anarchist and an enemy of class systems of all sorts. If there were any truth in any of the justifications that conservatives have come up with for the class system, I wouldn't exist. I'm supposed to be a day-laborer or something like that, coming from the working-class background I came from. And yet I've had dinner with the Rothschilds; I hobnobbed with the gentry at Hefner's mansion for five years. I've also seen enough of the middle class, God knows, because they're everywhere, and you can't get away from them. I just don't believe there's any genetic basis for class distinctions. It's all artificial; an organized form of brainwashing. I think without a class structure the increase in planetary intelligence would positively blind everybody with the dazzling light given off.

Take my brother. My brother would be considered, economically, a member of the proletariat. He never was anything else. He was a mechanic all his life. Yet he read things as diverse as Freud and Walt Whitman and was heavy into Spiritualism at the end of his life. He was so deep into astronomy that he built his own telescope. He built his own ham radio. His intellectual interests were wider than those of a lot of liberal arts graduates I've known. My brother was interested in science and literature and mysticism and you-name-it.

I don't think stupidity is a natural product. I think the class system deliberately stunts the intellectual growth of most of society. I don't mean there's a conscious conspiracy behind it; I mean that our kind of society just can't operate unless people are stunted to the mammalian level where it's possible to regiment them and herd them around like a bunch of cows and get them to do the stupid jobs at which most people spend their lives. If their intelligence was allowed to grow naturally, nobody would put up with that crap, going eight hours a day to do something utterly ridiculous to get rewarded every week or two with a piece of paper that entitles you to get the necessities you need to survive. B.F. Skinner's robot-psychology is perfectly true, within the context of authoritarian society.

Apel: That's one of the things we're interested in doing in this book; breaking down at least one more wall, which is the brick wall between science fiction and "serious literature."

Wilson: The people who erected that wall, the literary intelligentsia, comparatively speaking, are among the least likely to survive. When it comes down to knowledge that can be measured and demonstrated, they've got less of it than anybody. An ordinary factory worker has more intelligence than most of them.

The one thing literati really have in large quantities is narcissism. And they're usually wrong. They're not always wrong; even a stopped clock is right twice a day. But they're wrong so damn much of the time. What I mean by "wrong" is that insofar as you can measure anything in a subjective field like literature, their fads come and go and have very little effect on what actually lasts. And that's the only way you can measure objectively if something has real value—if it pleases more than a year, it's more than a passing fad. *The Count of Monte Cristo* is a classic in some sense, in that it's lasted over a hundred years. For over a hundred years, people have still gotten excited over reading it. I doubt Mickey Spillane will last that long. He just mirrored a particular mentality of paranoia that was around in the fifties and sixties. Of course, I could be wrong; maybe there is more in Spillane. I think Homer has lasted over three thousand years because he's so damned good, in every way. You look at the fads among the literary intelligentsia and what they were praising to the skies twenty years ago is forgotten already.

Apel: One of the things that interests me in science fiction is that it seems to be the branch of literature with the best tools. The archetypes of the collective unconscious, for instance. Science fiction, virtually since its inception, has been an archetypal literature.

Wilson: I don't know who first said, "Science fiction is the mythology of our time." An increasing number of occultists are realizing this and are incorporating science fiction into their rituals. Science fiction is the natural mythology of our time, as Jesus and Hermes were the natural mythologies of another time. To try to build up a faith in the metaphysics of Christianity or pop Hinduism is, I think, a deliberate stupidity. You can't do it, except through a process of stunting your own intellectual growth at around 1600 AD and deliberately deceiving yourself. Science fiction is the only mythology we can believe, and is the only mythology that is possible. We can't believe "God" knocked up a Jewish girl two thousand years ago, but we can believe, with Sir Francis Crick, that Higher Intelligence, in some form, designed the DNA code. Science fiction can give us models for that Higher Intelligence.

Briggs: *Illuminatus!* seems to be a conscious manipulation not just of archetypal mythology, but also of cultural mythology: the Kennedy assassination, Dillinger, and so on.

Wilson: Well again, this is part of my attack on the class definitions of literature. Lovecraft is very low-class, according to the certified saints of the sanctified lit-crit establishment. And yet I think Lovecraft is a hell of a lot more important an artist than Saul Bellow, for instance. When Pat Hurley got made a general, General Stillwell—who was one of the few generals I've ever really liked—wrote in his diary, "For Christ's sakes, couldn't they get Shirley Temple?" When they gave the Nobel Prize to Saul Bellow I thought of that quote.

Olaf Stapledon, I think, has done better modern mythos than anybody else. Stapledon's mythology, as a matter of fact, I do believe in, at least half the time. More than half the time. I don't think Stapledon really invented a damn thing. I think he turned on spontaneously, the same way a lot of great mystics of the past have done. Having his kind of scientific education he was able to put the experience into the metaphors of modern science. But it's the same basic experience, I think, that Buddha had, or Dante. But the metaphors of Buddha and Dante are out of date, and Stapledon's are still alive.

Apel: He described these far-reaching concepts with the best words available to him in his time and place, and with the best science available to him.

Wilson: And they're still the best we've got. Nobody since Stapledon has done better. I don't want to put Arthur C. Clarke down; I admire him tremendously. But he's the only one who comes close, and he doesn't do it; he hasn't yet done as well as Stapledon.

Apel: I was incredibly disappointed in his description of going through the Stargate in his novel, *2001: A Space Odyssey,* as "sort of a Grand Central Station to the stars." I read that line and thought, "Well, you've just completely missed the point there, Arthur. You've chosen the most mundane metaphor possible to describe the film's most mindbending segment. What's the use of writing the damn book if you don't understand it?"

Wilson: Yeah, Clarke has strange limitations. Of course, we all do. I think it's droll that he's so hostile to psychedelics. Intelligently used, psychedelics would help him to understand his own work better and he'd be a more intelligent writer. That's a prediction: if somebody can get that moralistic Englishman to turn on, he will understand his own work better, and write better books than he ever has.

I would like to add, in spite of everything I've said already, I think some of the traditional occult models are quite useful still. I think Kabbala is still a marvelous system. I think there's still a helluva lot in Kabbala. Kabbala was a thousand years ahead of its time when it was created. As a matter of fact, I know at least two physicists and one mathematician who are heavy into Kabbala.

Apel: Saul-Paul Sirag and Fred Wolf I know are...

Wilson: Yeah. And Mike Mohlé is the mathematician. I'm heavy into Kabbala myself. There's a hell of a lot of Kabbala in *Illuminatus!*

Briggs: If nothing else, the chapter headings are taken directly from the Tree of Life.

Wilson: The way it's organized is all based on Kabbala. I was just thinking how this would sound to some of the *Hudson Review*-type of literary critics. Through the first half of this interview I'm continually saying "up science" and downing the humanities department, then all of a sudden here I am talking about magic so casually. Both are terra incognita to literary types—so how can I get the science and the magic together?

Apel: Through the principle of complementarity!

Wilson: Exactly!

Apel: It's the only way. Equal opposites. You need both of them.

Wilson: My basic idea is from Aleister Crowley: "We place no reliance / On Virgin or Pigeon; / Our method is Science, / Our aim is Religion."

That dualism shows up again in the characters in *Illuminatus!*. For example, Hagbard and the Dealy Lama represent the basic conflict between the two schools of mystics. There have always been these two schools; the one which sees the Cosmic Joke and drops out, or goes off to enjoy Samadhi in a corner, and the ones who say, "Well, let's do something about it." Buddhism and Taoism are the extreme forms of the "dropout," and Christianity and Sufism are the extreme forms of "Let's do something about it." Especially Quaker Christianity, which is my favorite type of Christianity. If I had to be a Christian, I'd be a Quaker. Thank God I don't have to be a Christian. *(General laughter)* Anyway, Hagbard represents the Sufi or Gnostic Christian viewpoint, and Dealy Lama represents the Buddhist or Taoist viewpoint.

Apel: What is the Robert Anton Wilson standpoint?

Wilson: My position is undecided. The Dealy Lama speaks from the center of my being. I'm not at all sure that he's wrong, but I'm temperamentally on the side of the activists. As Gurdjieff said, "My way is against God and against nature." This is the rough sketch of a universe; it's our job to complete it and improve it, as freemasons in the true sense.

Briggs: Do you think that the border between the empirical sciences and mysticism is dissolving?

Wilson: Definitely. I think the importance of LSD historically will turn out to be that it opened the door to empirical experimental scientific mysticism. One of the things that Timothy Leary is going to be remembered for—and he's going to be remembered for a hell of a lot—is that he was the first one to see that. They'd been experimenting with LSD for about fourteen years, I think, when Leary came on the scene. He was the first one to see that this was our chance for experimental theology.

Briggs: Yeah, applied theology.

Wilson: And it's not just LSD; there are lots of other approaches. But LSD was the gate by which Leary made that discovery. Biofeedback and direct brain stimulation and a lot of other things are going to be playing a big role, too. Self-metaprogramming, in Lilly's term. We're living in science fiction. That came to me last year, in a blinding flash. I had just come back from Vancouver where I spent a week lobbying for the U.N. to recognize space migration as the answer to our energy problems—which is a theme out of the science fiction I was reading twenty years ago. And as soon as I got back here I was immediately involved again with Sirag and Sarfatti, who are trying to put parapsychology on a physical basis by creating quantum models to explain ESP and PK. Then I was involved again with Leary and his S.M.I^{2}. L.E. scenario—Space Migration, Increased Intelligence, and Life Extension—which is pure science fiction—and suddenly it hit me: "I'm living in science fiction!"

Then I got a new insight into what I had done in *Illuminatus!* — we're all living in a novel, and we've got a choice as to which kind of novel we're living in. I'm dreadfully sorry for the people who are living in naturalistic novels in the James T. Farrell tradition; you know, where everything comes to a bad end, and all there is injustice and stupidity in the world. People are living in that tunnel-reality because artists created it for them. And they were good artists, in that they were strong, they were powerful, they were influential, and so there are millions of people living in that reality. Then there are people who are living in the heroic Hemingway tunnel-reality still, and there are a lot of timid academic people living in a T.S. Eliot tunnel-reality. Most of the country is living in a television tube-reality. I'm delighted to be living in science fiction. It's one of the more open and exciting tunnel-realities to live in.

That was one of Joyce's great discoveries, that everybody is living in a novel. That's why *Ulysses* is an anthology of novels. It's a novel in the form of an anthology, and each of the characters is living in a separate tunnel-reality that's a mirror of the literature that's been programmed into their neurological circuits. Marshall McLuhan learned everything about media from Joyce.

Apel: This sounds like what Aldous Huxley said: "For better or worse, we all become our favorite character in fiction."

Wilson: I'm awfully opinionated tonight.

Briggs: Oh, that's all right.

Apel: That's what we want. Is there anything we haven't asked you that you'd like to talk about? This is your free speech minute...

Wilson: Okay. I think the most important decision confronting humanity is *life or death*. Norman O. Brown's book *Life Against Death* came out in the sixties, and I think he really pinpointed the most important issue of our times. On the one hand, we will soon have the potential for immortality. And on the other hand, we have a good chance for ending life on this planet, or ending human life.

To me, the two most important ideas around are pacifism and cryonics. Pacifism is saying, "No, we won't kill for you," and cryonics is saying, "No, we won't die for you." I favor total rebellion against death. This has never been presented favorably in the popular press; almost all the programming has been to accept death, and of course there's been tremendous brainwashing for centuries to accept death and war as our natural lot. I think the pacifism of the sixties was just an overture to a general rebellion against death. I think we're very close to scientific breakthroughs which will put an end to programmed senescence, aging and death, and we should be putting all our energies into that. As Alan Harrington says in *The Immortalist*, we should "hire the scientists, spend the money, and hunt down death like an outlaw." The fact that we're putting so goddam much time, money, and energy into creating bigger and better weapons with a greater and greater likelihood of killing all of us off is the major *dummheit* of our time. I think if there's one thing I'm trying to do in all of my writings—in my novels, in my articles, my poetry; every damn thing I do—it's saying yes to life and no to death.

Death and taxation are supposedly the two inevitabilities. Well, I reject them both.

Apel: Immortalist anarchist.

Wilson: Prometheanism sort of sums it up.

Apel: Thank you, Robert Anton Wilson.

AFTERWORD
to the 2014 Edition

by
D. Scott Apel

Why This Book?

Several questions might arise concerning this book. One is, Why publish a book of interviews some 40 years after they were conducted? Why promote conversations with minor genre writers, most of whom are long dead?

There are several answers, but all are quite simple.

One answer is that they *are* long dead. There are simply no longer any writers alive who lived and worked through the early years of science fiction, in the 1930s and '40s. There aren't any of their generation left to give any new interviews, to relate anecdotes, to inform us about those heady early days of writers creating a new genre. No future oral history of the field will be able to tap into their well of stories and relate them first hand. They live on through their work, but they themselves are "Read Only Memory" now.

The fact that so many of these pioneers have departed inspired another reason. Every few years when I reviewed this manuscript for possible small press publication, what struck me most was the intelligence and insight of these creative, articulate figures. These are people whose work shaped and defined an entire field of literature—a field that grew in cultural prominence during their lifetimes. They are writers who were devoted to their craft long before it was financially favorable to do so, and long before they received any attention from the mainstream literary establishment. They deserve to be remembered, their legacy deserves to be noted—and their works deserve to be kept alive.

Finally, on a personal note, the writers in this book are people who did my friend Kevin Briggs and I a kindness, taking two (and often more) hours out of their lives to discuss their work with young strangers and help them launch their own careers. Such generosity should not go unrewarded.

Why Isn't [Name of Your Favorite SF Author] In Your Book?

A true oral history of science fiction in the era we covered (1930-1980) should clearly contain interviews with its key figures; people like the Big Three—Robert A. Heinlein, Arthur C. Clarke and Isaac Asimov—possibly even Ray Bradbury or George Lucas (whose 1977 film *Star Wars* changed the nature of science fiction by catapulting it from cult pleasure to public prominence).

So why aren't these shining stars included?

Funny story. *Stories*, rather, and funnier now than when we were bending every effort to reach these notables and convince them to participate in this project but reaping only frustration and rejection. There are two ways to handle these funny stories. One is to ignore the fact that these shining stars were even considered for inclusion; to completely gloss over their contributions and existence; to pretend like we never had them in mind to begin with. Who'd miss what they're not told?

The other way is to relate the stories of why they are not included, regardless of the minor tarnish it might put on their public personas. Is it overly sensitive, self-serving, petty and vindictive to cast these great writers in a less-than-flattering light? Oh, for sure! But in some small way, by quoting them and allowing them to hoist themselves by their own petards, justice will be served. Justice, and, of course, revenge.

(At the end of the day, the bottom line is what does it really matter, since no one is ever going to read this shit anyway? If you are in fact reading this, consider this a personal connection: I am probably writing this for you alone. How ya doin'?)

While Briggs and I were eminently satisfied with the writers represented in this book, our agent (once we landed one; see the next section) informed us, flat out, that he would be unable to sell the book without a superstar name attached. His short list was clear and obvious: Arthur C. Clarke, Isaac Asimov, Robert A. Heinlein, George Lucas, Ray Bradbury. Without one of them, we would never sell. By implication, we would never have a career and would die in the gutter, poor, miserable, and unknown.

This demand presented us with a unique dilemma. When we began this book in 1975, we were barely out of college and still living the starving student lifestyle in that area of Northern California that would soon be known as "Silicon Valley." With essentially zero financial resources, we knew we could never afford to travel anywhere beyond driving range to conduct any of these interviews. Geography conspired against us to ever achieve a meeting with Clarke, who lived half a world away in Sri Lanka, or with Asimov, who was a Boston resident and rarely left home.

But there was one NorCal "neighbor" who might fit the bill: Robert A. Heinlein, who lived in the tiny town of Bonnie Doon in the Santa Cruz mountains, less than an hour's drive from our home in Santa Clara. Although he had a reputation as a recluse and had rarely been interviewed, we had to give it a shot.

We wrote him a letter detailing our project and the interview topics, a list of who we'd interviewed, and our agent's pronouncement that we'd never be published (and our careers would never begin) unless we obtained an interview from "The Dean of Science Fiction." We drove to his house and left the letter in his mailbox, to show how dedicated we were—rather than just mail him a letter, we were willing to go to the effort of hand-delivering it—and we prevailed upon Fritz Leiber, a friend of Heinlein's, to talk to him and suggest he do the interview.

As might be expected (since a Heinlein interview does not appear in this book), he ignored our request and a subsequent follow-up request. His wife, Virginia, eventually answered our letters, explaining that Mr. Heinlein has "so many" requests for interviews that he feels it's best to turn them all down. "If he gives even one, he'd have to honor them all." (We didn't know that's how it worked.) However, we considered ourselves lucky that he had a wife polite and considerate enough to reply, otherwise, she informed us, "your letter wouldn't have been answered at all."

She certainly appears a paragon of politeness compared to Isaac Asimov's terse response. When we discovered that Asimov would be traveling to our neck of the woods to deliver a lecture, we sent him a similar letter outlining our project and crediting him with the ability to get our book published and to start our careers if he could just spare an hour to be interviewed. "When I'm in the area," he wrote on a small piece of notepaper, "I'll be sightseeing. Let them buy my autobiography if they want all that stuff." End of note. We supposed one could not expect much verbiage from the author of only 200 books. And we wondered if we had contacted the same Isaac Asimov about whom Ben Bova wrote in his *Omni* magazine tribute, "Isaac is always ready to give beginning writers a helpful hand." He was certainly ready to give us the back of that hand.

George Lucas was another Northern California resident. Maybe it would impress him that we'd included Leigh Brackett in our interview lineup—after all, the week after we'd interviewed her, Lucas hired her to write the screenplay for *The Empire Strikes Back*. We could certainly travel to meet with him...if we could reach him at all. We ended up mailing five copies of our letter to five different addresses (including the *Star Wars* fan club). One actually got through to his secretary, who informed us that "George has a very strict policy of not giving interviews." We received that reply the week before George Lucas interviews appeared in *Rolling Stone, Time*, and several other publications. We assumed that he'd forgotten to mention these to his secretary...or that she'd forgotten to add a qualifying addendum to her statement, which would have read "George has a very strict policy of not giving interviews *to unknowns*." It's not like we were swell-headed enough to feel we deserved an interview. We *were* unknowns, and the demands on his time were no doubt intense. But we did resent being lied to.

Four down, one to go. Ray Bradbury lived in Los Angeles, only 350 miles away; we could stretch our budget to get there and conduct an interview with him if it would sell the book. Since he was our last shot, once we sent him our project-outline letter and interview request we called Ted Sturgeon, a friend of Bradbury's, and asked him if he would contact Ray and encourage him to meet with us, which he did, bless his heart.

One Saturday morning soon afterward, Ray Bradbury called me at home. We talked for nearly an hour, during the course of which he informed me that he'd just hired his own interviewer to do a book-length autobiographical interview with him. So he didn't want to talk to anyone else about his life or work. He echoed Asimov's sentiments ("Let them buy my autobiography if they want all that stuff") almost verbatim, and, like Lucas, he seemed to have selective memory about performing interviews, as Ray Bradbury interviews were prominently featured over the next few months in *Omni, Starlog*, and *Future* magazines, to name just a few publications.

So: no superstar, no book. But it's bad form to speak ill of the dead. They all have family, friends and fans who would defend them, and perhaps these failures to assist a pair of young writers were in fact the only social or professional mistakes they ever made during their distinguished careers. I should thank all these fine people for their support and encouragement on our project. Yes, I should.

What Took So Long to Publish This?

A funny thing happened on the way to the bookstore...

The obvious answer to this question is that it's a bad book and never deserved publication. If you've read this far, you can judge for yourself whether or not that is an accurate assessment.

There are a couple strikes against this theory, however. Many of the writers we interviewed were impressed enough with the results that they suggested we send the completed manuscript to their agents. The responses universally included solid praise punctured by a series of "but" holes.

Bantam Books' executive editor, for example, said the book is "nicely done," BUT "there's no place for it on our list."

St. Martin's Press informed us that "many here commented on the quality of the writing," BUT St. Martin's wasn't the right place to market it successfully.

The highest accolades came from Phil Dick's agent, Russ Galen (with whom I have maintained a life-long contact, and who was enormously helpful in my publishing *Philip K. Dick: The Dream Connection*), who praised it as "a terrific book and extremely publishable and worthwhile. I love the book...the Dick interview was one of the greatest things of its kind since Socrates" BUT "I'm afraid we won't be able to get involved at all."

A representative of the Scott Meredith Agency "admired your seriousness of purpose, was entertained and amused by the interviews, and was consistently impressed by the depth of insight, vitality, and originality of the minds of these men and women. The book's brilliance can be credited to the writers, but the credit for its balance and breadth must be yours." BUT "Sadly, then, I must tell you..." *aaaaaand* you know the rest.

Curiously, this detailed rejection letter went out of its way to negate its praise with some detailed criticism, mostly about the "deliberately 'chic,' 'in' attitude" they detected. "No one, I assure you, is interested in the fact that you smoke dope, sleep with women, etc." If I was to comment in today's parlance: WTF? Where did we talk about those things? Among the gems in this section is this charge: "Another objection we have is the catty, gossipy, and often cruel tone you take and encourage the authors to take." How odd that an agent doesn't realize that whenever writers gather together, the conversation often turns to trash talk about how they have been screwed by agents and publishers.

Speaking of which...one final story about why this book was never published decades ago. One of our authors insisted we send the manuscript to his literary agent—let's call him "Richard Move"—who agreed to handle the book. After signing the contract, we never received a further word from Mr. Move—no updates; nothing. We were minor clients, so we didn't want to bug him too often and piss him off so much that he'd drop the book. So we waited several months in silence, then queried him...and received no reply. Another couple months went by. We queried him again; again, no response. Another short, polite query; another non-response. This went on for over a year. Until this time, we figured that having any agent was better than having no agent. But eventually, since we were seeing no movement on our book and getting no response from our agent, we decided that we effectively had no agent. I wrote Mr. Move to let him know his services were no longer required and would he please return our manuscript. This letter, at least, received a prompt response, in which Mr. Move expressed his surprise, informing us that he'd stopped representing the book months earlier and had already sent back the ms. "Perhaps it was lost in the mail," he suggested. He made no mention of the other letters we'd sent him since he claimed to have dropped us. (Perhaps they, too, were "lost in the mail.") We called the author who'd recommended Move to report on this behavior; his response was, "Yeah, something's happened to him recently. He's grown fangs."

We had no idea how sharp those fangs were until a couple years later. Our book of interviews with science fiction writers was going to be the first of its kind, but another similar work made it into publication about this same time instead. This other volume was essentially the flip-side of our book: where our book concentrated on a few in-depth interviews, this other volume consisted of dozens of short, shallow interviews. Many of them were contentious in tone and dismissive or disrespectful in their description of the author or his work. Once they saw the published book, several of the interviewees publically complained that they had been mistreated or misquoted. One guess who the agent for that book was. Apparently, Mr. Richard Move received both manuscripts virtually simultaneously and chose to sit on ours and sell the other—and to ensure that this other book would have no competition.

And that, kids, was the real "Dick" Move.

From that time to this, *Science Fiction: An Oral History* has taken a back seat to numerous other projects—some successful; some not so much—as well as the exigencies of life such as work and family. Every time one of our authors died I considered adding this book to my small press (The Impermanent Press) catalog of publications. It didn't help move this project forward that Kevin Briggs died in 2007. But it did become one more reason to see that our project stayed alive.

This book fell into a metaphorical black hole about 1980, lamentably destined never to be read, or shared, or seen again. But Stephen Hawking now predicts that occasionally, under propitious circumstances, a small amount of radiation can in fact escape from the clutches of a black hole. This is it.

We hope you enjoyed the wit and wisdom of our authors, and—if you've read this far—the story of the odyssey of this 20th-century book into 21st-century print.

Bonus Interview

GENE RODDENBERRY

Interview conducted at the Marriott Hotel
Santa Clara, California
September 25, 1985

In September 1985, while employed at Lockheed Missiles and Space Company in Sunnyvale, California, I was approached by a representative of the LMSC Management Association and asked if I would like to attend a dinner in honor of *Star Trek* creator Gene Roddenberry. The dinner would be followed by a talk by Roddenberry, after which I would interview him for the Association's newsletter. I debated whether or not to accept the assignment for an entire picosecond before agreeing.

The following is a version combining my article for the Management Association Newsletter and my video column for the San Jose *Mercury News* dated October 18, 1985. While an interview with Roddenberry was never originally intended as part of this book, it seemed close enough in spirit to add it to the ebook release as a special bonus.

NB: To put *Star Trek* in context, at the time of this interview (1985), the original series had been off the air for 16 years, but had been rerun countless times on TV stations around the world. *Star Trek: The Motion Picture* had been released six years earlier; *Star Trek III: The Search for Spock* was the most recent feature release (1984); and *Star Trek IV: The Voyage Home* (1986) was in development. The sequel series, *Star Trek: The Next Generation,* would debut two years later, in 1987.

GENE RODDENBERRY

Gene Roddenberry's biography reads almost like an adventure novel itself. Far from being the typical deskbound writer, Roddenberry flew B-17 bombers in World War II, investigated air crashes for the Army Air Corps, and (as a pilot for Pan American airlines) crashed a plane in the Syrian desert. As a senior officer, he later received a Civil Aeronautics commendation for his rescue efforts.

After the war, he joined the Los Angeles Police Department and became a speechwriter, first for the Chief of Police and later for the mayor of L.A. After selling scripts to several drama anthology programs of the era, his writing overshadowed his other careers, and he left the force to become head writer on the television series *Have Gun, Will Travel.* Over the years, Roddenberry has been awarded many honors, including three honorary doctorate degrees and the first star on the Hollywood Walk of Fame awarded to a writer.

But his career could have turned out quite differently, he told the 330 guests at a Lockheed Management Association dinner. "I could have easily been sitting there with you tonight and listening to the speaker," he said. "As World War II was beginning, I was going to college [in California] and I heard that Lockheed was hiring people, so I went out and took an exam...which I failed. That kept us apart."

Optimism about the human future was the focus of Roddenberry's remarks to the group. "I hope to convince you that there really is, in front of our noses, much evidence supporting a positive human future...so much, in fact, that we often fail to see it." He cited such remarkable advancements in science and technology as the genetics revolution, the electronics revolution, and—most importantly to our future—the knowledge revolution. "It's difficult to believe that the universe could have created matter as complex as we are," he continued, discussing the "lovely mystery" of our brains. "We are a form of matter that is actually capable of thinking about itself. This is beyond Star Trek. Let's use this brain of ours to survive."

Why, then, if the future is so optimistic, are we facing so many crises today? "The answer could hardly be more obvious: Our species is now being tested. We show many signs of working out all that trouble. Despite what TV and newspapers say, the human future has much more good news in sight than bad news."

One of the brightest aspects of the human future, he continued, is space travel...but not necessarily the galaxy-roaming exploits of a Capt. Kirk or Mr. Spock. "The part of *Star Trek* that is true, however, is that this marvelous human creature will definitely soon be involved in spaceflight. For now, it doesn't matter how far away the stars are, because we have our own exciting, huge solar system only days or months away. It's a treasure house, one that includes a virtually inexhaustible energy source—the sun—and planets, moons, chemicals and metal ores enough to last us at least ten centuries, even if we continue developing as we are now. We very much need the challenges and thrills we'll experience over the centuries of mastering our solar system, to begin to mature into a truly adult life form. We will finally become adults who can be trusted to interact properly with the life we will almost certainly find out there in other solar systems. I look forward to the day when these humans, who are so much more than they realize, at last understand that the cosmos outside and the cosmos inside of themselves are one and the same."

Following his talk, I sat down for a one-on-one with Roddenberry, a soft-spoken and genial giant, where we discussed *Star Trek* in greater detail. How does he feel about its extraordinary success? "I am constantly flabbergasted by the whole thing," he admitted. "People say to me, 'Did you know this was going to happen when you were creating it?' But what kind of an idiot is going to sit down at the typewriter and say, 'Well, let's see. Today I think I'll create a legend.'?"

Why does he think *Star Trek* has attained such widespread popularity? "I believe it taps into our hopes about tomorrow," he replied. "And it does so with morality and decency."

As to his role in the production of the feature films, Roddenberry had this to say: "After the first movie, I decided that I just couldn't go on producing *Star Trek* the rest of my life. I have other things to do. So I made myself executive creative consultant and brought in other people." Is he happy with their work? "They do some things I don't particularly like. When they said they were going to crash the Enterprise, I broke out in a cold sweat. But when I produced, I wouldn't sit still for the network telling me what to do, so I can't really justify dictating to the new producers. The only time I would ever step in is if they broke one of our basic philosophies."

Also Available From
The Impermanent Press

Beyond Chaos and Beyond

The Best of Trajectories, Volume II

by Robert Anton Wilson

Edited by D. Scott Apel

For over a decade (1987-1997), Robert Anton Wilson, co-author of the *Illuminatus!* trilogy and author of *The Cosmic Trigger*, published a quarterly newsletter, *Trajectories: The Journal of Futurism and Heresy*, full of original articles, unpublished fiction and outrageous opinion. The 1994 book *Chaos and Beyond* collected the best essays from the first ten issues of the newsletter; this sequel, *Beyond Chaos and Beyond*, preserves the best of the final issues, including an excerpt from RAW's unfinished sequel to *Illuminatus!,* transcripts of audio and video issues, and transcripts of the several videos featuring RAW produced specifically for his globe-girdling fan base.

Additional material includes a rare 1977 interview with RAW; a major essay on Philip K. Dick, as well as RAW's comments from a PKD documentary; transcripts of RAW's 1978 PBS appearances discussing *The Prisoner*; and a 30,000-word essay by the editor detailing his 30-plus-year association with Wilson.

Beyond Chaos and Beyond is essential reading for hardcore fans of Robert Anton Wilson's extraordinary work and life.

Other Books by D. Scott Apel Available From The Impermanent Press

The Alex Smart Comic Mystery Trilogy

The Uncertainty Principle?
The Infinite Mistress
Detective, Comics

The Killer B's Film Guides

Killer B's
The 237 Best Movies on Video You've (Probably) Never Seen

Killer B's, Vol. 2: Son of a Killer B
237 MORE Great Movies On Demand
You've (Probably) Never Seen

Killer B's: The Hive
The 437 Best Movies On Demand You've (Probably) Never Seen*
**and a few TV Shows*

No Plan B:

The Adventures of a Carbon Unit in Silicon Valley

Famedroppings:

Close Encounters with 100+ Celebrities

Fourplay:

A Theatrical Quartet

Mein Summer Kampf

Or, Everything I've Ever Written That Was Funny, Almost

17673511R00145

Printed in Great Britain
by Amazon